Witold Koszela

Cruisers of the III Reich

vol. 1

Published in Poland in 2021
by STRATUS sp.j.
Po. Box 123,

as
MMPBooks,
3 Gloucester Close,
Petersfield
Hampshire GU32 3AX, UK
e-mail: office@mmpbooks.biz

http://www.mmpbooks.biz

ISBN
978-83-65958-84-6

Editor in chief
Roger Wallsgrove

Editorial Team
Bartłomiej Belcarz
Robert Pęczkowski
Arthur Juszczak
Matthew Willis

Cover
Artur Juszczak

Drawings
Colour profiles
Witold Koszela

Translation
Tomasz Besarabowicz

DTP:
Stratus sp. j.

PRINTED IN
POLAND

Table of contents

German Navy

11 November 1918 has gone down in history as the day that put an end to the four years of the Great War.

The conflict later referred to as World War One, which covered almost all continents, seas and oceans, ended in victory for countries supporting the Entente, while for the Central Powers it was a great tragedy, resulting in the collapse of their armed forces, governments and economies, and in the case of Austria-Hungary, the country's almost total collapse. Germany became the greatest "loser". Exhausted by a long and costly war, it could not fight on any longer and was forced to ask for an armistice.

This fact, considering the overall situation of the country where general dissatisfaction grew from day to day, meant de facto surrender and reliance on the grace of the Western powers, which, although also "tired" by war, still had the potential to perform a final blow.

As a result, Germany, one of the most powerful nations in the world, was almost on its knees, agreeing to the truce conditions imposed by the victorious states, and these very soon proved to be very severe and, in the opinion of many Germans, not entirely righteous. The signing of the extremely harmful Treaty of Versailles on 28 June 1919 imposed on the country, among other matters, the need to surrender to the victorious powers almost all overseas colonies and the loss of significant areas of the state.

The core of the German Navy were old battleships, which did not have any major combat capabilities.

One of the larger ships that were allowed to be kept by the Germans in Versailles was the battleship Hessen. *The ship presented herself menacingly, however, when she was serving with the* Reichsmarine, *she could not compare with this type of ship from other fleets.*

One of the most controversial provisions of the "Versailles dishonour," as the arrangement signed soon began to be called in Germany, was the practical liquidation of the armed forces. Simply put, the country was to be demilitarized by retaining only a force of 100,000 professional soldiers and banned from having aviation and armoured troops, and in addition all its fortifications were to be dismantled except for those remaining in the eastern borders of the country. The preservation of the latter was to be a possible defence against the predations of Soviet Russia, and probably only this threat allowed Germany to preserve some military potential at all.

A separate issue was the fleet which shared the fate of the land forces. It was extremely painful here as, at the end of the conflict it had enormous potential, including many very modern and powerful ships, which, according to the armistice, were to go to the British base in Scapa Flow and be interned there.

What is worse, Part V of the peace treaty provided that, after the ratification of the document by the German delegation, the ships in Scapa Flow would be transferred to the Allied countries, but after the British had taken care of the humiliation of the German commanders, that was too much for them and on 21 June 1919 Admiral Ludwig von Reuter, commanding officer of the interned fleet, ordered the ships to be scuttled. This move was certainly painful for the aforementioned admiral and other skippers, but it allowed the Germans to save their honour and prevent the seizure of their ships. It was also the end of the German fleet.

The Treaty of Versailles, which was later signed by German delegates, in accordance with Article 181 permitted them to keep only six battleships in active service and two more in reserve, six cruisers and two more in reserve, twelve destroyers and twelve torpedo ships. It would seem that this was quite a lot, but these ships were carefully selected and were relatively old vessels and for those times not offering any major combat capabilities. Also, their value can be evidenced by the fact that at the end of the war most of them were already in reserve, giving way to much more modern ships.

What was worse, subsequent provisions severely limited the displacement that newly built ships could have, and they could only be built with the intention of replacing old ships. The displacement of ships built to replace battleships was not to exceed 10,000 tons, for cruisers 6,000 tons, for destroyers 800 tons and for torpedo ships 200 tons. These restrictions were also followed by age limits, not allowing for the construction and commissioning of new ships before the expiration of twenty years for battleships and cruisers and fifteen years for destroyers and torpedo ships from the time of launching a given vessel.

As history has proved, these limits turned out to be completely unrealistic and, in a situation where the Germans wanted to build a ship representing some reasonable capabilities, they were practically forced to break the Versailles provisions by concealing some facts.

We can safely say that the allies were partly guilty of becoming victims of that fraud, which the Germans began to commit almost from the very beginning. Completely unrealistic restrictions imposed on the navy, the ban on the construction and acquisition of aircraft, tanks and the general expansion of the German armed forces, were very soon reflected in the actions taken. It quickly turned out that the Germans were not in any way going to fully go along with the Versailles arrangements, which seemed too far-reaching, and gave many officers a sense of hurt and bitterness.

Adolf Hitler, who was unknown at the time, called the Versailles provisions a "diktat". Having come to power, he quickly dealt with the treaty, officially rejecting it in 1935.

Meanwhile the fleet, itself with huge problems, began to function. Its first commander was Vice Admiral Adolf von Trotha, then later Admiral William Michaelis, Admiral Paul Behncke, Admiral Hans Zenker and finally Admiral Erich Raeder – a man who, together with Adolf Hitler, played a key role in the construction and subsequent service of the cruisers of the Third Reich.

However, those were extremely difficult days for Germany. Aside from the fact that political unrest could be felt at every step, the authorities of the country had to deal with serious economic problems. Rapid inflation and huge unemployment was reflected in spreading poverty, and this would not be without influence on a fleet requiring enormous financial resources.

The warships that were allowed to be retained by Germany needed modernisation, so despite the possibility of keeping, among others, six battleships and six cruisers, only some of them entered service and the rest had to wait for the proverbial "better times". As it was agreed, the fleet mustered five *Braunschweig* class battleships: *Braunschweig, Elsass, Hessen, Lothringen* and *Preussen* (German: *Preußen*) and three *Deutschland* class ones: *Hannover, Schlesien* and *Schleswig-Holstein*, with the aforementioned *Lothringen* and *Preussen* on the list as reserve vessels. Each of them was a relatively old ship. The dates of their launching were 1902–1906, and even worse was the fact that they were pre-dreadnoughts, i.e. ships built before a new ship entered service which set completely new standards in shipbuilding, namely the innovative British battleship HMS *Dreadnought*.

List of German battleships that Germany could keep according to the treaty provisions –

Name	Shipyard	Keel laid	Launched	Commissioned
Braunschweig	Germaniawerft, Kiel	1901	02.12.1902	15.10.1904
Elsass	Schichau, Danzig	1901	23.05.1903	29.11.1904
Hessen	Germaniawerft, Kiel	15.04.1902	18.09.1903	19.05.1905
Preussen	AG Vulcan, Stettin	04.1902	30.10.1903	12.07.1905
Lothringen	Schichau, Danzig	1902	27.05.1904	18.05.1906
Hannover	Kaiserliche Werft, Danzig	07.11.1904	29.09.1905	01.10.1907
Schlesien	Schichau, Danzig	1904	28.05.1906	05.05.1908
Schleswig-Holstein	Germaniawerft, Kiel	18.08.1905	17.12.1906	06.07.1908

The situation was even worse when it came to cruisers, which are the subject of this study, and which provided the foundations for the "The Third Reich Cruisers" later introduced into service. These were generally even older and belonged to two classes – *Gazelle* cruisers built in 1899–1903 and *Bremen* cruisers constructed in 1902–1905.

German ships on manoeuvres. Although outdated, they made it possible to train new personnel.

Battleships of the Reichsmarine. *At the very end of the line, the cruiser* Emden *can be seen.*

Both types, when they began their service with the *Reichsmarine*, left much – very much – to be desired in terms of combat capabilities, allowing for only the appropriate training of crews for modern class ships which would be built later. Interestingly, *Gazelle* cruisers, when they were built and commissioned into the *Kaiserliche Marine*, were considered to be one of the first "small" cruisers of considerable value, in which German engineers used much previous experience in the construction and operation of this type of ship.

They were widely regarded as relatively successful, so the whole series included as many as ten vessels: *Gazelle, Niobe, Amazone, Ariadne, Medusa, Nymphie, Thetis, Arcona, Frauenlob* and *Undine*. These ships were characterized by normal displacement in the range from 2,643 to 2,700 t and full displacement from 2,963 t to 3,180 t, and their hull dimensions were 105 m overall long, 12.2 m beam and 5.5 m draft.

Such significant differences in displacement were the result of changes in design introduced at the construction stage, such as different internal layouts and the use of different types of propulsion. For example, the drive for the prototype *Gazelle* consisted of two, four-cylinder steam engines and eight Niclausse boilers which supplied them with steam. It was similar in the case of the cruisers *Niobe, Nymphe* and *Thetis*, with eight Thornycroft boilers supplied for *Niobe* in pairs for the four-cylinder engines, and the Marine type for *Thetis* and *Nymphe*. However, different types were used in the latter: four double and one single. In the case of the remaining vessels, the drive was made up of two triple-expansion steam engines, supplied by nine Marine boilers each. Such variation in propulsion systems obviously resulted in achieving different output and speeds, calculated from 6,366 HP for the prototype to 7,972 to 9,010 HP for the remaining cruisers, and their speeds were in the range of 20 to 22.2 knots.

Interestingly, the ships were quite well armoured for their time, with armoured decks in thickness ranging from 20 to 25 mm with 50 mm slope. Added to this was much thicker armour in the area of the engine room, with a thickness of 80 mm. Command posts were shielded with plates of the same thickness with the exception of the roofs, the thickness of which was 20 mm.

The armament, consisting of ten 105 mm guns, ten-fourteen 37 mm guns and three 450 mm torpedo tubes, was also relatively powerful.

We will not describe here the fate of all the *Gazelle* class cruisers, and limit ourselves only to those allowed to be kept by the Germans after Versailles. There were six of these: *Niobe, Amazone, Medusa, Nymphe, Thetis* and *Arcona*.

These ships were built in various shipyards. *Niobe, Medusa* and *Arcona* were built at the A G Weser shipyard in Bremen, *Amazone* and *Nymphe* at the Germaniawerft shipyard in Kiel, and *Thetis* at the Kaiserliche Werft shipyard in Danzig.

List of *Gazelle* cruisers that took up service in *Reichsmarine* –

Name	Shipyard	Keel laid	Launched	Commissioned
Niobe	AG Weser, Bremen	30.08.1898	18.07.1899	25.06.1900
Amazone	Germaniawerft, Kiel	1899	6.10.1900	18.05.1901
Medusa	AG Weser, Bremen	1900	5.12.1900	26.07.1901
Nymphe	Germaniawerft, Kiel	1898	21.11.1899	20.09.1900
Thetis	Kaiserliche Werft, Danzig	1899	3.07.1900	14.09.1901
Arcona	AG Weser, Bremen	1901	22.04.1902	12.05.1903

They entered service between 1900 and 1903 and in the period preceding the outbreak of World War One operated mainly as training ships. The exceptions were *Niobe, Thetis* and *Arcona*, which were sent to serve in Far Eastern waters, where they carried out three-year tours. The other vessels operated mainly in the waters of the Baltic Sea and North Sea, performed training programs, visiting a number of ports both in the Scandinavian countries as well as further south, including Spanish ports.

During the war, all these ships operated mainly on the Baltic Sea. The war for the first of them – *Niobe* – was not marked by interesting events. Having participated in a series of more or less significant naval operations as part of the home fleet from 1916, she was used mainly as a residential hulk and a guard ship, and in fact the most interesting part of her story commenced after the war, when she found herself in the pool of ships that were allowed to remain with the German navy.

Interestingly, she did not take up active service with the *Reichsmarine* and took the first place on the list of German cruisers intended to be replaced by newly built vessels. Because of this, in 1925 she was decommissioned, having been replaced by the cruiser *Emden*. She did not go to the scrapyard, but was sold to Yugoslavia, where she was given the name *Dalmatia*. She underwent a thorough refurbishment, which increased her combat capabilities and extended her life for many years.

During World War Two, after the surrender of Yugoslavia, she was taken over by the Italian Navy, with which she served under the name *Cattaro*, and in 1943 she was taken over by *Kriegsmarine*, returning to her original name and performing operations alongside the allied Croats. She was sunk by British torpedo boats on 22 December 1943 in the area of the island of Silba after she ran aground. The wreck was demolished after the war.

During World War One the *Amazone* took part in a number of interesting actions. She carried out, among other things, surveillance duties in the Gotland region, and participated in one of the first offensive operations of the German fleet. She was part of the covering force of the squadron selected to block the Russian navy in the Baltic. The ship also participated in a deception landing operation in the area of Windau and took part in the rescue operation of the cruiser *Friedrich Carl*, which entered mined waters. An interesting action was also a failed raid to the Åland Islands. She spent the second half of the war as a hulk.

After the war, as one of the few cruisers preserved in the service of the German fleet, in 1921–1923 she underwent modernisation. During this her bow stem was re-shaped to a forward-leaning one and a number of changes were introduced in equipment and propulsion systems. She served with the *Reichsmarine* until 1930.

Her history from that period was not full of interesting events. The ship was mainly used as a training vessel. During this time, she visited a number of foreign ports, mainly in Scandinavia. In 1930 she was decommissioned, giving way to the newly built cruiser *Leipzig*.

She was later used as a hulk. She survived the war and only in 1954, over half a century (!) after she took up service with the *Kaiserliche Marine*, was she scrapped.

Not much can be written about the wartime history of the third *Gazelle* class cruiser, *Medusa*, considering that she was put into reserve even before the outbreak of the Great War. With the beginning of hostilities, she was restored to active service, but performed mainly auxiliary functions. She survived the turmoil of war and, based on the Versailles arrangements, found herself in the group of vessels that the Germans were allowed to keep.

The Reichsmarine *ships on the high seas.*

One of the few cruisers Germany was allowed to keep was Hamburg, *built in 1904.*

After renovation, together with the battleship *Hannover* and the cruisers *Berlin* and *Thetis*, she operated on the Baltic Sea under the command of the Baltic Sea Command (German: *Marinekommando der Ostsee*). She served as a depot ship for the mine sweeping forces, working on shipping routes in the waters of the North Sea. For some time, she was also the flagship of the commanding officer of the Search Forces, Commander Hugo von Rosenberg.

An interesting event was his service while he was briefly aboard, when he took the first president of the Weimar Republic, Friedrich Ebert, to East Prussia.

While performing tasks as a training ship, she visited foreign ports several times, including Sweden, Finland and Latvia. She ended her service with the *Reichsmarine* fairly quickly, as in September 1925 she gave way to the cruiser *Karlsruhe*. However, this did not mean her end. Over the following years, she was used as a hulk, and when World War Two broke out, she was rebuilt into a floating anti-aircraft battery.

After the work had been completed, which included removal of most of the superstructure, she had five 105 mm guns, two 37mm guns and six 20 mm cannons in her inventory, and in addition she had radar installed for detecting airborne targets. During the war, the ship was subordinated to the 222nd A-A Battery, staying on the so-called Vareler Tief in the southern part of Jade Bay.

Her end came on 19 April 1945, when she became the target of attacks by the Allied air forces. At that time, the ship suffered significant damage, and 23 crew members were killed on board, while 41 more were injured. Despite severe damage, her hull remained afloat.

After the war, she stood idle for a long time around one of the Wiesbadenbrücke bridges and only in 1950 did she reach Wilhelmshaven, where she was scrapped.

The service of the fourth *Gazelle* class cruiser, *Nymphe*, during World War One was very similar to the cruiser *Medusa* described earlier. At the beginning of the conflict, the ship operated mainly in the Baltic Sea, serving as a coastal defence vessel. In 1916 she was put into reserve and used as a hulk.

After the war, as one of six *Gazelle* cruisers, she was preserved in the German fleet and underwent extensive modernisation in 1922–1923, including reconstruction of the bow stem and replacement of her boilers for new ones. She served with the *Reichsmarine* mainly as a training vessel and, interestingly, as one of the few "old" cruisers in 1926–1927 she made a series of training cruises, travelling the waters of the Atlantic and Mediterranean. During her cruises she also visited a number of Scandinavian ports.

She was removed from the fleet list on 31 March 1931, giving way to the cruiser *Nürnberg*. She was scrapped in Hamburg in 1932.

Unlike the previous cruisers, the operational service of the fifth *Gazelle* cruiser – *Thetis* – was very interesting. Almost from the beginning of the war, the ship took part in a number of actions related to, among others, support for land forces in the area of Klaipeda, Palanga and Liepaja.

The ship was also the target of an attack by submarines, among which we can consider the most important the attack conducted by the British submarine E 9, commanded by Captain Max Horton, later the commanding officer of the Royal Navy submarine force.

Thetis took part in activities aimed at blocking the Russian fleet in the Baltic Sea. As a curiosity, it can be stated that she was the oldest German ship involved in crossing the Irbena Strait in August 1915. It was also then that she hit a mine, which led to significant damage. The cruiser underwent the necessary repairs, however, in the second half of the war she remained in reserve.

After the war, she underwent renovation and served with the *Reichsmarine* mainly as a training vessel. Together with the battleship *Hannover* and the cruisers *Berlin* and *Medusa*, she was subordinated to the Baltic Sea Command. For some time she was also the flagship of the 1st Torpedo Ship Flotilla. As a training ship, many times she visited foreign ports, mainly in the Baltic region.

Thetis was decommissioned on 27 March 1929, and was scrapped in Hamburg in 1930.

Of the six *Gazelle* cruisers which were allowed by the Versailles arrangements to be kept by the German fleet, *Arcona* was the youngest of them. The service of this ship can be called quite unusual, considering the fact that in 1911–1914 she was used for various types of experiments related to the use of naval mines and torpedo tubes, with the simultaneous removal of some of the original equipment.

There is not much to write about her wartime service except that she carried out minor tasks in the Baltic Sea. Later, like the others, she stood in reserve and only after being incorporated into the *Reichsmarine* did she return to active service.

Initially, together with the battleship *Braunschweig* and cruiser *Hamburg*, the ship was the core of the North Sea Command (German: *Marinekommando der Nordsee*). She performed tasks related to clearing shipping routes in the waters of the North Sea and served as a training ship, visiting a number of foreign ports. She was withdrawn from active service on 15 January 1931, after which she served as a hulk ship for several years.

With the advent of World War Two, she underwent a reconstruction similar to that carried out on her sister ship *Medusa*, and as a heavily armed floating anti-aircraft battery she was part of the Wilhelmshaven base defense system for almost the entire war. The ship was scuttled by her crew on 3 May 1945, and the wreck was cut into scrap in 1948.

The second group of cruisers permitted by the Versailles provisions were two ships belonging to the *Bremen* class, which were a kind of development of the *Gazelle* cruisers. They were slightly younger vessels, because they were put into service in 1904–1905, characterized by slightly larger dimensions and greater engine output. In external appearance the main difference between the classes was the third funnel, resulting from the increased number of boilers.

The series of cruisers of the *Bremen* class contained a total of seven ships named *Berlin, Bremen, Danzig, Hamburg, Leipzig, Lübeck* and *München*, with only *Berlin* and *Hamburg* serving with the *Reichsmarine*.

A kind of curiosity that had an impact on the cruisers described in the next chapter were the names of the ships mentioned above, which from this type began to refer to the names of German cities, thereby breaking the practice of drawing them from mythology.

List of Bremen class cruisers that took up service with the Reichsmarine –

Name	Shipyard	Keel laid	Launched	Commissioned
Berlin	Kaiserliche Werft, Danzig	1902	22.09.1903	4.04.1905
Hamburg	AG Vulcan, Stettin	1902	25.07.1903	8.03.1904

References give different characteristics for these ships. According to some, their normal displacement was 3,278 tons and the full displacement was 3,816 tons, but we can also find, for example, a full displacement of 3,756 tons. It was the same with the dimensions and power output.

We can guess that, as in the case of *Gazelle* class cruisers, one of the basic reasons for this, let us call it "confusion", was in a long series, various shipyards and changes introduced during construction, which in consequence made the characteristics of each of the ships a bit different.

Belonging to the Gazelle *class, the cruiser* Nymphe *looked nice on postcards, but in modern sea warfare she could not do much.*

Commissioned in 1905, the cruiser Berlin *with a rebuilt bow stem, which modernised her profile.*

In general, we can assume that the cruisers of the *Bremen* class had hulls 111.1 m long, 13.3 m wide and draft up to 5.6 metres, and their drive was two, 3-cylinder triple expansion steam engines with a power of 12,100 HP, to which steam was supplied by ten boilers.

Their armour was much stronger compared to their predecessors. The thickness of the armoured decks was in the range from 35 mm to 80 mm, and in the upper areas over the engine room they were 100 mm thick. The casemates and gun mounts were covered with 50 mm thick armour, while the command posts were 20 mm thick on the roofs and 100 mm thick on the sides. Basic armament was ten 105 mm guns, ten 37 mm guns and two 450 mm torpedo tubes.

As in the case of *Gazelle* cruisers, we will not describe the fate of all the ships belonging to the *Bremen* class, limiting ourselves only to those which entered service with the *Reichsmarine*.

As already mentioned, the first of these was *Berlin*, which began service with the *Kaiserliche Marine* in April 1905. It is worth adding that we can consider her as the youngest cruiser that began service with the *Reichsmarine*, but more on that later.

At first, *Berlin*'s service record was not the most interesting. Here, out of more interesting events, we can mention the activity as an escort to the imperial yacht *Hohenzollern*. The ship was used for operations in both the Baltic and North Sea waters. A noteworthy event took place only in July 1911, when *Berlin* was sent to Agadir, which had some link to the so-called "Moroccan Incident". Later on, major events include frequent participation in fleet manoeuvres, mainly as the part of the reconnaissance force.

It is also difficult to find more interesting events from her wartime history. Initially, the ship performed tasks in the Baltic as part of the 4th Reconnaissance Group. She carried out many more or less significant combat missions. She also took part in rescue operations providing, among others, help to the torpedoed cruiser *München* and to the cruiser *Danzig* which was damaged having hit a mine.

The end of the war found her in reserve, stationed for some time in Kiel and Swunemunde, and also brought – let us call it – a breakthrough in her current service after she found herself in the

A cruiser belonging to the Gazelle *class –* Arcona *– on a postcard issued before World War One.*

cruiser pool which was allowed to be retained by Germany under the treaty arrangements. After renovation, from 1922 she served in the ranks of the *Reichsmarine* as one of its most valuable vessels.

For a long time, together with the battleship *Hannover* and the cruisers *Medusa* and *Thetis*, she was subordinated to the orders of the Baltic Sea Command. Unlike the cruisers described above, her service with the Weimar Republic's navy abounded in many interesting events.

As part of her training tasks, the ship repeatedly visited a number of foreign ports, including Norway, the Netherlands, Spain and Portugal. As one of the first, she also began to perform distant training cruises, venturing to remote corners of the world. During the first of them she put to sea in 1924, heading to the Caribbean where she visited Cartagena, Colon, Veracruz, Havana, La Guaire and San Juan.

A similar voyage took place between September 1925 and March 1926. Then the ship sailed around South America, first passing through the Panama Canal. She visited ports such as Valparaiso, Montevideo, Buenos Aires, Rio de Janeiro, Bahia, St. Vincent and Spanish Vigo.

Undoubtedly, the most important event in her history was circumnavigating the globe, which lasted nearly fifteen months, for which she set off in December 1927. It is worth adding it was one of the few, and undoubtedly one of the most important, cruises by German ships at that time.

As a result of general wear and tear, *Berlin* was decommissioned in March 1929. She stood idle until 1935 when she began to be used as a residential hulk. In this capacity she was used during World War Two, which she managed to survive and it was only in May 1947 that she was scuttled in the waters of the Skagerrak.

The history of the second of the Bremen class cruisers, *Hamburg*, was similar. This ship began service with the *Kaiserliche Marine* slightly earlier than *Berlin*, in March 1904. In her case for almost the entire period preceding the outbreak of World War One she was subordinated to the submarine force as the flagship of the U-boats. She was assigned to escort the Imperial Yacht *Hohenzollern* several times, and in 1909 she took part, together with British and French ships, in operations in the Anatolia region.

After the outbreak of war, she participated in many naval operations in both the North Sea and the Baltic. One of the most important events was her collision with torpedo ship S-21, which as a result of the damage sank and 36 members of her crew perished.

Noteworthy was also her participation in the Battle of Jutland, during which she suffered serious damage caused by four direct hits, which in addition led to the death of 14 crew members and another 25 were wounded.

The rest of the war was not so abundant in tragic events. After renovation, the ship returned to service, but was mainly used as an HQ vessel for the submarine force, and in this capacity she survived until the end of the war.

In accordance with the provisions of the Treaty of Versailles, she took up service with the *Reichsmarine*, as one of its most valuable ships, being subordinated, together with the battleship *Braunschweig* and cruiser *Arcona*, to the orders of the North Sea Command. Initially, she performed tasks related to clearing shipping routes in the North Sea. Interestingly, she also found herself part of the mine sweeping force designated for similar operations far in the north, where, among others, mines laid at the entrance to Kola Bay were cleared.

Introduced into service in 1901, the cruiser Medusa *was one of the oldest cruisers that found themselves in the* Reichsmarine.

Like her sister ship *Berlin*, *Hamburg* also performed many tasks related to training cadets on a number of long-haul cruises. One of the most important was the one on which she set off in February 1926. Her route led around the world, covering the Canary Islands, Cape Verde, the Caribbean, and further through the Panama Canal, ports in Central America and the west coast of the United States, Hawaii, Japan, the Philippines, Dutch East Indies and Colombo, and on through the Suez Canal to ports in the Mediterranean and Vigo in Spain, after which on 20 March 1927 she returned to her home waters.

On 30 June 1927, she was put into reserve, and four years later she was removed from the fleet list. Over the following years and during World War Two, she served as a hulk, and her days came to an end when in 1944 she was bombed while stationed in Hamburg. The wreck was raised in 1949 and scrapping was completed in 1956.

Having become acquainted with the fate of the first cruisers incorporated into service with the *Reichsmarine*, it is easy to see that the navy, created on the ruins of the once proud *Kaiserliche Marine*, in the first years of its existence was a collection of completely outdated ships of doubtful combat capabilities.

To make matters worse, the situation in the country left much to be desired. Apart from the aforementioned economic problems, growing anarchy effectively inhibited all attempts to establish order, including activities carried out by the National Assembly of the Weimar Republic to the new German fleet.

The Reichsmarine *cruisers while in harbour.*

Entanglement in the political quarrels of many high-ranking navy officers, and above all the March coup d'etat attempt of 1920 commonly known as the Kappa Coup, could not be without influence on efforts to sort out the post-war chaos. Flames of rebellion then engulfed almost all major centres of the new navy, making matters worse. What is even worse, Admiral von Troth was arrested for overt support of the coup, and as many as one hundred and seventy other naval officers were arrested with him. This was too much for the beginnings of a fleet formed almost from scratch, and it was only the actions of the then Defense Minister Otto Gessler that managed to control the situation.

The Great Admiral Erich Raeder was a great advocate for the construction of large warships including cruisers.

It is worth adding that those were days when the careers of later *Kriegsmarine* commanders who had a lot to say about the term "The Third Reich Cruisers" began to crystallise. For example, the later Grand Admiral Erich Raeder, then with the rank of Commander, was at that time responsible for the implementation of tasks related to the reorganization of the *Reichsmarine* officer corps at the head of the Central Administration Department in Berlin.

His career, undoubtedly supported by the person of Rear Admiral Hans Zenker who commanded the North Sea force, looked very promising at that time. But not much later we hear about Admiral Raeder again when, as an advisor to Admiral von Trotha, he found himself in the circle of suspects participating in the said Coup. Only a quick transfer to the navy archives section, for which certainly Zenker was responsible, allowed him to survive this difficult period and once the situation calmed down, he continued his career with the *Reichsmarine*, rising successively to the ranks of Rear Admiral in 1922, Vice Admiral in 1925 and finally in 1928 Admiral, taking over the position of Chief of Staff of the Navy.

A similar problem had to be faced by the second of the famous *Kriegsmarine* commanders, Admiral Karl Dönitz, an extremely important figure considering the fact that he was appointed in the last days of World War Two as the successor to Adolf Hitler. While performing the duties of the commander of one of the torpedo boats, he was also caught up in the March coup and probably only thanks to a bit of luck he survived that dangerous time to later continue his service with the *Reichsmarine*.

The first armoured ship that entered service, Deutschland. *Together with the earlier cruiser* Emden, *she became a symbol of the revival of the German fleet.*

Much was also going on in the life of Adolf Hitler, without whom it would be difficult to talk about "The Third Reich Cruisers". As a thirty-year-old corporal at that time, he was entering the world of high politics, having left the ranks of the army only two weeks after the failure of the Kappa Coup and joining the German Workers' Party, in short the DAP (German – *Deutsche Arbeiter Partei*), known later as the National-Socialist German Workers' Party.

We all know about how his political career unfolded and what its effects were, but that is all politics, and we are interested in ships.

When this extremely difficult time for Germany began to stabilize, the *Reichsmarine* slowly began to function. The aforementioned problems prevented the entry into service of all the ships described above, so that in 1922 the German Navy could muster only the two battleships, *Braunschweig* and *Hannover*, and five cruisers, *Arcona*, *Berlin*, *Hamburg*, *Medusa* and *Thetis*.

With the vast German coasts stretching from the Baltic to the North Sea, they were only symbolic, to put it mildly, and to make matters worse they had to be divided into two groups. The battleship *Braunschweig* and cruisers *Arcona* and *Hamburg* became the core of the North Sea Command (German: *Marinekommando der Nordsee*), while *Hannover* and the cruisers *Berlin*, *Medusa* and *Thetis* were subordinated to the orders of the Baltic Sea Command (German: *Marinekommando der Ostsee*).

Admiral Karl Dönitz also had a lot to say about the activities of German cruisers. He took over the position of the commanding officer after the resignation of Admiral Raeder.

Considering what power the *Kaiserliche Marine* had presented a few years previously, for the remaining German commanders it was undoubtedly a bitter pill to swallow, but Germany was a nation that could always take care of itself. Despite struggling with many problems, according to one of the provisions of the Versailles Treaty allowing the replacement of old ships with new ones, only thirty months from the signing of the said document, in December 1921 a keel was laid for the first cruiser ship in post-war Germany, on the slipway of the Kriegsmarinewerft shipyard in Wilhelmshaven.

Undoubtedly, this was a great achievement for the German shipbuilding industry and the *Reichsmarine* commander – Admiral Paul Behncke. The ship herself, later known as *Emden*, was not the pinnacle of technology, in many respects giving way to constructions of cruisers built in other countries, but that was not the only thing at the time. Many Germans saw in her construction signs of a revival of the former power of the fleet, which made the shortcomings in her design and armament secondary.

Time went by and the possibilities of building new ships increased with it. In 1924 the keel was laid for the first destroyer, and in 1926 for three further cruisers named *Königsberg*, *Karlsruhe* and *Köln*, constructions not without flaws, but very innovative and with higher combat values, not comparable to *Emden*'s.

The keel laying in February 1929 for the first *Deutschland* class armoured ship, i.e. one of the three commonly known as pocket battleships, was a breakthrough.

List of major *Reichsmarine ships* 1919–1935

Battleships	Pocket Battleships	Cruisers
Schleswig-Holstein	*Deutschland*	*Amazone*
Schlesien	*Admiral Scheer*	*Arcona*
Hannover	*Admiral Graf Spee*	*Berlin*
Braunschweig		*Nymphe*
Elsass		*Medusa*
Hessen		*Thetis*
Lothringen – in reserve		*Emden*
Preussen – in reserve		*Königsberg*
Zähringen - converted to a hulk		*Karlsruhe*
		Köln
		Leipzig
		Nürnberg

The *Reichsmarine* was changing but slowly, and with time new ships were commissioned, namely the warships that broke the limitations which had been set in the Versailles Treaty.

Interestingly, the man who passed into history as the man who threw off the Versailles "shackles" – Hitler – was still far from such bold moves.

The Germans quickly began to disregard the Versailles limits in a calculated manner, and excellent proof of this was, among others, the "Lohmann affair". A former naval officer, Walter Lohmann, on the instructions of the fleet top brass conducted secret undertakings related to the implementation of military matters prohibited by Versailles. Many secret projects were carried out abroad. Banned types of weapons were secretly bought and Germans learned how to build them.

Germany and the mentality of many citizens of the country also changed. On 30 January 1933, Adolf Hitler came to power, taking up the positions of President and Chancellor of the *Reich*. In August 1934, he became Chief and Chancellor of the *Reich* in one.

In May 1935, the *Reichsmarine* was renamed the *Kriegsmarine*, and shortly afterwards in June, a maritime agreement was concluded in which Great Britain agreed to the development of the German Navy, which was not to exceed tonnage of 35% relative to the Royal Navy.

Following this, the expansion of the German fleet had gained momentum. From the slipways of the shipyards in Kiel, Wilhelmshaven and Hamburg, new ships with increasing displacement and more powerful armament began to descend onto the water.

This also applied to cruisers, although not many were built, but they entered service increasingly larger and stronger. Up until the outbreak of World War Two, the *Kriegsmarine* flag was raised on a total on seven such vessels and another two were put into service during the war.

They were classified as light cruisers: *Emden*, *Königsberg*, *Karlsruhe*, *Köln*, *Leipzig*, *Nürnberg*, and heavy cruisers: *Admiral Hipper*, *Blücher* and *Prinz Eugen*. Their fate we will learn in the following chapters.

Emden
The First One

The *Emden* can hardly be called a cruiser in the full sense of the word, but construction and commissioning into the *Reichsmarine* of a ship of this type was of great importance to the Germans.

It did not matter that the design of the ship was based on ideas from the World War One era, and that her armament left much to be desired. What was important that she existed at all, and gave the Germans hope to rebuild the power of a fleet that once equalled the Royal Navy. Just the building itself of this vessel, in a country overwhelmed by internal unrest in which inflation was breaking new records, which lacked materials for shipbuilding not to mention technical staff, was a real feat.

Not without significance also was the involvement in the political "scuffle" of many high-ranking *Reichsmarine* officers, which often manifested in the characteristics of mutiny, such as when a group of right-wing officers stood by the side of Wolfgang Kapp – a radical nationalist associated today with the so-called Kapp-Lüttwitz coup.

The flames of rebellion that engulfed Kiel, Wilhelmshaven and other naval bases at that time could not be without effect on the functioning or development of the fleet, whose core was obsolete ships with negligible combat value.

Once the situation in the country had been controlled and the post of Chief of Staff of the Navy had been taken over in November 1920 by Vice Admiral Paul Behncke, within the German fleet something started to happen. Germany, having realized that old and worn out cruisers, built

The Emden *was the first cruiser type ship to be built in Germany after World War One. It can be seen at first glance that her equipment left much to be desired, and the clouds of black smoke from coal-fired boilers testify to the not-so-innovative solutions applied as far as the propulsion is concerned.*

over twenty years ago and serving in the recent war, left much to be desired, decided they must be given priority.

First of all, it was necessary to modernize and renovate all the vessels that were allowed to be kept after Versailles, but their replacement was also taken into account almost immediately. On the short list was the cruiser *Niobe*, launched in 1899 – the technical condition of which was catastrophic and did not permit her to be operational in the full sense of the word.

But the design and construction of a new ship is one thing and the reality of the country that had lost the war is another. The problems faced by the head of *Marineleitung* would be encountered in every possible area.

Apart from the above mentioned ones, Vice Admiral Behncke could not count on his own research centre nor any of the privately-owned shipyards on which the expansion of the Kaiser's fleet had mainly relied upon earlier. According to the provisions of one of the points of the Treaty of Versailles, these were no longer allowed to build warships.

The largest state-owned arsenal to date was the *Kaiserliche Werft Danzig*, but due to being in the Free City of Gdańsk (*Freie Stadt Danzig*) it could no longer be taken into account, in the same way as the second "privatized" one in Kiel, which now operated as the Deutsche Werke.

Only the shipyard in Wilhelmshaven, with relatively low production capability, was available, but there was no other option. What is worse tonnage limits, limiting the displacement of the newly-designed ship to just 6,000 tons, did not allow the construction of a reasonably combat-worthy vessel, and its counterparts in other navies significantly exceeded this figure.

When starting work on the new ship, it was decided that it would be based on the design of the light cruisers of the *Cöln* class. It is worth noting this was one of the last ships of this type, which was introduced into service with the *Kaiserliche Marine* before the end of World War One[1]. These were ships whose displacement (standard one was 5,620 tons) and main battery (eight 150 mm guns) coincided with treaty restrictions, so seemed to be the most appropriate to be treated as the initial design.

In addition they were the most technically advanced vessels, reflecting the experience of German designers just a few years before. Of course, the newly designed cruiser was not to be a copy of the *Cöln* class ships, but rather that was a base on which the appropriate adjustments and improvements were made.

Interestingly, it was originally planned that the first cruiser of the Weimar Republic would be armed with eight guns placed in four twin-barrel turrets, arranged two forward and two aft. However, there was no consent for such a design from the committee supervising the project, in which the French, reluctant about the entire programme, had much to say, and they ruled out these plans.

A few images taken during the launching ceremony of Emden *on 7 January 1925.*

Finally, it was decided on a design that was used on *Cöln* class vessels, i.e. eight guns on single mounts "scattered" on the decks along the entire ship. This solution is today recognized as one of the main disadvantages of the *Emden*, which during the Third Reich period as well as World War Two was extremely outdated. This led the ship to be treated as a second-class vessel not destined for major tasks, thus limiting her role to a training ship.

Either way, in the days when the ship was designed and built, the *Emden* was a particularly valuable ship for the Germans, when compared with the much-to-be-desired cruisers in service, although it is worth noting that she came close to not being built at all.

When the matter of her construction and the allocation of appropriate funds appeared in the *Reichstag* forum, anti-war parties sharply criticized the project, wanting to spend the money necessary for her construction on other matters related to the reconstruction of the country, which it is worth

1 Only two of the eight planned vessels of the *Cöln* and *Dresden* classes, entering service in January and March 1918, were completed. Both ships were scuttled by their own crews after internment in Scapa Flow in June 1919. It is worth adding here that in some accounts you can also find information that the *Emden* project was based on the cruisers of the *Königsberg* (II) class, built as a series preceding the *Cöln* type.

remembering was at that time in a catastrophic state. The political struggle lasted a long time and it was only in March 1921 that the *Reichstag* finally approved the funds that allowed the signing a contract with the *Reichsmarinewerft* shipyard in Wilhelmshaven, under which she was to be the first warship built in Germany's post-Great War history.

The keel for the new cruiser, designated at that time as "*Kreuzer* A" or "*Ersatz Niobe*", was laid on 8 December 1921 on slipway No. I of the said shipyard, which – it is worth adding – soon changed its name to *Marinewerft*, and the construction received the shipbuilding No. 100.

Interestingly, the aforementioned contract was not signed until 20 February 1922, when the first outlines of the hull appeared on the slipway, but the pace of the works themselves, despite the enormous interest of both public opinion and fleet representatives, was not the quickest. It was a time when the war that had ended not long ago was still taking its toll. Everything was unavailable.

Building materials, personnel, tools and, of course, money, which was sometimes worthless immediately after it had been issued as a result of rampant inflation.

The cruiser's hull slipping onto the water.

There was also a problem with subcontractors, many of whom had not yet managed to shake off the post-war turmoil and ensure regular supplies, and strikes that were breaking out in various regions of the country, leading to unplanned stoppages.

It was also important that the French were occupying the Ruhr, from which the Krupp factories supplied steel for shipbuilding, and they did not make it easier for Germany to build a new ship by supposedly blocking, among others, the turrets we mentioned above[2].

Finally, after more than three years of construction, on 7 January 1925, the hull of the cruiser *Emden* floated on the water. It was a huge event, which would not be short of high state dignitaries, invited guests and navy officers with the new head of *Marineleitung* – Admiral Hans Zenker – at the helm and huge crowds of inhabitants of Wilhelmshaven. Also, these were times when no one had yet heard of the Third Reich and the Nazis associated with it, and so many sought in lofty speeches the first signs of the rebirth of Germany.

The godmother of the ship was Mrs. Jutta von Müller, widow of the World War One *Emden*'s skipper Karl von Müller, who by the traditional breaking of a bottle of champagne against her hull gave the newly built ship the famous name *Emden*[3]

It cannot be denied that the launching of the ship was a great achievement for the aforementioned Admiral Behncke and his staff, who managed to develop and later push through the cruiser's design, leading to a keel laying only thirty months after the signing of the Versailles Treaty (!). Now not much was needed to complete it.

Name of the ship

The name of the cruiser came from the city of Emden, located in north-western Germany at the mouth of the River Ems. Its origins date to around 800 AD and the current number of inhabitants was estimated at about 50 thousand people. The city itself is now one of the largest and one of the most important industrial centres and one of the Volkswagen plants is located there. During World War Two it suffered severely, having been on the route of Allied air raids on Germany.

Interestingly, unlike the hull construction, the fitting out works were carried out at a truly express speed and on 15 October 1925 the cruiser officially entered service. Despite many shortcomings, obviously caused by the Versailles restrictions already mentioned, the *Emden* was an extremely interesting vessel.

2 The French occupation of this region was to be a form of pressure on the German government in the event of non-payment of war reparations and a way of controlling orders placed, among others, at the Krupp plant – the main weapon manufacturer.

3 The cruiser *Emden* described in this chapter was the third German warship to be given this name, although undoubtedly the most famous was *Emden* (I) built in 1906–1909, belonging to the Dresden class (4,268 t, dimensions 117.9 m long, 13.5 beam and 5.5 draft).

This vessel has gone down in history as one of the most effective German raiders during World War One, sinking 16 merchant vessels with a total tonnage of over 70,000 tons (three more were taken over as prizes). She ended her life on 9 November 1914 under the fire of the Australian cruiser *Sydney*.

The second *Emden* was the Königsberg class cruiser built in 1914–1916 (displacement 7,215 t, 151.4 m long, 14.3 m beam and 6.0 m draft). This ship was not so spectacularly successful, although her service was also marked by many interesting events. It came to an end on 21 June 1919 at Scapa Flow, where the ship was seriously damaged during the scuttling operation of the German fleet.

Her hull, with beautiful and harmonious shapes, was characterized by a slightly forward sloping bow, cruiser type stem and the set-off on 1/3 of the length of the decks.

Overall length was 155.1 m, length on the waterline 150.5 m, beam 14.3 m, the draft, depending on the displacement, ranged from 5.15 m to 5.38 m, and the hull broadside height reached 8.96 m.

The construction was based on the longitudinal-transverse bonding system, which divided it into 23 compartments.

The double bottom, where the fuel tanks found their place, stretched for 2/3 of the length of the hull between frames No. 22 and No. 90

A kind of curiosity is the fact that it was during the construction of the *Emden* that the Germans for the first time widely used an innovative method of joining elements using electric welding, which was later commonly used in the construction of subsequent ships.

This, of course, resulted in significant weight savings, so necessary for the construction of ships subjected to the treaty displacement limitations, and yet the *Emden* as well as later K class cruisers or the famous "pocket battleships" were just such as they were.

One of *Emden*'s main disadvantages was her propulsion, partly based on coal-fired boilers, which at that time could have been be considered a kind of technological step backwards criticized by many specialists.

It consisted of two sets of Brown-Boveri & Cie steam turbines, manufactured at the BBC plant in Munich, with a total power of 45,900 HP driving two propellers with a diameter of 3.75 m. Each of the units consisted of high and low pressure turbines and reduction gears.

Ten boilers supplied them with steam, of which six were Schulz-Marine type fired with liquid fuel.

These were boilers with a total heating area of 3,009 m^2 supplying steam with an operating pressure of 16 atm.

The other four boilers also belonged to the Schulz-Marine type, with the difference that they were coal-fired and their heating area was 1,629 m^2.

The maximum speed of *Emden* was estimated at 29 knots, although on trials she accomplished 29.4 knots, while the sailing range with liquid fuel supply of 300 t and 875 t coal was 5,290 NM at 18 knots, and 6,750 NM at 14 knots.

A kind of curiosity is the fact that some power generators, generating 220 V electricity with a total power of 420 kW, were placed in a compartment at the very bow part, quite far from the engine room and boiler room described earlier.

The ship was of course also equipped with armour, although it is difficult to speak of armouring in the full sense of the word.

For a length of about 120 metres, the hull was covered with a 2.9 m wide and 50 mm thick armour belt, of which 1.3 m was below the waterline.

The transverse bulkhead was 40 mm thick, similar to the "armoured" deck in the midships area above the ammunition magazines. In the remaining parts it was only 20 mm thick.

The thickness of the armoured decks, sloping at a 40° angle, varied between 20 and 40 mm. The sides of the command post were 50 mm thick, the roof 20 mm, while the communication shaft leading to it formed a pipe with a wall thickness of 100 mm.

The ship's armament is also perceived as one of its main disadvantages.

Despite the original proposal of having the cruiser equipped with fully enclosed main battery turrets, the *Emden*'s armament eventually comprised of eight old SK C 16 150 mm L/45 guns, installed on single MPL C 16 mounts in semi-open mounts.[4]

It was quite an old weapon, developed during the Great War, characterized by a range of 20,000 m and muzzle velocity of 835 m/s.

The barrel elevation was in the range from -10° to +27°, while the weight of the entire gun without protective shields was 11.4 tons.

---

4 At this point, it is worth noting that the names of guns we usually apply i.e. the type first, and then the calibre in millimetres. However, the Germans used a slightly different scheme, first giving the calibre of a given gun in centimetres, then the type with the abbreviation "SK" from the German *Schiffs Kanone* and finally the date of building expressed by the capital letter "C" – from the German *Construktionsjahr* (in 1940 the abbreviation SK – *Schiffs Kanone* – was replaced by the abbreviation KM – *Kanone Marine*). For example for the 380 mm guns on the *Bismark* and *Tirpitz* it looked like this: 38 cm SK C/34 – i.e. 380 mm *Marine Kanone* (SK) Model 1934 (C/34). In addition, the armament of all major German ships of World War Two was divided into four basic groups: main battery "SA" – *Schwerer Artillerie* – 280 mm and 380 mm, medium guns "MA" – *Mittel Artillerie* – 150 mm, heavy anti-aircraft artillery "*SFlak* "of 88 mm and 105 mm calibres and light anti-aircraft artillery "*Lflak*" of the two basic calibres 20 mm and 37 mm.

A commemorative postcard issued for the launching of Emden.

The arrangement of these guns' location on board the *Emden* was almost a copy of what was on the *Cöln* class cruisers. The first two were on the bow (one on the deck, the other on the superstructure), the next two were on the broadsides about 1/3 of the length of the hull from the bow. The next pair was also on the sides a little further aft, while the last pair were on the stern deck arranged like the bow guns – one on the deck and the other on the aft superstructure.

The main battery was complemented by two SK C 13 88 mm L/45 guns mounted on the main superstructure deck behind the second funnel, based on the MPL C13 mounts and equipped with very characteristic semi-circular protective armour shields, also known as masks.

Like the main battery, they were not the newest weapons with a range, muzzle velocity of 790 m/s and barrel elevation angle of + 43° with a range of 14,100 m. The entire setup was complemented by two 500 mm twin-barrel torpedo tubes placed on the sides by the fore mast.

It is worth adding at this point that originally it was planned to equip the ship with four such sets, two of which were to be found more or less where the third pair of 150 mm guns was eventually located. However, due to subsequent changes in the design and abandoning the main battery turrets, there was no space for the additional torpedo tubes.

To direct the cannons were three rangefinders with a 4-meter base at the top of the mast and two on the bow and stern superstructure, and two rangefinders with a 3-metre base intended for directing the torpedo tubes.

Let us now leave the description of the ship's construction for a while and focus on its history, which, as we remember, was interrupted on 15 October 1925.

Commander Richard Foerster was appointed the first commander of *Emden* – a man with vast experience whose career with the navy began long before the start of World War One, and ended many years later as an Admiral. It was under his orders that the most important of the *Reichsmarine*'s ships set off for the first sea trials to find out her true value, and unfortunately it turned out almost immediately that *Emden*'s designers had got it wrong.

Towering over the entire silhouette, the characteristic tubular mast housing the fire control station at its top turned out to be too high and heavy, leading to the creation of quite significant listing even in relatively calm seas. It was not long after that the ship was again at the shipyard quay where her tangent mast, protruding over 34 metres above the water as built, would be shortened by 7 metres.

In the next months, the ship went out to sea every now and again to carry out further tests, and above all to train the crew, which consisted of almost five hundred men.

The first interesting event can be noted in the spring of 1926, when the *Emden* took part in fleet manoeuvres as the flagship of *Befehlshaber der Seestreitkräfte in der Nordsee*, in English "Commander of the North Sea Maritime Force". As one can easily guess, the cruiser, although she could not boast of too many revolutionary design features, powerful armament or modern engines, at that time was the most important ship of this era.

In the summer, the ship's activity was mainly focused on training duties and, interestingly, in September she was officially reclassified as a training cruiser, which, as you can easily guess, can be traced to her deficiencies mentioned many times above.

There is no deception that, beyond propaganda, the construction of this ship for action in a modern sea engagement no longer made sense, unless her service would immediately involve the training of the future *Reichsmarine* and of course the later *Kriegsmarine*. If we would like to approach the matter this way, it can be safely said that the *Emden* was quite good at it.

After all, the main battery guns on semi-open mounts, plus both coal and oil-fired boiler rooms, were great for training purposes, giving future officers, gun crews etc., an excellent opportunity to learn in practice the features and operation of such equipment.

In October, the *Emden* went to the shipyard again, in which, apart from a typical check, several changes were introduced that significantly affected her appearance. The height of one of the funnels was changed, and the fore mast, which had been rebuilt once, was equipped with a 16-metre

The profile of Emden *from the initial period of her service.*

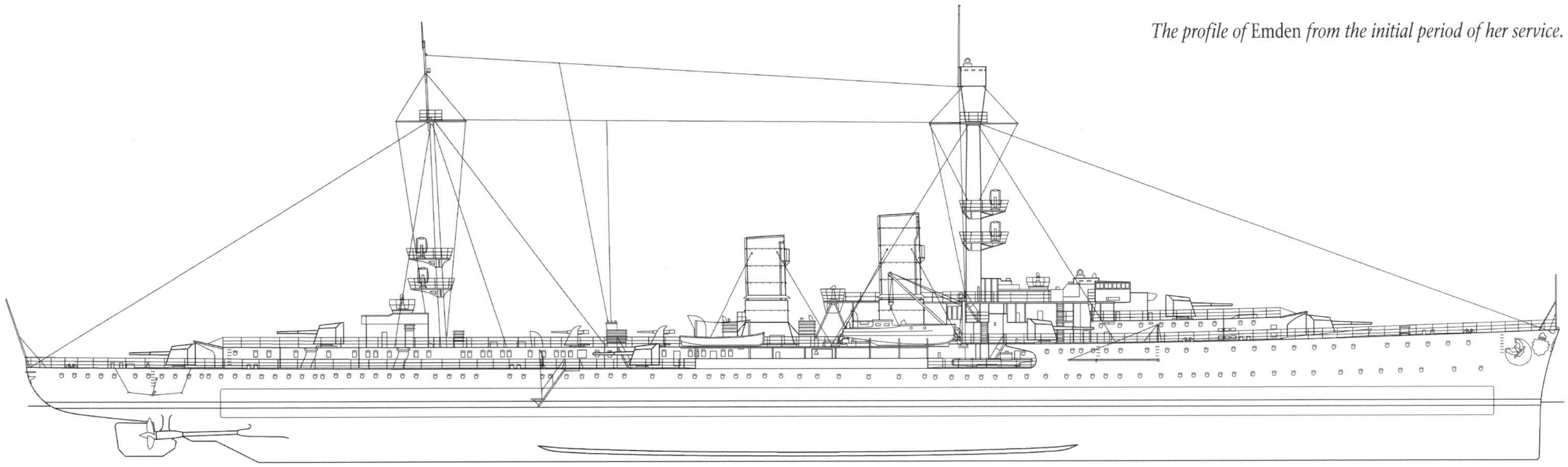

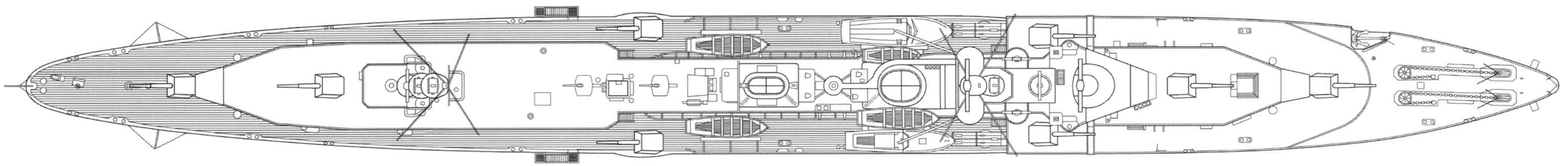

A simplified sectional drawing depicting the internal layout of the Emden.

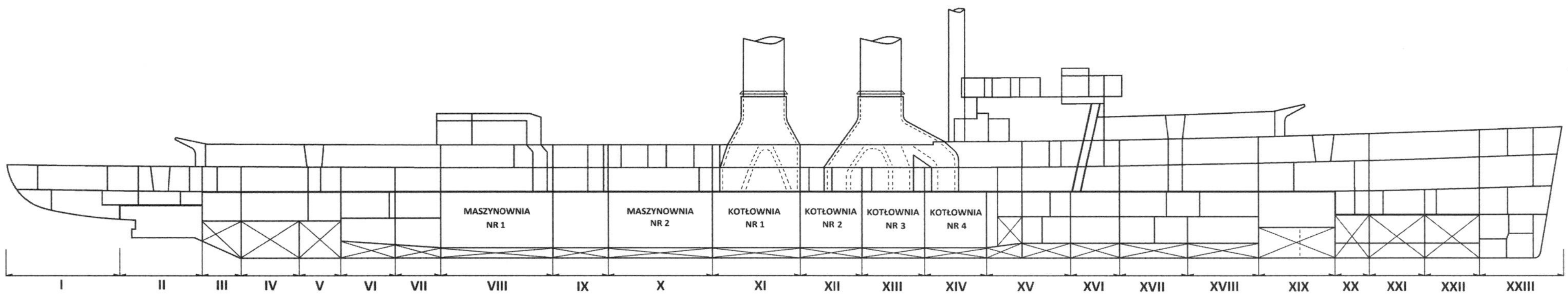

jib-boom, and the aft one was lowered. This was the second modernization of the ship in just one year of service, which can only testify to the imperfections of the entire project, but let us leave that to the specialists.

Shortly after she had left the shipyard, *Emden* received an extremely interesting task, which was a distant tour, and as it would later turn out, was going to be the longest cruise in her history. Her route, on which she set sail on 14 November 1926 from Wilhelmshaven, led successively through Spain, the Canary Islands and then circling the African continent, the island of St. Helena, Cape Town and Mombasa via the Indian Ocean to Saban and Padang.

The pride of the Reichsmarine *entering service.*

Undoubtedly, one of the most important places to which the cruiser called during this cruise was the Cocos Islands, where she found herself on 14 March 1927, and the reason for visiting this place was that her predecessor, the cruiser *Emden* (I), had been sunk there on 9 November 1914 after an unequal fight with the larger and better-armed Australian cruiser *Sydney*.

After a solemn mass at the wreck of the ship commemorating 134 German sailors killed in this engagement, the *Emden* moved on, visiting the islands of Java and the Celebes, then ports in Japan, the Aleutians and finally the United States.

The further route led south to Mexico, Ecuador, Peru and Chile, and then, rounding Cape Horn, she headed for the Falkland Islands – another important place for the Germans, where on 8 December 1914 the force of the East Asian Cruiser Squadron of Vice Admiral Count Maximilian von Spee was crushed by the Admiral Doveton Sturdee's Squadron.

Here the memory of the fallen was also honoured, and later the cruiser went on, visiting ports in Argentina, Brazil and Haiti, and then the Azores and again Spain from where she went directly back to Germany, reaching at Wilhelmshaven on 14 March 1928.

It is easy to recount the cruise, of which can be said that it was one of the longest in the *Reichsmarine*'s training ships history. It lasted over 16 months and, apart from the obvious injection of a large dose of priceless experience for the trained crew in such a long sailing, it also brought a lot of good for German foreign relations, as after losing the war they were pushed to the proverbial side track.

The *Emden* herself was welcomed enthusiastically back home, where the press wrote about her unusual voyage and, although perceived as a hero, the ship required a thorough refurbishment. In the end, the ship had circumnavigated the world and her extensively used engines required major repairs, and the crew and the officers needed rest.

Little can be written about the history of the *Emden*'s service over the next few months.

Only in September can we note another interesting event, which was the change in command of the ship, when on 24 September 1928 Commander Lieutenant Lothar von Arnauld de la Perière-took took over from the outgoing Commander Foerster. He is another interesting figure, perceived as one of the most distinguished, although many historians are of the opinion he was the most outstanding U-boat commander of World War One with 194 merchant ships of a total tonnage of over 453,000 BRT – a result worthy of many urban legends.

Could one choose a better character for the position of commander of a training ship staffed with a large group of cadets, for whom he was undoubtedly a man worthy to follow? Rather not. Therefore, when on 5 December 1928 the *Emden* put to sea on another long voyage, for many members of the cruiser's crew it was a major experience, giving them a sense of both great adventure and the acquisition of skill under the orders of the great hero.

The route of the cruise itself, in terms of distance as well as the exotic nature of the places visited, was not far behind the previous one. Having left Wilhelmshaven, she headed as before for Spain, and then, rounding the Iberian Peninsula, she entered the Mediterranean Sea, calling in turn at Cartagena and Naples, and later visited the ports of Greece and Turkey and finally passed through the Suez Canal to visit Aden and Mombasa in turn.

Her further route led through the waters of the Indian Ocean to the Dutch East Indies, and later Australia, New Zealand, Fiji and finally Samoa – the former German colony lost to Britain as war reparations after the Great War.

Of course, this was not the end of the "trip" and having left the archipelago, the *Emden* went on, heading to Hawaii and further to San Diego, from where she lined up at the entrance to the Panama Canal, through which she passed as one of the few cruisers of the later Third Reich to do so.

The further route led to the Caribbean, then the Canary Islands and directly to Wilhelmshaven, where the ship arrived on 9 December 1929, after not much more than twelve months of extremely interesting sailing.

Less interestingly, the next such cruise *Emden* undertook started on 13 January 1930, after visiting the shipyards as any necessary maintenance was carried out. However, it was a much shorter cruise compared to the previous ones and significantly different from them even in terms of the direction, which now included the ports of Madeira, and then further west to the Caribbean Sea to St. Thomas, the Gulf of Mexico and New Orleans.

Further on, the route led to Jamaica, Puerto Rico and Charleston in South Carolina, from where the ship headed east to the Canary Islands, Las Palmas and Santa Cruz, then back on 13 May 1930 to Wilhelmshaven. In the homeland, as usual, time was then largely passed at the shipyards.

It was not until 11 October that we can note anything interesting, again connected with another change in the position of the skipper which was now taken over by Cdr. Lieutenant Robert Witthoeft-Emden – another extremely interesting character. He could boast of, among others, participation in the battle near the Cocos Islands on board the first *Emden*, for which he was awarded the Iron Cross and the right to add the second part to his name, i.e "*Emden*"[5].

It is worth noting here that from a group of sixteen skippers who would later be given command of the *Emden*, as many as twelve achieved high promotions to the ranks of two Rear Admirals, seven Vice Admirals, two Admirals and one Grand Admiral – that is, the highest rank in the military naval forces in the officer force of the *Reich*'s Navy.

Commanders of the ship:

- 15 October 1925 – 23 September 1928 – Cdr. Richard Foerster
- 24 September 1928 – 10 October 1930 – Cdr. Lt. Lothar von Arnauld de la Perière
- 11 October 1930 – 21 March 1932 – Cdr. Lt. Robert Witthoeft-Emden
- 22 March 1932 – 1 April 1933 – Cdr. Werner Grassmann
- 29 September 1934 – 21 September 1935 – Cdr. Lieutenant Karl Dönitz
- 21 September 1935 – 25 August 1936 – Cdr. Johannes Bachmann
- 26 August 1936 – 19 June 1937 – Cdr. Walter Georg Lohmann
- 20 June 1937 – 27 July 1937 – Cdr. Lieutenant Bernhard Liebetanz
- 28 July 1937 – 15 June 1938 – Cdr. Lt. Leopold Bürkner
- 15 June 1938 – 5 May 1939 – Cdr. Paul Wever
- 8 May 1939 – 28 August 1940 – Cdr. Werner Lange
- 29 August 1940 – 19 July 1942 – Cdr. Hans Mirow
- 20 July 1942 – 9 September 1943 – Cdr. Friedrich Traugott Schmidt
- 10 September 1943 – March 1944 – Cdr. Hans Heningst
- March 1944 – January 1945 – Cdr. Lieutenant Hans-Eberhard Meisner
- January 1945 – March 1945 – Cdr. Wolfgang Kähler
- March 1945 – April 1945 – Cdr. Lieutenant Ernst-Ludwig Wickmann

For her next, and fourth, long distance training cruise the *Emden* set off on 1 December 1930, heading to the port of Vigo on the west coast of Spain, and then through the Gibraltar Straits to the Mediterranean, and then via the Suez Canal she entered the waters of the Red Sea. After a short stop in Aden, she headed across the Arabian Sea to Ceylon, visiting the ports of Colombo and Trincomalee en route.

Further along the ship's route were Bangkok, Shanghai, Nanjing and Japan, with the harbours of Nagasaki, Osaka, Nii Jima, Tsuruga, Hakkodate and Yokohama visited.

Later, the *Emden* headed south for Guam, and then to the west, to the Dutch East Indies, from where she was not far from a place that was significant, above all for the ship's commander, the Cocos Islands.

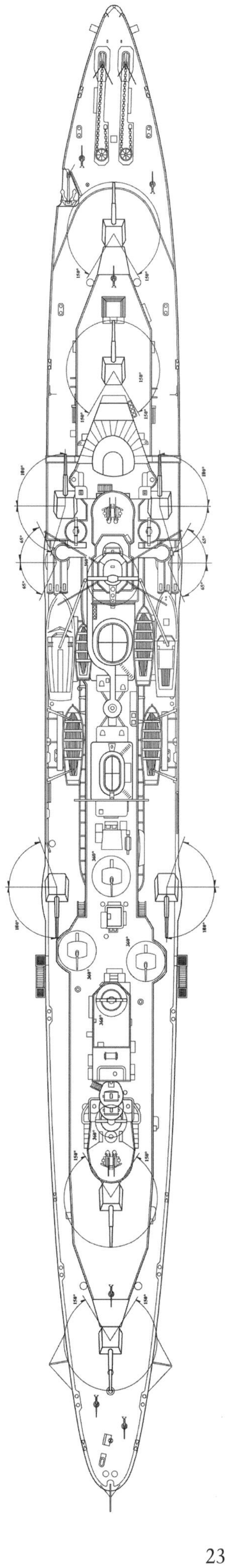

A simplified scheme of the range of angles at which individual gun positions could fire.

5 Cdr. Lieutenant Robert Witthoeft-Emden was at the time torpedo officer on the *Emden*.

In the interwar period, the Emden's *profile often became an inspiration for postcards issued at that time.*

Heading further west through the Indian Ocean and Mauritius, the ship reached Durban and East London, and then, circling the African continent, visited Lobito, Luande, and Freetown, St. Vincent, Las Palmas and Santander, from where she headed back on 8 December 1931, when she called again into Wilhelmshaven.

Back home, as usual, the ship was sent for shipyard inspection and then, unlike previous years, she did not embark on another cruise, giving way to the new cruiser *Karlsruhe*, which from May 1930 had made long-distance international cruises similar to the *Emden*'s.

According to the orders of the fleet command dated 1 January 1932, the *Emden* was again transformed into a combat-worthy ship with her assignment to the reconnaissance force led by Rear Admiral Conrad Albrecht, *Befelshaber der Aufklarunskräfte*. In this new role, the ship took part in a series of exercises in the waters of the North Sea and Baltic Sea, cooperating with the cruisers *Koln*, *Königsberg* and *Leipzig*, among others.

An important event was another change in the position of commander of the ship, which was taken over by Cdr. Grassmann from the outgoing Cdr. Lieutenant Robert Witthoeft-Emden.

Quite interesting was the *Emden*'s cruise in the Atlantic Ocean between 21 February and 15 March 1933, when she was accompanying the newest *Reichsmarine* cruiser *Leipzig*, which was conducting a series of broadside and fire control system tests at that time. Both ships then visited Funchal and Las Palmas.

In April, she went back to the shipyard, where she underwent quite an extensive modernization.

Its scope included, among others, modernization of the propulsion consisting of replacing the coal-fired boilers with much more efficient and less troublesome liquid fuel boilers. This allowed improvement to the ship's stabilty by shortening the height of both funnels by two metres, and the coal bunkers, occupying a lot of space, were rebuilt into technical, magazine and crew rooms.

The shortening of the funnels was not the only change in the silhouette of the ship. In order to improve seaworthiness, the bow stem was re-designed again, as well as the foremast being lowered, and small yardarms on the funnels for radio antennae were installed. The aft mast also changed its appearance, but most importantly changes also occurred in the armament. The existing 500 mm torpedo tubes were replaced with the newer 533 mm type with a supply of six torpedoes each.

At the beginning of December, the *Emden* found herself at the shipyard again, this time to modernize her weaponry, thus preparing her for another operation. In the period from 2 December to 3 January 1940, two sets of 20 mm AA guns, commonly known as *Vierling*, were installed on the aft superstructure. In addition, a demagnetizing cable was provided around the hull about halfway up the waterline, providing protection against magnetic mines.

Later, February and March were spent on patrols until *Emden* was deployed in Operation *Weserübung* – Exercises on the Weser River – which for Norwegians and Danes meant an invasion of their countries and long years of occupation. Of course, we are talking here about the Norwegian campaign and the joint attack by the *Kriegsmarine* and *Wehrmacht* on Denmark and Norway, which, as we know, ended in the disgraceful defeat of the Allies and the occupation of these countries by German troops.

Emden *and her crew. We must admit that both photographs look extremely interesting.*

Apart from *Emden*, the heavy cruisers *Lützow* and *Blücher* also became part of one of the groups of ships designated for this operation, called Group V. The *Blücher* became the flagship of Rear Admiral Oskar Kummetz, and this group also contained the torpedo ships *Möwe, Albatros, Kondor* and seven minesweepers, on board which there were 2,000 troops in total.

Undoubtedly, this was the largest combat operation the *Emden* participated in, given that there were six such groups, and the total number of troops on board the ships was almost 8,000 men.

On 7 April the troops began to embark, the next day the force sailed north.

Blücher was in the lead, followed by *Lützow* and *Emden* and then the other ships, and the group's route led through the Langeland Belt, Great Belt, Kattegat, Skagerrak and finally Oslofjord.

Accomplishing the task, however, did not go smoothly. When the force was in the Skagerrak area, at 1906 hrs it was attacked by the British submarine *Trident*, the torpedo salvo from which almost led to serious complications.

Emden *on the high seas.*

On 9 April 1940, *Emden* and the other vessels found themselves at the entrance to Oslofjord, where at 0300 hrs the torpedo ships *Kondor*, *Albatros* and two minesweepers departed, heading for the Horten area.

Meanwhile, the leading *Blücher*, followed by *Lützow* and *Emden*, went on and at 0500 they were detected by the Norwegian defences, for whom holding the bay was undoubtedly crucial. A dozen or so minutes later, the 280 mm guns of the Oscarerborg fortress rang out, and their accurate fire seriously damaged the *Blücher* and soon also focused on *Lützow*, which at the same time fired at the Norwegian batteries together with *Emden*.

Unlike the flagship *Blücher*, for which fate turned out to be extremely cruel – we will learn more about this in one of the following chapters[6] – and *Lützow*, which followed her, the *Emden* remained unscathed and on 10 April at 1145 hrs the force, now led by *Lützow*, entered Oslo.

Interestingly, unlike *Lützow*, which, having disembarked the troops set off on her way back, *Emden* remained in the area of operations for quite a long time, where she served as a communication hub for the German troops fighting in that area.

The ship with her extensive social facilities also performed the function of the headquarters of the Oslo harbour commanding officer, Commander Friedrich Rieve, as well as the commander of the security forces himself, the ship's skipper Commander Werner Lange.

An important event in the story of the cruiser was also the visit of the head of the *Kriegsmarine*, Grand Admiral Erich Raeder, who arrived on board the ship in Oslo on 19 May.

In total, *Emden* remained there until 7 June, when her commander received an order to return to Germany, which she reached the next day, calling at Swunemunde.

Undoubtedly, this was the most important operation in which *Emden* had the opportunity to participate and, more importantly, despite many deficiencies she coped well with it, which allowed for speculation that the ship could be directed to further tasks.

Meanwhile, during a stop in Wilhelmshaven on 29 August her new skipper was appointed – Commander Hans Mirow, a very experienced officer who had been in charge of, among others, the cruisers *Karlsruhe* and *Leipzig*.

In November, *Emden* was directed to the shipyard where, in addition to the standard maintenance, her armament was once again increased. This time four individual 20 mm cannons were installed on the vessel, located in pairs in the area of the navigation platform and aft superstructure. The works were completed on 15 February 1941, after which the ship continued patrol duties.

In June, Cdr. Mirow received an order to move to Norwegian waters, where for the next two months the cruiser operated, based in the ports of Oslo and Horten. A curiosity is that at this time the ship sported a very interesting side camouflage pattern, consisting of white and black stripes, similar to those on the battleship *Bismarck* during her famous Operation *Rheinübung*.

At the time *Emden* remained in Norway, Hitler was already realizing his next crazy dream, hidden under the name "*Barbarossa*". After the intervention in the Balkans, where German troops, following the plan to occupy Greece, had to "pave" their way through Yugoslavia, it was time to break the famous Ribbentrop-Molotov pact and invade the USSR.

6 *Blücher* was hit twice by torpedoes at 05.32, which together with the 280 mm rounds fired from the Oscarerborg fortress earlier, sealed her fate. The *Lützow*, which followed her, also suffered severe damage.

The route of one of Emden's *long-haul cruises is shown on a postcard issued for this occasion.*

We all know what the course of this largest and most important operation in the history of Germany looked like, and also about the fact that virtually all operations took place on the vast territories of the Soviet Union. This meant that the naval operations associated with the invasion were limited only to the Baltic region and did not have any spectacular actions.

Of course, Hitler, initially not seeing the need to engage the *Kriegsmarine*'s major ships, did not consider the use of battleships and cruisers, even issuing a specific order in which he stressed that larger naval operations should be avoided at least until the capture of Leningrad.

Everything changed at the beginning of September, when Riga fell and *Wehrmacht* troops stood on the outskirts of Kronstadt – the main base of the Baltic Fleet, where the battleships *Marat* and *Oktyabrskaya Revolutsya* were moored. Both ships posed a serious threat, which Adm. Raeder notified to Hitler, who therefore agreed with the plans of the Grand Admiral, which were to create a force of heavy ships called *Baltenflotte* and commanded by Vice Admiral Otto Ciliax.

Its main task was to blockade the Soviet battleships in the Gulf of Finland, and *Emden* together with the battleships *Tirpitz* and *Admiral Scheer*, cruisers *Köln*, *Leipzig* and *Nürnberg*, three destroyers and five torpedo ships were assigned to the task.

Emden *seen from the starboard side while approaching the quay.*

The Emden's *starboard view.*

What is interesting, the *Emden* and the entire force did not have much to do, because by the time it had taken up position at the Åland Islands on 24 September, it turned out that three days earlier German aircraft managed to damage the battleship *Oktyabrskaya Revolutsya*, and on 23 September they sank the *Marat*.

After *Tirpitz* and *Admiral Scheer* had left the formation and the rest of the ships had been regrouped, the *Baltenflotte* took on slightly different tasks. Having been transferred to Libau, the *Emden*, along with the cruiser *Leipzig*, was assigned to Operation *Weststurm*, and were to bombard Soviet positions on the Sworbe Peninsula.

On 26 September, almost all day long, both cruisers supported German troops, firing a total of 582 150 mm and 48 88 mm rounds, of which 255 150 mm and all the 88 mm ones were fired by *Emden.*

Emden *at the shipyard. Clearly visible is the ship's bow with its decorations.*

The next day, *Emden* and *Leipzig* continued to bombard the enemy positions as part of Operation *Weststurm* II. This time, there was a lot of trouble when the force was attacked by a group of Soviet torpedo boats, commanded by Captain-Lieutenant V.P. Gumenko. Fortunately for *Emden*, the enemy ships failed to launch an effective attack and disengaged with the loss of one boat.[7] It was also the last major event of *Emden*'s *Baltenflotte* activities.

After the dissolution of the force, *Emden* found herself in Gdynia and only in November can we note a more interesting event, which was her inclusion in the *Ausbildungsverband der Flotte* (Squadron), which also included *Köln*, *Leipzig* and *Nürnberg*. Thus, *Emden* again became a training ship, operating mainly in the Baltic Sea.

It is actually hard to find any exciting events at this time. Over the next months, the cruiser embarked on short cruises and trained various specialists on board without taking part in any major actions.

It was not until June 1942 that more interesting events came along – she was directed to the Wilhelmshaven shipyard for installation of the only FuMO 21 radar in her history, whose characteristic antenna, measuring 4 x 2 m and commonly called the "mattress", was mounted on the platform of the fire control mast[8] At this point, it is worth mentioning that during *Emden*'s stay at the shipyard, in the German high command a rather interesting project for

7 This was the TKA 83 topedo boat commanded by Lt. N.N. Kremeskiy

8 It was a 8 kW radar, working at 368 MHz frequency of a range of 14 to 16 km. Some references claim that another radar was installed – the FuMB (?)

Emden *in a colour postcard depicting her in Holtenau.*

re-configuring the ship appeared, consisting of removing the aft 150 mm guns and replacing them with two twin-barrel 88 mm sets. After that, another three 150 mm guns were to give way to two 37 mm gun sets, one 20 mm cannon set and at least four single 20 mm mounts.

As history has shown, the plans did not take effect, and *Emden*, which would undoubtedly have gained a lot from it, becoming something like a AA ship that could co-operate with other major *Kriegsmarine* vessels. The reasons for abandoning this project can be traced to the person of Adolf Hitler and his controversial directive, but more on that later.

During her stay at the shipyard, on 20 July once again – for the twelfth time – her skipper changed, the newly appointed one was Commander Friedrich Traugott Schmidt.

A very interesting event took place on 7 November, when the ship, once she left the shipyard, was the first major *Kriegsmarine* vessel to pass through the newly opened lock IV Raeder-Schleuse – part of an extremely daring and at the same time sophisticated construction, whose task was to cut off the water between the internal, and external areas of the harbour[9].

The significance of the event may be evidenced by the fact that on this occasion even Grand Admiral Erich Raeder arrived on board the cruiser, adding splendour to the whole event.

Unfortunately, it was one of the very few events of that time in the story of the ship and despite the ongoing war, there is not much to write about the *Emden*'s activities.

Having left Wilhelmshaven, the cruiser found herself in Gdynia again – it is worth adding this was then one of the main Kriegsmarine bases – and from there she went out on short training cruises, not leaving the waters of the Baltic Sea. This was more or less the case in the whole of 1943, in which we can note only two somewhat exciting events.

The first occurred in February and it would be best to remain silent of it as the ship, during her stay in the waters of the Gulf of Gdańsk, was hit by a torpedo fired... from her own tube! Although it was a training torpedo, it still caused serious damage, which meant that the ship had to go to Danzing and remain in dock.

As the second major event we can consider a change in the position of the skipper – Cdr. Friedrich Traugott Schmidt was replaced by Commander Hans Henigst on 10 September. And actually that would be all as far as the *Emden*'s 1943 story is concerned.

After a series of defeats in naval operations involving major *Kriegsmarine* ships, Hitler in his madness demanded from the commanders the immediate disarmament and decommissioning of almost all large ships, and *Emden* was one of them. In his mind, despite many spectacular successes from the beginning of the war, these ships did not mean much, and only wasted their crews which could be useful elsewhere.

As a result, in January 1943 he dismissed Admiral Erich Raeder[10], replacing him with the current commander of the underwater forces, Admiral Karl Dönitz – a man whose mind was focused on submarines.

9 Its construction commenced in 1936 and until the very end of war was never fully completed

10 Admiral Raeder resigned on 30 January as he could not have agreed with the decision of the ships' disarmament

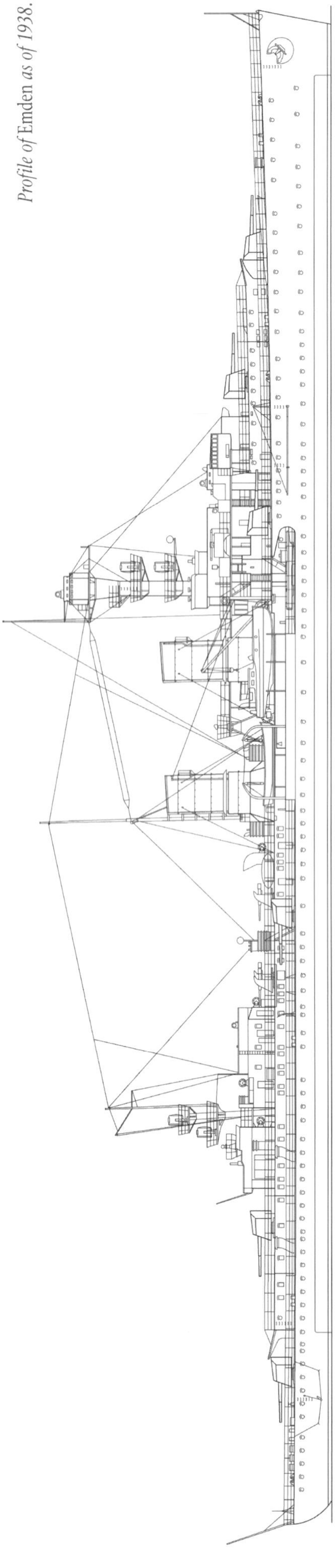

Profile of Emden *as of 1938.*

As history has shown, thanks to the efforts of *Kriegsmarine* commanders including Adm. Dönitz himself, this kind of "pogrom" never happened, but it cannot be hidden that for the German battleships and cruisers another task was found far in the north – Norway – which for Hitler, was one of the most important regions worth keeping at all costs.

Anyway, in his frantic directives, he repeated more than once that every large *Kriegsmarine* ship that was not in Norway was in the wrong place, because it was this country that would stand against an Allied invasion.

Emden was saved by the fact that she was a training ship, so regardless of the situation she was needed, which is why her decommissioning was never really taken into account. On the contrary. in the summer of 1944, she was even transferred to the shipyards where she underwent quite significant modernization of her armament.

Despite the status as a training vessel, the archaic guns of World War One vintage were not even suitable for training purposes. In any case *Emden* was a warship, and at at any time she could be ordered to perform a combat task, and with a main battery of poor ballistic parameters she could not do very much. That is why, after seventeen years of service, the ship finally underwent a significant modernization of armament.

The old SK C 16 150 mm L/45 guns were replaced with new TBK C 36 150 mm L/48 ones, weapons of the same calibre, but of much better characteristics[11]. Guns of this type were designed for large destroyers of the Model 1936, also known as the *Narvik* class. With muzzle velocity of 835 m/s, the range of these guns was 21,950 m with a barrel elevation angle +30°, while the rate of fire was estimated at 5–6 shots per minute.

Even the older 88 mm AA guns were replaced by three SK C 32 105 mm L/45 guns on MPL C 32 mounts. This was a weapon that could not even be compared with the inefficient 88 mm guns, capable of firing at airborne targets at a ceiling of 6,300 m, and their rate of fire was 10 shots per minute.

Interestingly, a lot of changes also took place in light AA weaponry. The ship was equipped with two new 37 mm L/83 Flak C 30 guns on MPL C 30U mounts and two Flak Bofors 28 40 mm L/56 guns. In addition, the single 20 mm AA cannons were replaced with twin-barrel 20 mm L/44 FlaMG C 38 sets.

With this weaponry *Emden* gained a lot, having become a notably more capable ship of which, after all, the *Kriegsmarine* was running out of. Only the *Tirpitz* remained in service of the most valuable battleships, whose days were already numbered, as well as the cruisers *Lützow*, *Admiral Scheer*, *Prinz Eugen*, *Admiral Hipper*, *Leipzig*, *Nürnberg* and *Koln* – almost all heavily worn out.

Having left the shipyard, *Emden* was sent to where Hitler demanded, namely Norway. At that time, her new skipper was Commander Lieutenant Hans-Eberhard Meisner, appointed to this position in March.

After she had moved into Norwegian waters, *Emden* operated from the Horten base and became the flagship of the mine-sweeping force in September, and such tasks were associated with her service for months to come, focusing mainly on the waters of the Skagerrak.

For example, between 19 and 21 September, *Emden* covered the operation of laying the minefield marked as XXXW – Operation "*Klaudius*". On 1 and 2 October she participated in Operation "*Caligula*", laying the minefield called XXXIIb, and a few days later between 5 and 6 October the minefield XXXIIa – "*Vespasia*".

On 14 October she was also supposed to take part in the mining operation codenamed "*Augustus*", but due to increasing attacks by the Allied air force it was cancelled.

Later, the ship operated in the Oslofjord waters escorting transports.

In mid-November she took part in joint exercises in the waters of the aforementioned fjord with the cruiser *Köln*, and it was there where on 9 December she ran aground, suffering damage. This damage however was not serious, but reports from the engine crew about numerous problems and the need to carry out maintenance of the power unit caused the ship to be repaired.

11 Some references are silent on this fact, which may raise doubts if the 150 mm guns were ever replaced

Emden *in all her glory.*

As a result, on 23 December *Emden* left Oslofjord and headed for the motherland to arrive in Königsberg on 25 December, where at the Schichau Werft shipyard she was to undergo the necessary renovation. Despite the almost immediate commencement of work, the situation on the front line did not allow for their completion.

At the beginning of January 1945, the situation of the *Wehrmacht* in East Prussia was, to put it mildly, "dramatic". The retreating German troops were not able to stop the overwhelming forces of the Red Army, which was approaching the outskirts of the city very quickly.

For this reason, it was impossible to continue the work and on 23 January the order was issued to immediately evacuate the ship. After command of *Emden* had been taken over by Commander Wolfgang Kähler, within several dozen hours and in a hurry the shipyard workers loaded on her decks elements of dismantled armament, propulsion and other equipment.

It is impossible not to mention the special cargo loaded onto *Emden* on 25 January. They were coffins with the remains of the *Reich* President Paul von Hindenburg and his wife, who died in 1934, which Germany, not wanting to allow profanation by Soviet soldiers – which would undoubtedly have happened – evacuated from the Hindenburg Mausoleum[12].

Undoubtedly, this was one of the most important tasks that *Emden* experienced during her longest service among all German cruisers, and no doubt quite difficult considering the fact that at that time

12 From 7 August 1934, the remains of Paul von Hindenburg were in the Mausoleum located between today's Olsztynek and the village of Sudwa, originally as a monument to the Battle of Tannenberg, (German: Tannenberg-Denkmal) in one of the towers of the Honorary Yard. After the evacuation of his remains, the retreating *Wehrmacht* troops blew up the entire building, the ruins of which were removed in the mid-1950s.

Emden *seen from the starboard side.*

One of the most significant crew members was the brown bear visible in the photograph.

the ship's engine was partly dismantled, which did not make it possible to leave port on her own. Even worse, the Russians could launch an air raid at any time, the target of which could have been *Emden* – a ship armed with 150 mm guns that could bombard their positions when attacking the city.

For this reason, the cruiser left Königsberg on 25 January at 0300 hrs at night, accompanied by the clearly-audible sounds of salvos of enemy artillery, and assisted by tugs she went to nearby Pilau, where the coffins were transhipped on board the converted passenger vessel *Pretoria*, which almost immediately headed west.

Cleaning work on the foredeck.

Emden herself remained in Pilau for several days, during which the shipyard workers managed to start one of the engines and restore the ship's ability to sail on her own.

However, it was a time when the *Wehrmacht* could only dream of fighting in the full sense of the word. The offensives of the Soviet troops left no illusions about the future. It was clear that East Prussia would soon be lost and that the population living there should be evacuated as soon as possible, as well as anything that presented both historical and material value.

Panic escape from those regions, with thousands of victims in its process, meant that the Germans decided on evacuation by sea using almost everything that could float, which is why *Emden*, though with not fully operative propulsion, was a very valuable vessel that could embark a large number of refugees on board.

It is difficult to determine who and in what quantity was taken, but there is no doubt that when the ship left Pilau on 1 February heading west, her decks must have been overcrowded with refugees, wounded and the like.

It is worth remembering that it was a time when ships such as *Wilhelm Gustlof* went to the bottom hit by the Soviet torpedoes, when according to the latest estimates 9,600 people perished! And the transport *Goya* with an equally frightening number of over 6,000 victims.

The same fate could have happened to *Emden*, which was sailing slowly and actually defenceless in this situation, and the journey to Kiel, which was less

Another postcard with Emden *as a star.*

than seven hundred kilometres away, took as long as six days. It is not known exactly how this cruise progressed, but we can guess that, like other *Kriegsmarine* ships involved in the evacuation, the cruiser would call in to Gdynia and Swunemunde.

Interestingly, according to the original schedule, *Emden*, having arrived in Kiel which took place on 6 February, was to go to the shipyard for renovation, but taking into account the realities of those days and the hopeless situation of the dying state, it is rather difficult to say that it made sense.

German factories, railways and the most important shipyards were being turned into ruins almost every day and were not able to function normally, let alone the air raids directed directly at warships, which, if operational, had nowhere to flee and which were in Kiel as well as Wilhelmshaven in the last days of the war, became targets of attacks.

This was also the case with *Emden*, which, although she did not present major combat capabilities, could not be ignored by the Allied air force, the more so as some time later, the cruisers *Admiral Scheer* and *Admiral Hipper* stood at the Deutsche Werke shipyard. This could not go unnoticed and air raids were carried out on almost a daily basis.

Despite attempts to repair *Emden*, not much was happening on her, and one of the most important events those days was the last change in the position of the commander, who in March became Lieutenant Commander Ernst-Ludwig Wickmann.

Emden *in an interesting photograph taken from the bow while approaching a quay.*

Emden *at her berth. One of the torpedo tubes and various boats on the deck are clearly visible.*

Air raids that were almost regularly carried out, gradually demolished the ship. For example, after the raid of 11 March, a raging fire ruined a significant part of the fore superstructure, and given the massive damage to the quays and shipyard installations, there could be no question of any repairs.

The worst came in April, when the attacks by the Allied air forces reached their peak. In the raid of 3 April, the ship, similarly to the above-mentioned *Admiral Hipper*, received one direct hit, which destroyed the midship superstructures and completely ruined the fore funnel.

It was even worse at night on 9/10 April, when another of the countless formations of British bombers appeared over Kiel – in this case Lancasters, which, taking into account the almost symbolic AA defence, once again devastated the city and port, not sparing the already massacred ships. It was then that the explosions of bombs dropped into the shipyard basins sent the cruiser *Admiral Scheer* to the bottom and seriously damaged *Emden*'s stern.

Three days later, after another attack, the effects of which can be guessed, the heavily damaged *Emden* was towed from the shipyard basin to the waters of the Heikendorfer Bay, where due to serious damage she found herself on the bottom with a 15° list to the port side.

It was the end of the ship.

On 26 April, after nearly twenty years of service, *Emden* – the longest serving cruiser in the Third Reich – was removed from the fleet list. At that time, most of the crew were no longer on board and were directed to land operations. For some time, only a skeleton crew of 20 men remained on the ship, who on 3 May 1945 had the task of placing explosives and scuttlingthe ship. The *Emden* sat on the bottom at 52° 22" N and 10° 10" E, eventually completing her story.

After the war, the wreckage was systematically dismantled, which came to an end in 1950.

Tactical and technical characteristics of the cruiser *Emden*

Type A

- *Reichsmarinewerft* Shipyard, Wilhmshaven
- Construction No. 100
- Date of laying the keel – 8 December 1921.
- Launch date – 7 January 1925.
- Date of commission – 15 October 1925.
- Standard displacement 5,689 t
- Combat displacement 6,990 t
- Overall length 155.1 m
- Length on the waterline 150.5 m
- Beam 14.3 m
- Draft (standard) 5.1 m
- Draft (full) 5.9 m
- Propulsion – 6 oil-fired Schulz-Marine & Cie boilers, 4 coal-fired Schulz-Marine & Cie boilers, 2 sets of Brown Boveri turbines with a total output of 45,900 HP, from 1934 onwards 10 oil-fired Schulz-Marine & Cie boilers.
- Maximum speed 29.4 knots
- Fuel supply 875 tons of coal and 300 tons of oil, from 1934 onwards, 1,266 tons of oil
- Range 5,290 NM at a speed of 18 knots, 6,750 NM at a speed of 14 knots
- Ship's company (1925) 19 officers and 464 NCOs and naval ratings
- Armament (1925) 8 (8x1) 150 mm guns, 2 (2x1) 88 mm guns, 4 (2x2) 500 mm torpedo tubes, 4 (2x2) 533 mm torpedo tubes
- Armament (1938) 8 (8x1) 150 mm guns, 3 (3x1) 88 mm guns, 4 (4x1) 37 mm guns, 4 (2x2) 533 mm torpedo tubes
- Armament (1940) 8 (8x1) 150 mm guns, 3 (3x1) 88 m guns, 4 (4x1) 37 mm guns, 12 (2x4, 4x1) 20 mm cannons, 4 (2x2) 533 mm torpedo tubes
- Armament (1944) 8 (8x1) 150 mm guns, 3 (3x1) 105 mm guns, 2 (2x1) 40 mm guns, 2 (2x1) 37 mm guns, 12 (6x2)) 20 mm cannons, 4 (2x2) 533 mm torpedo tubes
- Armour – 50 mm broadsides, 20–40 mm decks, 20–50 mm command post, 40 transverse bulkheads

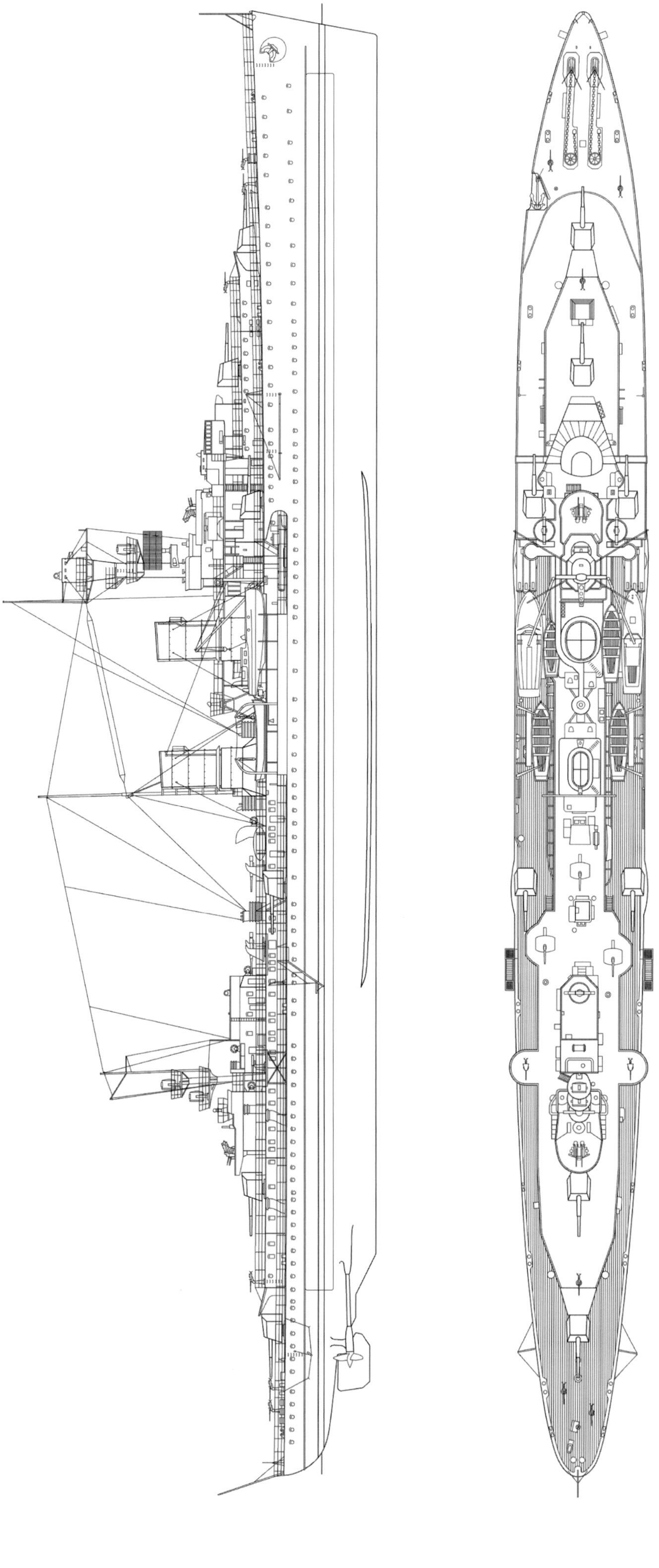

Profile of Emden as of 1942.

Emden *on the high seas.*

Emden *at her berth.*

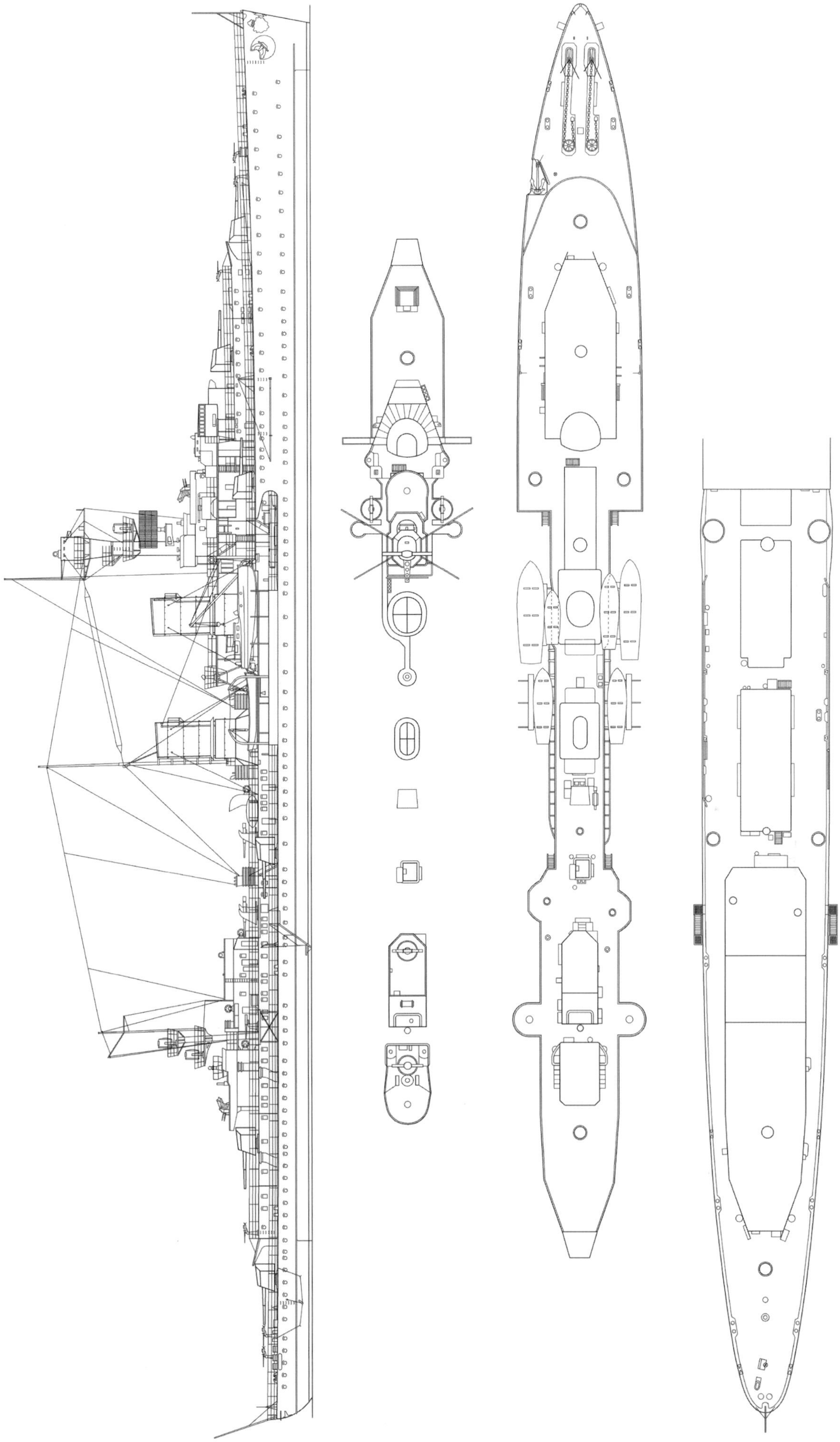

Diagram of the Emden's superstructure layout.

Königsberg
A Modern Cruiser

Having familiarized ourselves with the story of the *Emden* in the previous chapter, it is easy to see that her design and construction, which began only thirty months after the signing of the Treaty of Versailles, was of great propaganda importance. The same cannot be said about her combat value.

The construction of a ship armed with outdated guns in semi-open mounts and, what was even worse, with coal-fired boilers, did not arouse enthusiasm among officers who not so long ago had the opportunity to serve aboard much more modern ships of the once proud Navy of the German Empire.

Almost everyone, commanders, navy officers, designers and shipyard workers, were aware of *Emden*'s deficiencies, which is why even before her construction had been completed in 1924, a team of German designers led by Eng. Albrecht Ehrenberg began work on a new project.

Interestingly, given the difficult economic situation in the country and the unflagging voices of opposition from leftist parties, reluctant to finance the construction of warships in a situation when millions of its citizens were struggling with unemployment and hunger, they had initially designed the new cruiser based on *Emden*, taking into account all her flaws. However, it quickly became apparent that there were too many of these disadvantages to base a modern ship's design on.

When compared to the Emden, Königsberg *was a much more modern ship, which also had better combat capabilities.*

Not without significance was the construction of the *Duguay-Trouin* cruisers in France, with a displacement of 8,000 tons and main armament consisting of eight 155 mm guns placed in

The Königsberg *as seen from the bow. In the foreground the ship's emblem is clearly visible.*

enclosed, twin barrel turrets. So once all pros and cons had been considered, it was decided to go in a completely different direction so that now a real cruiser could be put into service, able to face her counterparts from other fleets.

Only one "but" remained...

Since the Versailles Treaty had been signed, which has already been mentioned many times, nothing had changed, and when designing a new cruiser German ship constructors had to bear in mind the main armament not exceeding 150 mm calibre and 6,000 tons maximum displacement. While the former could still be reconciled, it was impossible to fit the construction in the unfortunate tonnage limit if one wanted to build a capable ship.

It is no secret that the Germans quickly started mocking the above limits, which is why at the design stage of the new ship it was decided to exceed the "treaty" displacement and to conceal this fact. It is worth noting here that this took place many years before the National Socialists came to power headed by Adolf Hitler, who many historians credit with the main responsibility for breaking and subsequently rejecting the Versailles provisions.

Meanwhile, in the German high command there was no shortage of officers who disregarded the treaty arrangements, trying to circumvent them at every step and thus express their opposition

Königsberg *depicted in one of many post-cards published in peacetime.*

to – according to themselves – the unjust conditions of ending the Great War. But that is politics and we're interested in the ship.

By choosing the path of a completely new ship design, which, unlike *Emden* was to be a more capable vessel, the team of Eng. Ehrenberg developed a design for a cruiser, or rather a series of cruisers, designated as *Kreuzer* B, C and D, later called the K-class ships. This time they were to be cruisers in the full sense of the word, the peculiar feature of which was to be the location of the main battery in enclosed turrets – just as in the original *Emden* design.

This testified to the enormous progress of German engineers who, having drawn conclusions from the construction and service of the unsuccessful ship, developed a cruiser project for which now they did not have to be ashamed – on the contrary, because it was considered a first-class cruiser with main armament placed in modern enclosed three-gun turrets[1].

After approval of the project by the High Command of the *Reichsmarine* had been granted and the allocation of appropriate funds in the *Reichstag*, in which, it is worth adding, there were no opposition votes, the construction of the cruiser "B" (*Ersatz Thetis*) or the future *Königsberg*, numbered 108, began on 12 April 1926 on the slipway of the *Marinewerft* shipyard in Wilhelmshaven. The newly built ship was to replace the old cruiser *Thetis*, built in 1900 and belonging to the *Gazelle* class, whose combat capabilities left much to be desired.

The construction itself, in contrast to the construction of *Emden*, went extremely smoothly and after less than thirteen months the hull was ready for launching, which took place on 26 March 1927. As you can guess, there was a huge celebration in Wilhelmshaven, which could not have been missed by high-ranking dignitaries with the Commander-in-Chief of the Navy at the forefront, invited guests and huge crowds of the city's inhabitants.

Among the most important guests was the then Mayor of Königsberg, Dr. Lohmeyer, who on this occasion had the honour to give a speech, while the godmother was the widow of the last commander of the cruiser of the same name from World War One, Lt. Cdr. Max Looff, who by the traditional breaking of a bottle of champagne on the the ship's bow, gave her the name in honour of the capital city of East Prussia, *Königsberg*[2].

The hull slipped majestically onto the water to the sounds of the national anthem and cheering crowds, turning the entire ceremony into a magnificent spectacle, but she was still far from entering service.

Name of the ship

The name of the cruiser was given in honour of the city of Königsberg in East Prussia on the Pregola River. At that time it was the capital of East Prussia, and in the mid-thirties of the previous century its population was estimated at about 950,000 inhabitants. In the Third Reich, it was one of the largest German cities, constituting an important industrial and commercial centre. It was also an important sea and river harbour.

During World War Two it was ruined, with some areas virtually levelled, and after the end of hostilities it found itself within the boundaries of the USSR. In 1946, its name was changed to Kaliningrad. Currently, it belongs to the Russian Federation, constituting a large military base, and its population is estimated at about 500,000.

Once the hull was towed to the shipyard quay, the fitting out works commenced. Over the next 24 months, superstructure, funnels, masts and most importantly the armament and fire control systems appeared on the ship. At the end of spring 1929, the shipyard workers announced the completion of their work and the readiness to begin hand-over tests, and finally on 17 April 1929 the banner was solemnly raised for the first time.

As the *Königsberg*'s first commander, Lieutenant Commander Wolf von Troth was appointed, and the crew of more than five hundred men mainly came from the cruiser *Nymphe*, de-commissioned the day before. The ship herself cost the German taxpayer 38 million *reichsmarks*, and looked extremely impressive.

Her hull, structurally based on a transverse-longitudinal system of construction, was divided into 16 watertight compartments, and measured 174 metres in overall length, 169 m on the waterline and 15.2 m in width. At first glance she was very similar to *Emden*, but in reality she featured many new ideas, including the transom stern which was quite unique at that time.

1 The Germans were slightly ahead of the Americans in this respect, who in 1926–1930 built a series of cruisers of the *Pensacola* class, equipped with three barrel and twin main battery turrets.

2 Lt. Cdr. Max Looff commanded the cruiser *Königsberg* built in 1907, which after several successes in German East African waters was scuttled by its crew at the mouth of the Rufidji River in July 1915 as a result of damage suffered during an engagement with British ships.

The Königsberg*'s profile from the initial period of her service.*

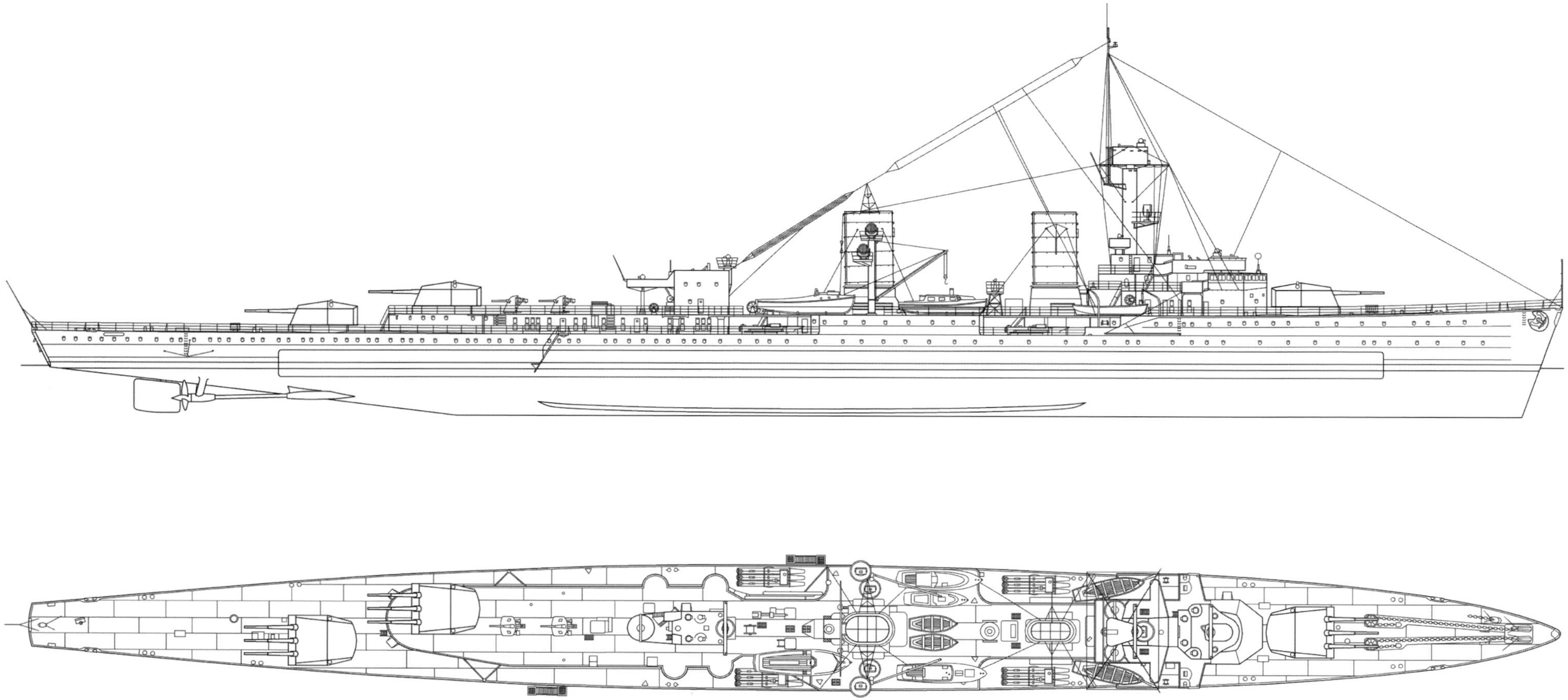

A peculiar feature of the Königsberg *and her sister ships was the asymmetrically placed aft gun turrets.*

Interestingly, as in the case of *Emden*, the method of electric welding was used to join elements on a large scale – a technique that was very innovative at the time, which unfortunately in the case of the K-class vessels had a very negative impact on their seaworthiness. The fixing of more than 80% of all hull plates, whose construction – it is worth remembering designed with tonnage limits in mind – with new technology which was still in the trial and experiment phase, caused problems with its strength. Numerous deformations and cracks, which later were observed during the

Königsberg *on the high seas performing a sharp turn.*

operations of *Königsberg* and the other two "K" cruisers, negatively affected their combat capabilities very quickly, thus limiting their areas of activity mainly to coastal waters.

It was a huge disadvantage of these ships, but what else could have been done if the German engineers wanted to build a powerfully armed ship and at the same time had to consider tonnage limits when constructing the ship?

Anyway, as it turned out later, although officially the "K" cruisers were within the imposed limit of 6,000 tons of standard displacement, in fact once they entered service they had 6,380 tons, which of course was a clear violation of the Versailles conditions. However, this did not change the fact that *Königsberg* had to deal with this problem for almost the entire period of her operational service.

Equally it was similar in the case of armour, which in many places had to give way to armament. Also in this respect, opinions among specialists are divided and it is very common to find the opinion that the protection was far from adequate.

At this point, however, we must remember that, considering the limit of 6,000 tons displacement, it is rather difficult to talk about the armour of a cruiser, which according to preliminary design criteria was to be something of a reconnaissance ship, adapted to ocean-going raids in which crucial factors were to be speed and armament.

Anyway, the total weight of the armour used on each of the "K" cruisers was 988 tons, and it consisted of 126 metre long armour belts, 50 mm thick, on both sides of the hull extending a height of 2.5 m above the waterline and 1.3 m below. It is easy to see that lowering the armour belt just over a metre below the waterline was far from ideal and did not provide the ship with sufficient underwater protection, but there was no other solution.

The armour belts ended at the levels of the "A" and "C" gun turrets, where they were closed by transverse bulkheads 70 mm thick, while the anti-torpedo bulges running parallel along them were 15 mm thick, and on sloping areas this decreased to just 10 mm. Protection from above was provided by a 20 mm thick armoured deck, while in the areas of the ammunition compartments its thickness reached 40 mm. The thickness of the armour covering the command post measured from 30 to 100 mm, while the main battery turrets were covered with 30 mm thick armour from the front and 20 mm in other areas.

An extremely interesting and at the same time innovative matter was the ship's propulsion system, which was based on four sets of steam turbines produced at the F. Schichau Werft plant in Elbing, to which steam of 16 kg/cm^2 operating pressure was supplied by six Marine Schuls-Thornycroft water-tube boilers. The total output of the power unit was estimated at 65,000 HP, while this turned out to be significantly exceeded during tests, reaching 66,350 HP and giving a speed of 32 knots.

Interestingly, for sailing at an economical speed of 10.5 knots and manoeuvring, the ship was equipped with two type W10V28/33 diesel engines produced at the Maschinenfabrik Augsburg-Nürnberg (MAN) plant in Augsburg, with the affectionate names of "Max" and "Moritz" given by the crew, and total output of 1,800 HP. It was a very innovative solution, unfortunately not without flaws because both drives could not work together and, in a situation when the diesel drive was to be changed to turbine drive, the crew had to stop the engines and switch over, rather than make use of the complicated clutch system, which took about 10 minutes!

It is worth adding at this point that in the later years of service, the total abandonment of the diesel engines and their removal were taken very seriously into account, which would leave the drive to rely completely on the steam turbines which performed much better.

It cannot be overlooked that *Königsberg* was not without flaws, but it must also be remembered that she was a prototype ship, very innovative for its time and, more importantly, built according to strict limits, which of course had affected her design. But no matter how it looked the new cruiser towered over the design applied in the construction of *Emden*.

The fuel supply that was bunkered in *Königsberg* was 1,239 tons of fuel oil for the boilers and 139 tons for the diesel engines, although later these values increased to 1,300 tons and 150 tons, respectively.

The cruising range at 19 knots was 5,700 NM, and at 17 knots it increased to 7,300 NM, while at 10 knots and with diesel engines it was 8,000 NM. The propulsion sets were supplemented by power units, which consisted of three 360 kW turbo generators and two 180 kW turbo generators driven by diesel engines and producing 220 V DC.

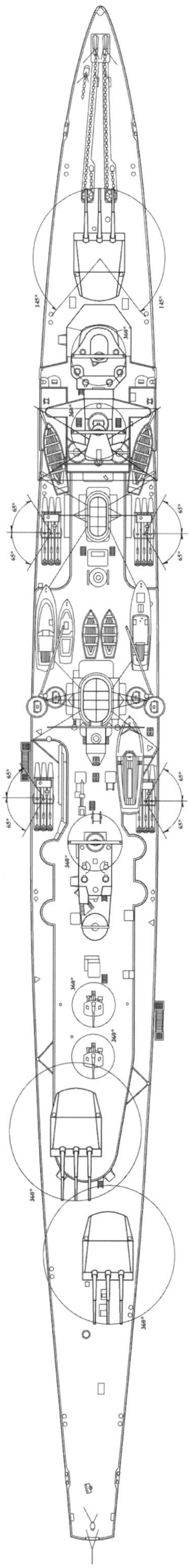

A simplified diagram depicting the angles of fire of the guns.

Königsberg *as seen from the stern. The hull details as well as the name plate are clearly visible.*

The issue of armament is extremely interesting, though it was quite obviously dictated by the Treaty of Versailles. It consisted of nine 150 mm SK C/25 guns L/60[3], interestingly from the Rheinmetall-Borsig plant in Düsseldorf. This was a very modern weapon designed in 1925, and featured quite good ballistic properties. The weight of a single gun with breech was 11.9 tons, while the total length was 9,080 mm, which corresponded to a length of 60 calibres. With a muzzle velocity of 960 m/s and a barrel elevation angle of +40°, the guns' range reached 25,700 m, while at +10° it dropped to 14,100 m.

However, this was not the most important thing.

As you can easily see in the images depicting *Königsberg* as well as the other K-class cruisers, the arrangement of the LC/25 gun turrets is noteworthy, especially in the aft part. The German engineers wanted to achieve the largest possible angle of fire towards the bow, so decided on their unusual and at the same time innovative solution in the aft part by locating them asymmetrically in relation to the hull's centreline.

This was, of course, a consequence of the decision to set only one turret in the fore part, which in the event of a chasing an enemy vessel could be inadequate, but as the designers had also anticipated

3 The actual calibre was 149.1 mm.

Konigsberg *in a fine view from her bow.*

The aft main battery turrets of Konigsberg.

the cruiser performing tasks on her own as a reconnaissance ship, or a "classic" raider, which in certain circumstances could be forced to fire during retreat, it was the most optimal solution.

Spreading the aft turrets to the broadsides (in the case of the "B" turret by 225 cm from the hull's axis to port, and the "C" turret by 195 cm to starboard) had made it possible to increase the field of fire towards the bow significantly, and enabled them to fire above the tops of the funnels and foremast in extreme cases. The firing angle of the fore turret, marked "A", was 290° (i.e. 145° to each side) so let us call it typical, however, the aft "B" and "C" turrets could, at least theoretically, fire within a range of 360°!

It is difficult to determine what it looked like in practice, but considering the blasts of salvos fired towards the bow, which undoubtedly had to cause a lot of damage to the fragile elements of the superstructures, the practical angle of fire of the aft turrets was rather similar to the fore one, as evidenced by later abandonment of this solution when designing subsequent cruisers. However, this does not change the fact that the entire idea was extremely interesting, just like the LC/25 turrets specially designed for these cruisers[4].

As far as their most important data is concerned it should be mentioned that their total weight was 136.9 tons, while the maximum elevation was +40° to -10°. The vertical barrel elevation speed was 6°/s and they rotated horizontally at 6–8°/s, while the rate of fire was determined at eight shots per minute, although in practice it was limited to about five.

Interestingly, each of the turrets on *Königsberg* was given its own name, which referred to the names of *Kaiserliche Marine* ships – from the bow SMS *Von der Tann* ("A" turret)[5], SMS *Lützow* ("B" turret) and SMS *Seydlitz* ("C" turret)[6].

Of course, the 150 mm guns were not the only weapons that the cruiser was armed with, although in the initial period of service they were the only modern ones. They were complemented by two SK C/13 88 mm L/45 guns on MPL C/13 mounts with half-round shields, almost the same as those found on *Emden*. As we were able to find out in the previous chapter, it was a weapon that still recalled the days of World War One with rather mediocre ballistic values, but at that time the only one of its kind in *Königsberg*'s armament. The guns were complemented by four triple 500 mm torpedo tubes, which were spaced in pairs on the sides in the midship area with a supply of 24 torpedoes.

An unusual detail is the fact that the aforementioned transom stern, characteristic of the K-class cruisers, was not a coincidence but a carefully thought-out feature allowing the ship to be used

4 The Swedes decided to apply a similar solution on their *Tre Kronor* class cruisers.

5 Many authors stress that the "A" turret's name is not 100% certain, but no-one provides any information on the alternative name.

6 In the German Navy the main battery turrets were called as follows – "A" for *Anton*, "B" for *Bruno*, "C" for *Caesar* and "D" for *Dora*. On the major ships the turrets were given additional names, related to ships or historical events.

The Königsberg *during one of many visits to the port of Pilau in East Prussia (today Baltyisk, Russia), 1937.*

as a mine-layer after unfolding the mine tracks on the stern deck. Approximately 120 sea mines[7] could be carried.

To control the main battery fire, the ship was equipped with three rangefinders with an optical base of 6 m, installed on the top of the mainmast and fore and aft superstructure, and another three with a base of 3 m intended for the 88 mm guns, installed on platforms on the sides of the aft mast and aft superstructure.

A kind of curiosity is also the fact that despite the current ban on German military aviation, both the *Königsberg* and the other K-class cruisers provided space for a catapult and floatplane, which eventually found their way onto the ship in 1935 in the form of Heinkel He 60 aircraft and later the much more modern Arado Ar 196.

Here, we will leave the ship's description for a while and focus on her operational history.

As we have already found out, *Königsberg* officially entered service on 17 April 1929, but it took a long time before she reached full operational readiness. According to German methods, the ship had to be tried and subjected to appropriate tests in order to learn her actual combat values, but primarily to train and rehearse the crew, without which even the most modern and best-armed ship would not be worth much.

For the first test trip, whose route led to the Heligoland region, *Königsberg* set off on 27 May, and two weeks later she sailed to the waters of the Baltic Sea, where trials and training continued.

The first interesting events in her story can be noted on 22 June, when during a stop in Swinemünde she was visited by the Commander-in-Chief of the *Reichsmarine,* Admiral Erich Raeder, a man who was soon to have a lot to say about the major ships of the German fleet including *Königsberg.*

Also, around the same time there was also the first change in the position of the ship's commander – from Lt. Cdr. Wolf von Troth it was taken over by Lt. Cdr. Robert Witthoeft-Emden, who has already been mentioned in the previous chapter.

July and August followed with plenty of further tests and training, but it is worth noting that the ship stayed between 22 and 26 August in Königsberg – a port important to the ship due to its name. Later, in September and October, the cruiser stayed in Wilhelmshaven, where at the shipyard she underwent regular maintenance combined with the installation of still missing equipment.

More importantly, the stay at the shipyard was also aimed at preparing her for quite an unusual task, which was to represent Germany during the world exhibition in Barcelona. Considering that it was a very prestigious task during which the ship was to be made available to the public, in addition to crew training specially conducted for the occasion the cruiser increased the number of all types of equipment for the purposes of display. Added among others were carpets, ashtrays, candlesticks,

7 The K-class cruisers were supposed to be equipped with two kinds of mines – *Einheitmine* C (EMC) contact mines of 112 cm diameter and 1,300 kg weight and *Einheitmine Fernzündund* (EMF) magnetic mines of the same diameter and weight.

Crewmen cleaning a barrel of one of the main battery gun barrels.

wall portraits, plates, flower pots, etc., while every smallest spot of rust was painted over and almost every element of the ship's equipment was polished to make the best impression.

Finally, it must be remembered that *Königsberg* was one of the most important ships of the *Reichsmarine* at that time and it was she which carried the main burden of representing the German colours with dignity.

On 12 October Rear Admiral Walter Gladisch, who was responsible for the ship's visit to Spain, embarked on board, and on the same day *Königsberg* left Wilhelmshaven heading west. Six days later, having encircled the Iberian Peninsula and entering the waters of the Mediterranean, the ship called at Barcelona on the north-east coast of Spain.

There, for the next eight days, at this extremely prestigious exhibition – organized since 1851 – the ship represented her country as one of the greatest achievements of German marine engineering open to the public.

Königsberg *on the high seas.*

Interesting view of a part of the ship's deck, demonstrating the main battery turrets.

Well, despite the many shortcomings that the K-class cruisers faced, it must be said that for its time with non-typical propulsion, welded hull and armament grouped in three-barrel gun turrets, *Königsberg* was a ship worthy to show off and to impress visitors, among whom one would have undoubtedly found specialists in the area of shipbuilding. In total, her stay in Barcelona lasted until 26 October, and she returned to Wilhelmshaven on 1 November.

Until the end of the year, little can be said about events related to the ship. Most of that time was still largely spent on tests and training of the crew, which finally came to an end on 7 December and only ten days later *Königsberg* officially became the flagship of the Commander of the Baltic Sea Forces, and at the same time the Commander of the Reconnaissance Force.

Interestingly, on 1 January 1930, both formations were combined under the uniform command of the reconnaissance force in which, besides *Königsberg*, there was also the old cruiser *Amazone*, the 1st and 2nd Torpedo Ship Flotilla and 1st Mine-sweeper Flotilla. Together with the entire force, *Königsberg* took part in various tasks, priding herself as the most important ship not only within the reconnaissance force, but the entire *Reichsmarine*.

Without a doubt the commanding officer of the cruiser, Lt. Cdr. Witthoeft-Emden, was envied by many German skippers, considering the fact that at that time the only modern and capable ships

Königsberg *accompanied by the cruiser* Leipzig.

Port side view of the *Königsberg*. The catapult and a Heinkel He 60 floatplane are clearly visible between the funnels.

of the German Navy were *Emden* and *Königsberg* introduced less than five years ago. Although it is worth noting that at that time her sister ship *Karlsruhe* was undergoing a series of trials – she was put into service in November 1929.

Commanders of the ship

- 17 April 1929 – 19 June 1929 – Lt. Cdr Wolf von Troth
- 24 June 1929 – 26 September 1930 – Lt. Cdr. Robert Witthoeft-Emden
- 27 September 1930 – 25 September 1932 – Lt. Cdr. Hermann Densch
- 26 September 1932 – 24 September 1934 – Lt. Cdr. Otto von Schrader
- 25 September 1934 – 26 September 1935 – Lt. Cdr. Hubert Schmundt
- 27 September 1935 – 15 February 1937 – Lt. Cdr. Theodor Paul
- 16 February 1937 – 2 November 1938 – Cdr. Robin Schall-Emden
- 3 November 1938 – 26 June 1939 – Cdr. Ernst Scheurlen
- 27 June 1939 – 15 September 1939 – Cdr. Kurt Caesar Hoffmann
- 16 September 1939 – 10 April 1940 – Cdr. Heinrich Ruhfus

It cannot be hidden that at the turn of the twenties and thirties of the 20th century, the German fleet presented quite modest combat potential. based mainly on outdated battleships and cruisers, whose replacement by new ones was just gaining momentum.

But for now the most important was *Königsberg*, for which there was no shortage of tasks.

Between 1 and 4 February, the ship was subordinated to the Commander of the Naval Gunnery Experimental Section, and the crew took part in specialized training. In March, *Königsberg* briefly went to the shipyard, where she underwent maintenance after nearly a year of service. Unfortunately, not much is known of what was happening to the ship at that time, although in some publications you can find information that, apart from the standard inspection, a platform was added in front of the fore battle mast[8].

At this point, it should also be mentioned that the stay at the shipyard was aimed at preparing the ship for the first foreign cruise – very similar to those at the time repeatedly mentioned above, and performed by *Emden* with the status of a training ship, which was then on her way back from the Caribbean Sea and Central America ports.

Remembering the description of these cruises from the previous chapter, it is easy to see that they were extremely interesting "expeditions", having been a kind of adventure for crew members, for which young cadets set out with undisguised willingness. This was also the case with the *Königsberg*

8 It cannot be determined with 100% certainty whether this modification took place during this stay or during the so-called winter refurbishment. Many references which mention this fact refer generally to 1930 without being specific.

Königsberg *during the only pre-war visit to Gdynia, Poland, in August 1935.*

crew, who took on the task given to the ship with great enthusiasm, the more so that their ship was commanded by a real hero, which was already mentioned in the previous chapter.

Interestingly, before the ship left Wilhelmshaven, on 2 April in the area of the light-ship *Weser* she took part in joint exercises with the battleships *Schlesien*, *Schleswig-Holstein*, *Hannover* and *Hessen*, and vessels from the aforementioned torpedo ship flotilla. At that time, on board was the commander of the Reconnaissance Force, Rear Admiral Gladisch, who led the ship westward once the manoeuvres ended.

On the *Königsberg*'s route, the first stop was a Spanish port located at the north-western edge of the country, Vigo, and then having encircled the Iberian Peninsula and entering the waters of the Mediterranean Sea she called at picturesque Almeria. Later, the cruiser headed east, visiting successively Catania (Italy) and Argostoli (Greece), as well as Split (Yugoslavia) on the Adriatic.

From there she started her journey home, again visiting more of the ports of Spain – Port Mahon in Menorca and as the last one Lisbon, from where she returned to Kiel on 19 June.

Little was happening to the ship over the following weeks. In August, the cruiser was sent for naval gunnery tests, and in September she participated in the *Reichsmarine*'s autumn manoeuvres.

Then the commander of the ship changed, on 27 September it passed to Lt. Cdr. Herman Densch. It is worth mentioning here that the former skipper, Lt. Cdr. Robert Witthoeft-Emden, was directed to take the position of commander of the cruiser *Emden*, which was to set off on another long training voyage soon after.

For *Königsberg* herself, the change of commander was no longer associated with such interesting events. By the end of the year the most important ones that are worth mentioning was sending the crew to a training course at the School of Naval Specialists in Kiel, which took place from the end of September to the first half of November, as well as the ship's temporary assignment to the School of Torpedo Weapons and Communications Equipment.

In 1931, *Königsberg* started an almost three-month stay at the quay of the Deutsche Werke shipyard in Kiel, in which, apart from a standard maintenance, she underwent a minor modernization.

At the end of March she participated in a series of firing practices, and on 13 April, along with other ships, she took part in the spring fleet manoeuvres.

An interesting event was the participation of the cruiser in the celebrations related to the launch of the first modern battleship of the *Reichsmarine* – although it would probably be more correct here to use the expression "armoured ship" – named *Deutschland*, which slipped into the water on 19 May[9].

9 *Deutschland* was the first vessel of three, commonly known as the "pocket battleship" class. The keel was laid on 5 February 1929, and she was commissioned on 1 April 1933. After the outbreak of World War Two she was re-classified as a heavy cruiser and re-named *Lützow*.

Another photograph taken during the cruiser's visit to Gdynia.

It was an extremely interesting event during which almost all the major ships of the German fleet arrived at Kiel, and presented a full naval gala. The whole ceremony was honoured by the most important personalities of the state, with the President of Germany Paul von Hindenburg and the *Reich* Chancellor Dr. Heinrich Bruning at the head.

At this point, it is impossible not to mention that, apart from such important personalities, the ceremony was very special due to the fact that it had been the first of its kind since the end of the Great War in which a battleship was launched. According to many it was almost a symbol of the rebirth of the power of the German Navy.

Anyway, excellent evidence of this was over 60,000 people who came over to the shipyard for this ceremony, and *Deutschland* herself a few years later became almost a symbol of the Nazis and the Third Reich. In April 1934 Commander-in-Chief of the *Reichsmarine* Adm. Erich Reader, Minister of *Reichswer* Col. Gen. Werner von Blomberg and the Head of the land forces Werner von Fritsch, who all gathered on board of *Deutschland*, almost "offered" absolute power to Hitler when he was pursuing his aspirations to take over Germany. It was then that he consulted with them, asking for support in his efforts to become the President of the Reich, in exchange for a promise to eliminate Ernst Röhm and his SA, who posed a huge threat, which has been recorded in history as the "Pact aboard *Deutschland*".

However, this was politics, though it had a huge impact on the history of the ships described in this book, but let us return to the *Königsberg*'s story, on board which arrived the aforementioned President of Germany, Marshal Paul von Hindenburg, the following day.

The purpose of his visit was to participate in fleet manoeuvres organized for this occasion, which the most important person of the state closely observed from the deck of "our" cruiser, which also allows us to speculate about the status that *Königsberg* enjoyed at that time.

At the turn of May and June, the ship briefly went to the shipyard in Kiel, where, apart from a minor maintenance, she was docked. Shortly afterwards, on 10 June, *Königsberg*, together with the torpedo ships *Albatros*, *Falke*, *Greif* and *Möwe* went to Liepaja (German: Libau) where she took part in the celebrations related to the tenth anniversary of the Latvian Navy.

Another interesting event is the participation in fleet manoeuvres conducted in the Skagerrak area between 15 June and 3 July, then a visit to Swinemünde between 18 and 19 July and to Königsberg on 22 and 23 July.

In the following weeks there were various kinds of exercises interspersed with insignificant though interesting events, such as participation in the rifle firing competition of navy crews (3–6 August) or participation in the deck boat regatta in Kiel on 8 August.

This was the case until the end of the year, but considering the lack of space, we will not focus on each event of this type, referring interested parties to the specialist literature on the K-class cruisers.

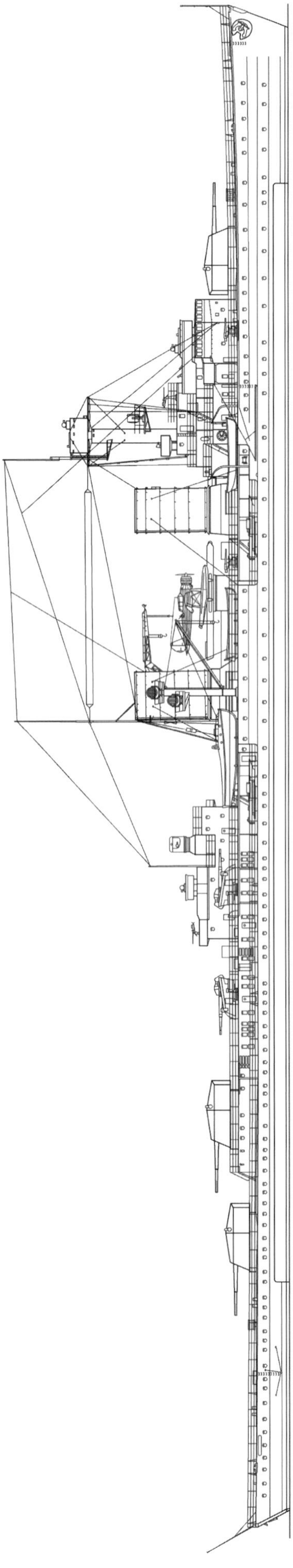

The Königsberg's profile as of 1939.

Königsberg, as usual, began 1932 with a stay at the shipyard which lasted until 13 February, and less than a week later served as a target ship for the gunners of the battleships *Schlesien* and *Hessen*.

Only in April can we note a more interesting event, which was the participation between 9 and 22 April in the spring fleet manoeuvres, during which, among others, she went to Swinemünde.

In May she operated in the North Sea, and from June began a series of visits to the Baltic ports. The first of these was Stockholm, which she visited on 11–17 June with the torpedo ships *Falke*, *Greif* and *Möwe*, and later to Königsberg in East Prussia on 8–11 July, Kranc (German: Cranz) on 12–15 July and Rosity (German: Rossitten) on 15–17 July.

In the first half of August, *Königsberg* stayed at the shipyard in Kiel, then between 20 and 21 August she visited Travemünde, and on 26 September her commander changed – Lt. Cdr. Otto von Schrader was appointed on that day.

It is easy to notice that the service of the training ship began to be slightly monotonous and deprived of events to write about, but we must mention at least the more important ones. There were only a few by the end of the year.

For almost all of October, the ship's activity was limited to various kinds of training, with the exception of a stay on 25–26 October in Swinemünde, where the Commander of the Reconnaissance Forces, Admiral Conrad Albrecht, paid a visit.

Quite interesting was the training cruise on which the ship set out on 31 October from Swinemünde together with a team of ships from the 1st Mine Sweeper Flotilla. Their route led north through the waters of the Great Belt and further around the northern Jutland headland through Doggerbank, south to Helgoland and later to Wilhelmshaven.

Later again there is not much to write about because the ship's service was focused mainly on training activities in home waters. That was until the end of the year and throughout almost the whole of January 1933.

On 16 February, the cruiser found herself at the Deutsche Werke shipyard in Kiel, where she underwent the traditional winter maintenance. I April she took part in team exercises, in which the battleships *Schleswig-Holstein*, *Schlesien* and *Hessen*, cruiser *Leipzig* and ships of 1st and 2nd Torpedo Ship Flotilla, as well as the 1st Trawler Flotilla, also participated. This is the only major event in the story of the ship in early 1933.

At this point, however, it is worth paying attention to the fact that in Germany a lot was happening and – as everyone knows – exactly then Adolf Hitler himself came to power, whose aggressive policy was also to have an impact on the German fleet and its ships.

Anyway, it did not take too much time since this event as on 22 May on the Kiel Roadstead, *Königsberg*, together with almost all major warships, took part in the ceremonial naval review organized in honour of the new Chancellor of the Reich, thus giving a foretaste of the madness of Nazism, which was soon to embrace Germany.

For now, however, the war was still far away, and *Königsberg*'s service followed a familiar path, focused primarily on training activities, of which the most interesting events can be mentioned about participation in joint exercises with the cruiser *Leipzig*, which both ships held on 29 May.

From the history of the ship from that period, it is quite difficult to find events that were not related to training activities, which lasted practically until the end of the year. We can only mention here a short visit on 8 June to Warnemünde where the cruiser found herself with the battleships *Hessen* and *Schlesien*, and then a rather interesting cruise between 26 July and 6 August. The route of this led far north to Norwegian waters, namely to the extremely picturesque Geiranger fjord located in south-western Norway.

Another noteworthy event took place only in November – more precisely on the 27th – when the ship's crew took part in the celebrations related to the funeral of the retired Admiral Victor von Harder, one of the many German heroes of the Battle of Skagerrak, better known to us as the Battle of Jutland.

And so much for the service of *Königsberg* in 1933, which ended on 18 December by mooring at the quay of the Deustche Werke shipyard in Kiel.

Königsberg *while approaching a quay.*

Interestingly, this time the stay at the shipyard lasted much longer than normal, due to the quite significant modernization which strongly influenced the silhouette of the ship.

One of the more important changes that were made on the ship during the almost three-month renovation was the replacement of the port side boom with a powerful truss crane, that would perform its task much better. Most importantly, new armament was installed on the ship in the form of two 88 mm guns, which were placed on the sides of the aft superstructure. Although not the most modern weapons, they still increased the ship's combat potential.

In addition, the appearance of the superstructures had changed. The platform was removed from the battle mast, with the simultaneous enlargement of the platform on the bottom bridge of this mast, and the steering deck was extended to the fore funnel.

In total, all these works, together with later sea trials, lasted until the end of March. Shortly after she left Kiel on 11 April 1934 the ship embarked on a foreign cruise, whose route, as before, led far north to Norway, where the ship arrived on 13 April in the southern extremes of this state, to Kristiansand.

Königsberg *seen in another post-card.*

More importantly, this was not the only port on the ship's route, which, having left the Norwegian port, headed north-west to half-way between Scotland and the Faroe Islands, Fair Isle, and later to the port of Peterhead, but undoubtedly the most interesting place that the cruiser visited during this cruise was the Royal Navy's Scapa Flow base, which *Königsberg* had the opportunity to visit, one of the few German ships of that era to do so.

Anyway, there is no doubt that during such cruises selected crew members closely watched what all installations, building and the entire infrastructure of visited ports and bases looked like, providing valuable information to the intelligence services and the High Command, including of course the Navy. It is worth noting here that at that time not only Germany's ships, but all fleets – including the Polish Navy[10] – visited foreign ports, and prepared documentation that could be useful in the case of an armed conflict.

An example of such reasoning can be the great success of Günther Prien – the commander of the submarine U-47 – who perfectly acquainted himself in the specifics of the base at Scapa Flow, and struck the British a sharp blow when he managed to sink the battleship HMS *Royal Oak* at the base on 14 October 1939[11]. Undoubtedly, it was one of the greatest successes of the *Kriegsmarine*, to which German propaganda gave unprecedented publicity, maximizing the humiliation of the British while demonstrating the ability and knowledge of the Germans about their enemy's military installations.

Yet another view of the Königsberg *during her visit to Gdynia in 1935. Note the recognition sign for aircraft painted on top of the main battery turret.*

Of course, it is difficult to say whether Prien's success had been influenced by the visit to Scapa Flow a few years earlier made by *Königsberg*, but it undoubtedly allowed the Germans to get acquainted with the peculiarities and features of this most famous Royal Navy base of that time.

Interestingly, *Königsberg*'s visit to Scapa Flow was not the only one of its kind that she made this year. Having returned from the first cruise, on 24 April, she took part in the annual spring fleet manoeuvres in mid-May and paid several visits to Swinemünde, Königsberg and Warnemünde. On 9 July *Königsberg* set off on another such journey, whose route this time led to Portsmouth, another strategically important naval base in Britain.

Moreover, *Königsberg* was not alone because she was accompanied by the cruiser *Leipzig*, with which she visited Portsmouth from 11 to 15 July, and later they sailed through the Irish Sea, then around the Orkneys and across the North Sea. She returned to Kiel on 20 July.

This was also the last major event of 1934, not counting the series of training cruises in home waters, as well as a visit on 26–30 July to the Estonian port of Tallinn (German: Rewel), crew participation on 29 August in annual rowing competitions, autumn fleet manoeuvres, and the visit to the ship on 29 September by the BdA Commanding officer, Rear Admiral Herman Boehm.

The last saw also a change in the position of the ship's commander. The outgoing Lt. Cdr. Otto von Schrader was replaced by Lt. Cdr. Hubert Schmundt, on 25 September. The latter was a very experienced officer, who began his service with the *Kaiserliche Marine* in 1908.

---

10 The Polish Navy before the outbreak of World War Two had no training ships in the full sense of this word at its disposal. But Polish NCOs practicising aboard French ships had also been given orders to prepare appropriate reports on the ports and bases they were visiting.

11 HMS *Royal Oak* belonged to the *Revenge* class, also known as the R-class. The keel was laid on 17 November 1914, and she was commissioned on 1 May 1916. Her standard displacement was 29,000 t and full 33,500 t. The ships's main battery consisted of eight 381 mm guns.

Königsberg *during a naval parade.*

As usual, *Königsberg* commenced a new year, 1935, with a stay at the shipyard – this time a very short one, because it lasted less than two weeks. Later, as usual, training cruises, the most interesting of which was that on 2–3 February from Wilhelmshaven to the English Channel and back.

Later, it is difficult to find out more interesting information until June, when after a short stay on 5–11 June in Königsberg, in the last days of this month the cruiser served as a representative vessel at the prestigious *Kieler Woche* (Kiel Week) regatta. More importantly, the event was interesting because at the same time, on 26–29 June, the Polish destroyers ORP *Wicher* and ORP *Burza*[12] were in Kiel. Polish seamen visited, among others, *Königsberg* and the battleship *Deutschland*, and a group of Polish officers took part in the regatta.

It is impossible not to remark here that the visit to Kiel of Polish ships was the first of its kind in history and, more importantly, was associated with a return visit, to which, less than two months later, none other than *Königsberg* was appointed.

Well, these were strange days in which Poles were warmly welcomed and properly hosted, but also times in which it was impossible not to notice the growing mutual hostility fuelled by the hatred of Nazism, which was already spreading throughout Germany. It should be remembered that for almost a year now, Hitler had full power, holding both the positions of President and Chancellor of the *Reich*, and *Königsberg* herself from May this year had belonged to a new military formation, which was the *Kriegsmarine*.

The red colours with the black swastika ominously waving on the cruiser's mast quite eloquently testified that the times *Königsberg* served began to change, bringing the ship a completely different future compared to her past we have seen so far.

So far, however, it has not yet been that bad, although it was now clear that all training cruises, exercises and other activities would be reflected in the impending conflict. The first such exercises *Königsberg* took part in were in July, while on 20–21 July she was in Warnemünde, and 27 and 28 in Swinemünde.

In early August, the ship's crew took part in the annual rowing competition, then again in a series of team exercises in torpedo and gunnery practices. Finally the time had come for the aforementioned return visit to Poland – it is worth adding, an official friendly visit of the German ship, and more importantly the first of its kind since Poland had regained independence in 1918. It took place from 22 to 25 August in Gdynia, and the ship herself was moored at the French Quay next to the sea station.

It must be admitted it was a strange visit, enjoying considerable interest especially among the city's inhabitants, but almost continually demonstrated a certain distance, which both sides kept. After all, *Königsberg* was a ship belonging to a state whose authorities did not hide their hostility,

12 The destroyers *Burza* and *Wicher* were the first ships of the Polish Navy with some real combat capability. They were built at the Chantier Naval Francais shipyard in Balinville, and for several years were the backbone of the Polish fleet.

Painting works on one of the main battery turrets.

and in the Polish press it was difficult to find any loud voices of delight.

Anyway, in the report made for Berlin by the *Reich*'s ambassador Hans Adolf von Moltke in Warsaw, he said, among other things, that despite the relatively warm reception "*it was difficult not to notice some moderation*".

Either way, it was the only such visit, although another topic with a similar one planned for 1939 is very interesting, but more on that later.

After she had returned home, *Königsberg* continued training, also in the waters of the North Sea and Skagerrak. On 27 September, her skipper changed again. Lt. Cdr. Theodor Paul was appointed, and a little later the ship's crew underwent significant personnel changes, as some went to man newly built ships.

All in all, for the following months the only information worth mentioning is on various exercises and a short stay at the shipyard to install a floatplane catapult. This year's service of the ship traditionally ended on December 30, when she moored at the quay of the Deutsche Werke for another inspection.

The beginning of 1936 turned out to be quite sad for *Königsberg*. Having left the shipyard on 22 February she ceased to be the flagship of the BdA commander, and becoming a training ship of the Naval Gunnery School. And actually for the first months of this year this was the most important event.

From 13 to 15 June we can note a courtesy visit to Helsinki, quite important as it was the only foreign visit of this kind of cruiser held in this year. Later, as usual, there were training cruises as well as gun and torpedo firing exercises, mainly in Baltic waters. Noteworthy is the modernization the ship underwent this year, by removing the antenna from the second funnel and replacing it with a yardarm antenna, reconstructing the aft superstructure, and most importantly replacing the old 88 mm guns with more modern twin guns of the same calibre.

It is only in the autumn that more interesting events follow the outbreak of the Spanish Civil War. On 17 July an anti-republic military coup had erupted in this country, led by Francisco Franco Bahamonde, better known as Franco. The armed conflict that began to spill over the whole country entailed the need to ensure the safety and evacuation of foreign nationals, especially Germans, of whom there were quite a lot over there. For this reason, almost all major *Kriegsmarine* ships, including the *Königsberg*, were put on standby, although unlike the other ships which arrived in the region in July, she was only sent to Spain at the end of November. Why was it so late? Enough ships had been sent in the summer, and the *Königsberg* was to replace her sister ship *Köln*, so on 25 November the cruiser left Kiel and headed west through the Kiel Canal. It is worth mentioning that there were problems encountered en route due to heavy fog, the ship had to interrupt its cruise and anchor on the Elbe. It was not until 28 November that the cruiser arrived at El Ferrol on the north-western Spanish coast – incidentally, the port city where General Franco was born. Her activity in Spanish waters was not spectacular, although it must be stressed that the civil war in Spain, however, continued and took on a more and more bloody character. The *Königsberg* herself remained in these waters for quite some time, guarding German interests and progressively engaging in the conflict.

It should be noted here that the war in Spain very quickly met with reactions from European states, including Nazi Germany and Fascist Italy, which declared for General Franco who was a perfect candidate for Hitler's ally. Similarly, other states also acted with the only difference that the Soviet Union and France openly backed the Republican government, while the UK, while officially maintaining neutrality, also supported the government. The *Königsberg* initially performed patrols in the Gibraltar area visiting, among others, Cadiz, Tangier and Lagos. An interesting event can be noted in January 1937, when the *Königsberg* was in the process of detaining the Republican merchantman s/s *Soton* which was supposed to be a response to the government's seizure of the German

Poor quality but very interesting post-card published on occasion of the Königsberg's *visit to Pilau.*

merchant vessel s/s *Palos*. The cruiser failed to capture the Spanish ship as her crew managed to run her aground. However, on the same day, the *Königsberg* seized another ship, s/s *Marie Junquer*, which after manning her with a German skeleton crew was eventually handed over to the Nationalists. It is easy to note that the service of the ship did not have much to do with the security of citizens of foreign nationalities or keeping order. The *Königsberg*'s tasks, as well as the other *Kriegsmarine* ships operating in that region, were somewhat different and were aimed at discreet and later open support for General Franco's rebels and the protection of convoys carrying supplies for them. Hitler did not fear that Germany's involvement in the conflict could lead to international incidents and, according to Admiral Reader, who, after the events of August, when Republican ships detained German merchantmen and forced them back to the Atlantic, insisted on providing "effective support" – he decided to assist the rebels and get involved directly in the conflict. From this time on there was an escalation in the German involvement in this extremely bloody war. In addition, the formation of the famous Condor Legion was already in full swing, so that by November it contained more than 5,000 fully-equipped troops, and throughout the war 20,000 men served with it! Such a force could only be sent to Spain by sea and here the task for the *Königsberg* and the rest of the German ships was to secure the route that carried tens of tons of military equipment.

Well, "Hitler's struggle with the Communists," who dominated the government forces, had flared up for good and there were no sentiments – it was simply a war and Germany was one of the warring sides. But let us leave politics and focus on the *Königsberg*, which a few days after the actions with the s/s *Soton* and s/s *Marie Junquera* was recalled home and on 11 January was replaced by the *Köln*.

The cruiser returned to Kiel on 15 January and after brief routine maintenance she returned to a somewhat monotonous service, completing the interrupted previous year's training program which focused primarily on gun and torpedo firing. In February was she also testing new models of communication devices. It is also worth noting the fact that the new commanding officer of the ship, appointed on 6 February, was Commander Robin Schall-Emden, one of the German heroes honoured with the Emden suffix, was of course related to the history of the World War One cruiser *Emden*. Interestingly, the *Königsberg*, unlike other major warships, did not return to war-torn Spain, but operated in home waters. Why? There is absolutely no certainty, but among writers dealing with the history of the *Kriegsmarine* one can find the opinion that the ship was poorly suited to such tasks due to her not quite successful construction. On long cruises, especially because of the effects of turbulent waters on both the *Königsberg* and the other K-class ships, many cracks and other damage were observed on the hull and superstructure, which made a group of *Kriegsmarine* officers convinced that these ships were unsuitable to operate in distant waters, especially in the sometimes very dangerous Atlantic. An excellent example of this would be the sister ship *Karlsruhe*'s journey in 1936 to the Pacific Ocean, where after entering the hurricane zone, construction defects almost led to actual catastrophe. It was a clear sign that the construction of the K-class cruisers left much to be desired, and their service should be based only in relatively safe coastal waters. And thus was the *Königsberg*'s further service. After a short stay in the shipyard on 13–27 May she continued to implement the training programme. Interestingly, in June she served as target ship for the 1st U-boot

Königsberg *as seen from her stern.*

"*Weddigen*" Flotilla – a formation that was interesting because it was the first of its kind which was set up in Germany after World War One, on 27 September 1935[13]. Also worth noting was the cruise on which she departed on 12 June, and her route led north to Norwegian waters. She then visited the fjords of Sulen, Stor, Summelo and Giranger and returned to Kiel on 28 June. The following months continued with countless exercises until the end of the year and did not stand out as anything special. F inally, on 5 December, she arrived at the shipyard for refurbishment and modernization.

1938 was almost a repeat of the previous year, when the most important events were training cruises. We will not describe every training or firing practice here, but merely mention that they were primarily based on co-operation with submarine flotillas and firing at target ships, mainly the downgraded battleship *Hessen*. Unfortunately, in this year there are also a lot of inconsistencies about what was actually happening to the ship. In several references we find information that in May the cruiser visited the Swedish port of Visby, and on 22 August participated in the launching ceremony of the cruiser *Prinz Eugen*[14]. It is more certain that in the summer on the occasion of training cruises she visited, among others, Wernemünde, Sassnitz, Travemünde, Grömitz and Swinemünde. There is also some information about the change in commander's position – on 3 November Commander Ernst Scheurlen took over the ship.

At the beginning of 1939, despite Hitler's increasingly noticeable aggressive policy in Europe, there were no spectacular events. Despite another triumph for the Third Reich, which the occupation of Memel (today Klaipeda, Lithuania) undoubtedly was, the *Königsberg*'s service, as she was not included in the force tasked to seize the port, continued to be based on training. In February-May the *Königsberg* was in the shipyard. On 11–15 May she visited the Finnish port of Vaasa, and from 17 to 19 May Visby in Sweden. On 27 June (briefly, until September only), Commander Kurt Caesar-Hoffman was appointed as the new commander of the ship.

At that time it was already noticeable that difficult times were coming for Europe. The Nazi insanity that haunted the whole of Germany and the hatred spread by the country's leader, Adolf Hitler, had to finally find its outlet. June, July and August were the months when more and more

13 After the World War One the Treaty of Versailles completely forbade the construction and possession of submarines by Germany.

14 There are many inaccuracies in both cases, and quite contradictory information is often found in professional literature.

people began to realize that the outbreak of war was inevitable. The only mystery was when would it happen.

Today in retrospect, we all know that it officially took place on 1 September 1939 when the battleship *Schleswig-Holstein* opened fire on the Polish military transit depot on Westerplatte Peninsula. Interestingly, it is relatively little known that, according to the initial plans of the German headquarters, the first shots at the little Polish garrison were not to be fired by the battleship *Schleswig-Holstein*, but by the *Königsberg*! The initial plans were very similar to those we know from the history of the battleship *Schleswig-Holstein* and assumed a visit by the cruiser to Danzig (today Gdańsk, Poland) on the pretext of taking part in the anniversary celebrations to commemorate the sinking of the cruiser *Magdeburg*.

The *Königsberg* with her status of a training ship which, more importantly, once visited Poland as we have seen before, seemed almost perfect for this task. Interestingly, the first signals from Berlin about the intention to send the *Königsberg* to Danzig were notified as early as in May. It was then that the German embassy in Warsaw, in accordance with the provisions agreed in Versailles, informed the Polish side of these intentions and later the details were discussed[15]. It is not known when exactly these plans were changed, but as the preparations for the *Königsberg* to set sail were fully completed on 23 August, orders from Berlin arrived to cancel the mission which would instead be performed by the *Schleswig-Holstein*. This was, of course, a violation of the arrangements with the Polish side, which was not informed about the change or given an explanation of its reasons. Why did Germany make this decision at the last minute? It is difficult to say, but it can be expected that the 280 mm guns of the battleship were much better suited to fire at the Polish defences rather than the 150 mm main battery of the *Königsberg*[16]. It might also have been connected with the uncertainty at which wharf the much smaller cruiser could be moored after potential steering of the ship by a Polish pilot boat and this would complicate the entire operation, and in the case of the much larger battleship her mooring was more predictable. All these are mere speculations – and although reasonable, there is no doubt that the person responsible for the change of plans had to be Adolf Hitler and probably no one knew what was going on in his brain...

The foredeck. Note the recognition sign for aircraft painted on top of the main battery turret.

Anyhow, for the *Königsberg* such a task would undoubtedly have made her one of the most famous ships in history but in fact has become only a "curiosity" worth mentioning when describing her story. Her participation in the September Campaign was to be limited only to taking part in a long line of distant surveillance blockading the Polish coast, for which she was assigned on 1 September. However, on the same day she was ordered to abort this mission and head to the waters of the North Sea where, as part of Operation "*Westwall*" and together with the cruisers *Köln*, *Emden* and *Leipzig* participated in laying mines from the coast of the Netherlands to Skagerrak. This was the case for almost the whole of September, and the only more interesting event of the month was another and – as it turned out later – the last change in the position of the commander of the ship, when on September 16 she was taken over by Commander Heinrich Ruhfus.

By the end of the year, despite the ongoing war, as regards to the *Konigsberg's* activity it is hard to write anything interesting, except that she was alternately operating in the Baltic Sea and North

15 According to the Treaty of Versailles provision, the Germans were obliged to inform the Polish side of every visit of their warships to Danzig.

16 In some publications one may find information that the main reason for the change was the 280 mm guns of the *Schleswig-Holstein* could fire at the Polish positions and coastal batteries on Hel Peninsula.

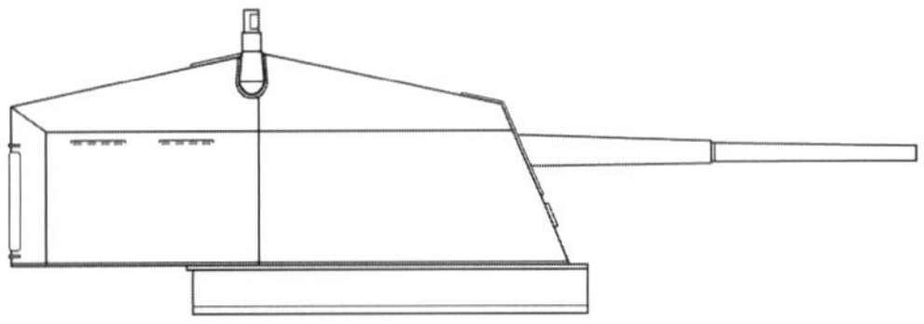

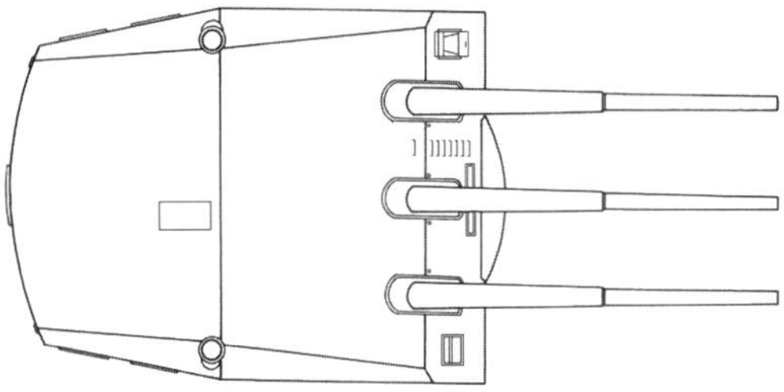

The main battery turret with 150 mm guns.

Sea, where she participated in exercises and mine-laying operations. Later she was sent to a shipyard where, because of the effect of sever frosts, she was literally "entombed", and in which, apart from the standard inspection, she underwent a minor modernization consisting in the reconstruction of the wings of the bridge and fitting a demagnetization installation.

March was marked by preparations for the *Weserübung* operation, which was aimed at occupying Denmark and Norway. This was a great challenge for the *Kriegsmarine* to carry out, involving over 100,000 troops and almost all the major warships the Germans had at their disposal at that time. The *Königsberg* was assigned to Group 3 (out of six) under the command of Rear Admiral Hubert Schmidt. In addition to her, there were the cruiser *Köln*, the training gunship *Bremse*, the torpedo ships *Leopard* and *Wolf*, 1st Torpedo Boat Flotilla (S19, S21, S22, S23, S24) along with the depot ship *Carl Peters* and auxiliary vessels *Schiff* 9 and *Schiff* 18.

The target of the formation was Norway's second largest city, Bergen, which was of great economic and strategic significance, located at the western tip of the country where the North Sea and Norwegian Sea meet. On 2 April the *Königsberg* was still in Wilhelmshaven and troops embarked and some equipment was loaded. On 7 April the entire force moved north. An interesting fact to note is that, as part of the activities aimed at keeping the destination of German ships secret as long as possible, each of them in the event of premature detection by the Norwegians was to fly a British flag and, if requested, give one of the names of British ships. The Norwegians were expecting a formation of Allied ships designated for the defence of Bergen. In the case of the *Königsberg* she was supposed to pretend to be the British cruiser HMS *Calcutta*, her sister ship *Köln* was the HMS *Cairo*.

Initially, the mission was carried out according to plan and the passage from Germany went undisturbed. On 9 April at about 0200 hrs the force arrived at the entrance to the Karsfjord fjord. Here the formation was detected by the Norwegians. The *Köln* which was leading was asked for identification. According to the German plan, the name HMS *Cairo* was sent back in response – the Norwegians believed this and remained unalarmed. Everything seemed to run almost perfectly. At dawn, the force found itself in Byifjord, where the *Köln* and the torpedo ships halted in order to disembark the troops who were to eliminate the Kvarven battery guarding the approaches to Bergen. The *Königsberg*, along with the rest of the ships, went on to Bergen directly and shortly thereafter received the first hits from this battery, which, contrary to the original schedule was not immediately suppressed. Before it was finally silenced by German troops it fired a series of accurate salvos. Now with the *Königsberg* in the lead, which was the largest ship and in the eyes of the Norwegians

Opinions of the specialists on Königsberg *as well as other K-class cruisers vary, nevertheless as far as their silhouettes are concerned, they were very peculiar vessels.*

The last photographs of Königsberg. *The ship is burning at the quay of Bergen harbour, 10 April 1940.*

the greatest threat, had become the main focus of the Norwegian gunners, who managed to hit the cruiser three times. Two rounds hit the starboard side, of which one in the area of engine room No. 1 caused serious damage, and one exploded on the deck, severely damaging the 37 mm guns and deck equipment as well as killing and wounding several crew members[17].

In spite of these problems that led to the damage of the engine, the *Königsberg* arrived in Bergen early in the morning, where the troops disembarked and captured the harbour and city. Unfortunately for the cruiser, due to the damage that affected its mobility, her future did not appear too bright. The force commander Admiral Schmundt ordered the *Königsberg* to stay at the wharf where she was supposed to repair the damage while providing support to the troops ashore and the remaining ships were about to head back home. For the effects of this decision one did not have to wait too long. After all, these were the first days of action in Norway, during which the situation of the Allies in France was not so bad and they could assist in the defence of the country. News of the Germans in the Bergen area arrived very quickly to the British, who wanted to know the situation and sent into the air many reconnaissance aircraft, which, among others, identified two cruisers (*Königsberg* and *Köln*) in the port. Interestingly enough, on the same day 12 Wellingtons of 9 and 125 Squadrons RAF and 12 Hampdens of 50 Squadron RAF bombed the German-held port. The raid did not cause any major damage to the Germans, but made Admiral Schmudt aware that another air strike could seriously damage his ships, so regardless of her problems the *Königsberg* was ordered to join the rest of the force and leave Bergen as quickly as possible and return to Germany. At this time, the British were preparing for another attack, which would have a tragic effect on the cruiser.

Early on the morning of 10 April, 16 Blackburn Skua bombers of 800 and 803 Squadrons RAF, led by Naval Lieutenant W.P. Lucy, took off from the Hatston base on the Orkney Islands, 500 kilometres from the coast of Norway. They headed for Bergen to resume the attack on the harbour and the German ships there[18]. Given that these single-engined aircraft had to fly over a long route in harsh night-time conditions and, more importantly, operate at the limits of their range, the mission was extremely difficult and dangerous, as evidenced by the fact that one of the machines went missing on that flight.

Meanwhile another day was dawning in Bergen.

In spite of the fighting around the city, in the port itself it was relatively quiet, and on the lone *Königsberg* the crew struggled to repair the damage so that the ship could set off as quickly as possible for Germany. Unfortunately, no repairs were completed. At 0730 hrs came the first anti-aircraft alert, which was later cancelled, but half an hour later it was re-announced. This time the bombers were over the port and the *Königsberg* as the only large ship became the main target of the attack. Amid a roar of engines from the attacking planes and anti-aircraft gun fire, the first of the bombs dropped hit the cruiser at 0805 hrs, followed shortly thereafter by two more. The poor design of the ship, whose armour was inadequate, could not resist the 227 kg bombs which easily penetrated the thin armour and exploded inside the ship. The powerful explosions inside the ship and the next three in the near vicinity left no doubt that her fate had been sealed. Interestingly, the precision of the British airmen, which deserves the highest praise, means that there has been no certainty to this day as to the order and damage caused by the bombs dropped. In the references on the K-class cruisers and the *Königsberg* herself, we can find information that, as well as the three direct hits, the cruiser received yet another, but this is very difficult to verify. It does not change the fact that the shattered ship quickly caught fire and was covered with black smoke, then leaned over to her port side at 1051 hrs. Almost three hours after the raid, and despite the heroic struggle of the crew to save the ship, she capsized and sank.

It is worth noting here that the destruction of the *Königsberg* on 10 April 1940 meant she was the first cruiser during World War Two sunk by aircraft – certainly not the last.

Despite a series of very serious hits, the ship's crew did not suffer very severe casualties. In fact on the short list of victims there were only 18 killed and 24 wounded, adding to the number of nearly 5,300 German military personnel who perished during the entire campaign in Norway.

Besides the *Königsberg*, the total *Kriegsmarine* losses in the campaign were three cruisers (including "*Königsberg*"), ten destroyers and 38 other warships and transports.

It is also interesting to note that the British airmen, despite such a spectacular attack, lost only one aircraft, and were still not sure about the effects of their raid, so the next day the whole operation was repeated, but the *Königsberg* was not there any more..

---

17 As a result of this fire, the *Bremse* and *Carl Peters* following the *Konigsberg* also suffered serious damage.

18 The Blackburn Skua was a single-engined fighter-bomber aircraft also classified as a dive bomber. Its overall length was 10.85 m, wingspan of 14.08 and height of 3.81 m. Engine was a Bristol Perseus XII of 902 hp which provided a top speed of 362 km/h. The crew was two, and the armament consisted of five 7.7 mm cal machine guns.

The Königsberg*'s wreck for several months stayed on its side.*

One of the last photographs of Königsberg, *taken during dismantling works.*

There is a lot of contradictory information about the *Königsberg*'s further fate. In some publications we can find information that the Germans took up her recovery as late as in 1942, which seems to be a bit strange due to the fact that the ship sank in shallow waters at the port quay which would not make such work too complicated. More reliable information mentions 1941 as the year of recovery, after which the ship was used as a floating base for U-Boats.

In September 1944, still in the Bergen area, she sank again and her wreck was dismantled after the war ended.

The cruiser *Königsberg* (Kreuzer "B") specification[19]

Type K

- Shipyard Reichsmarinewerft, Wilhmshaven
- Construction No. 108
- Keel laid 12 April 1926
- Launched 26 March 1927
- Commissioned 17 April 1929
- Standard displacement (official) 6,000 t
- Standard displacement (actual) 6,380 t
- Total displacement (official) 6,750 t
- Total displacement (actual) 7,700 t
- Overall length 174.0 m
- Waterline length 169.0 m
- Beam 15.2 m
- Draft (full) 5.4 m
- Power unit 6 x Marine Schuls-Thornycroft boilers, 4 x steam turbine sets, 2 x diesel engines total output 68,150 shp
- Maximum speed 32.0 knots
- Fuel supply 1,239 tons for boilers and 139 tons for diesels
- Range 5,700 NM at 19 kn 7,300 NM at 17 kn 8,000 NM at 10 knots (diesels)
- Crew 514–614 men
- Armament (1929) 9 (3x3) 150 mm guns: 2 (2x1) 88 mm guns, 12 (4x3) 500 mm torpedo tubes
- Armament (1933) 9 (3x3) 150 mm guns: 4 (4x1) 88 mm guns, 12 (4x3) 500 mm torpedo tubes
- Armament (1934) 9 (3x3) 150 mm guns: 4 (4x1) 88 mm guns, 12 (4x3) 533 mm torpedo tubes
- Armament (1935/36) 9 (3x3) 150 mm guns: 6 (3x2) 88 mm guns, 8 (4x2) 37 mm guns, 8 (8x1) 20 mm cannons, 12 (4x3) 533 mm torpedo tubes
- Armament (1940) 9 (3x3) 150 mm guns: 6 (3x2) 88 mm guns, 8 (4x2) 37 mm guns, 8 (8x1) 20 mm cannons, 12 (4x3) 533 mm torpedo tubes
- Armour 50 mm broadsides: 70 mm transverse bulkheads, 20–40 mm decks, 30–100 mm command post, 20–30 mm main battery turrets
- Aircraft equipment 1 x pneumatic catapult Type FL22 1–2 floatplanes Heinkel He 60, later Arado Ar 196

19 There are a number of discrepancies in terms of the ship's parameters, which makes quoting them with absolute certainty extremely difficult and one should be aware that they may not match the data from other references.

Layout of the *Königsberg's* superstructure in her initial period of service.

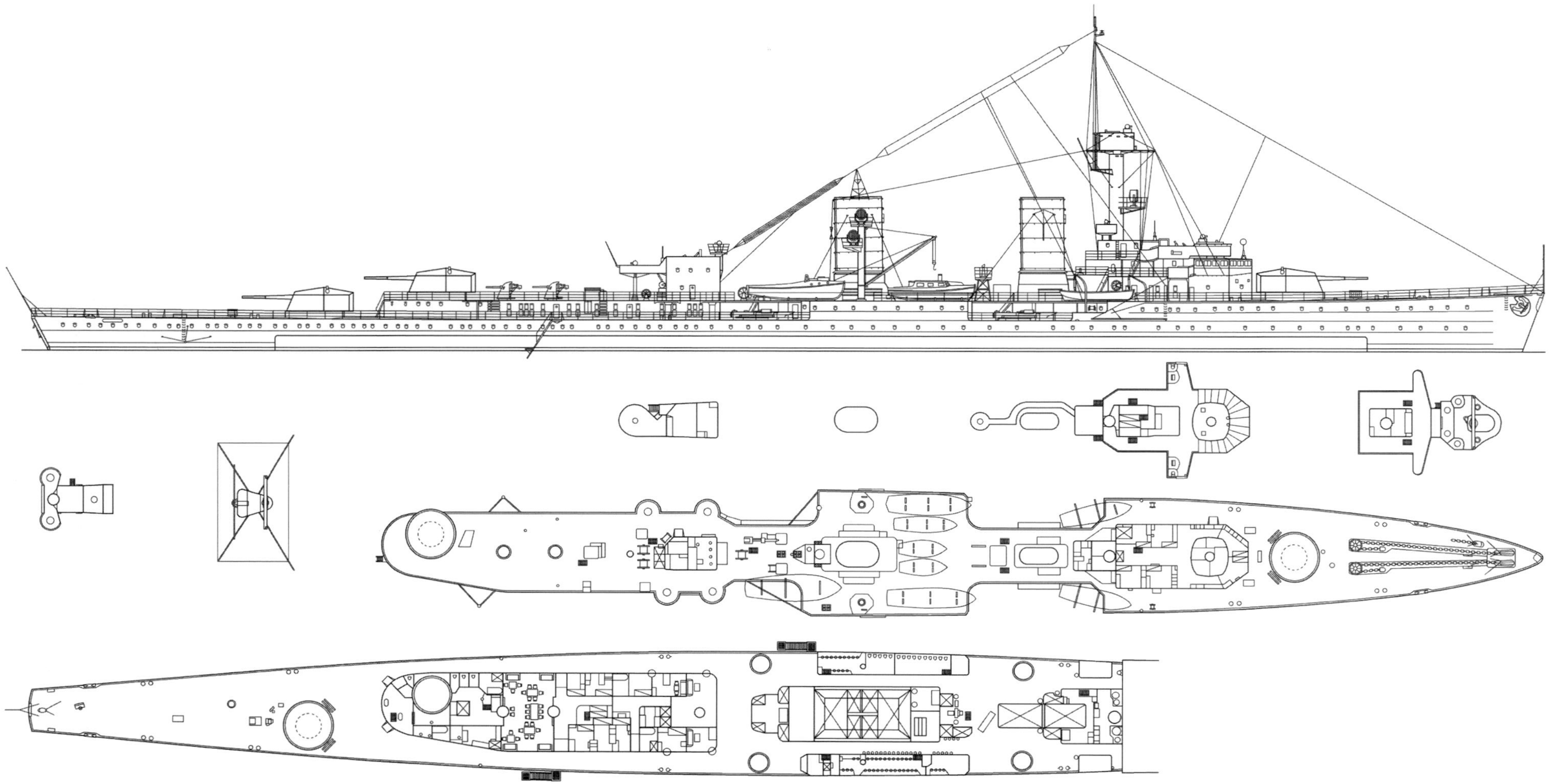

Karlsruhe
A Victim of One Torpedo

Just over three months after the construction of the *Königsberg* in Wilhelmshaven had commenced, on 27 July 1926 the keel was laid at the Deutsche Werke shipyard in Kiel for the third cruiser-type ship in Germany's post-war history.

Designated as "*Kreuzer C*" in accordance with the implementation of the plan to build a series of K-class cruisers, which like the *Königsberg* described in the previous chapter and the next sister ship *Köln*, was to replace an old cruiser. In her case the *Medusa*, built in 1901 and no longer representing any useful combat capabilities.

The *Karlsruhe*, because this name was to be given later to the cruiser under construction, was a relatively good ship considering the reality that her constructors had to face. Innovative weapons layout and a powerful turbine-diesel drive enabling her to achieve a slightly higher than average operating range meant that, like the cruisers mentioned in previous chapters, she would turn out to be a unique vessel with many interesting features.

Placing of the main battery guns in enclosed turrets, and their location asymmetrical to the plane of symmetry, made her one of the first cruisers in the world which featured such a design. Similarly,

Karlsruhe *was the third and the last of the K-class cruisers that served with the* Reichsmarine, *and later with the* Kriegsmarine.

Launching ceremony of Karlsruhe *on 20 August 1927.*

we can say the same about the propulsion system and the wide-scale use of electric welding, which, with a view to saving weight, was used to connect elements of the hull structure and superstructures.

Undoubtedly, these features distinguished her from the other cruisers of that time, however, they also became her curse, having a direct impact on her stability and hull strength. These were serious shortcomings, but when she was built that was not the most important detail.

When in 1924 the duties of the Chief Commanding Officer of the Navy were taken over by Admiral Hans Zenker, his main goal – among others – was to commission as soon as possible modern cruisers able to face their counterparts from other fleets.

Of course, given the almost impossible to meet restrictions imposed on the German Navy in the peace treaty, there could be no cruiser ship with perfect armament, armour, etc., though it can easily be said that the team of engineers led by Albrecht Ehrenberg designed a series of excellent

Karlsruhe's *profile as seen in a postcard.*

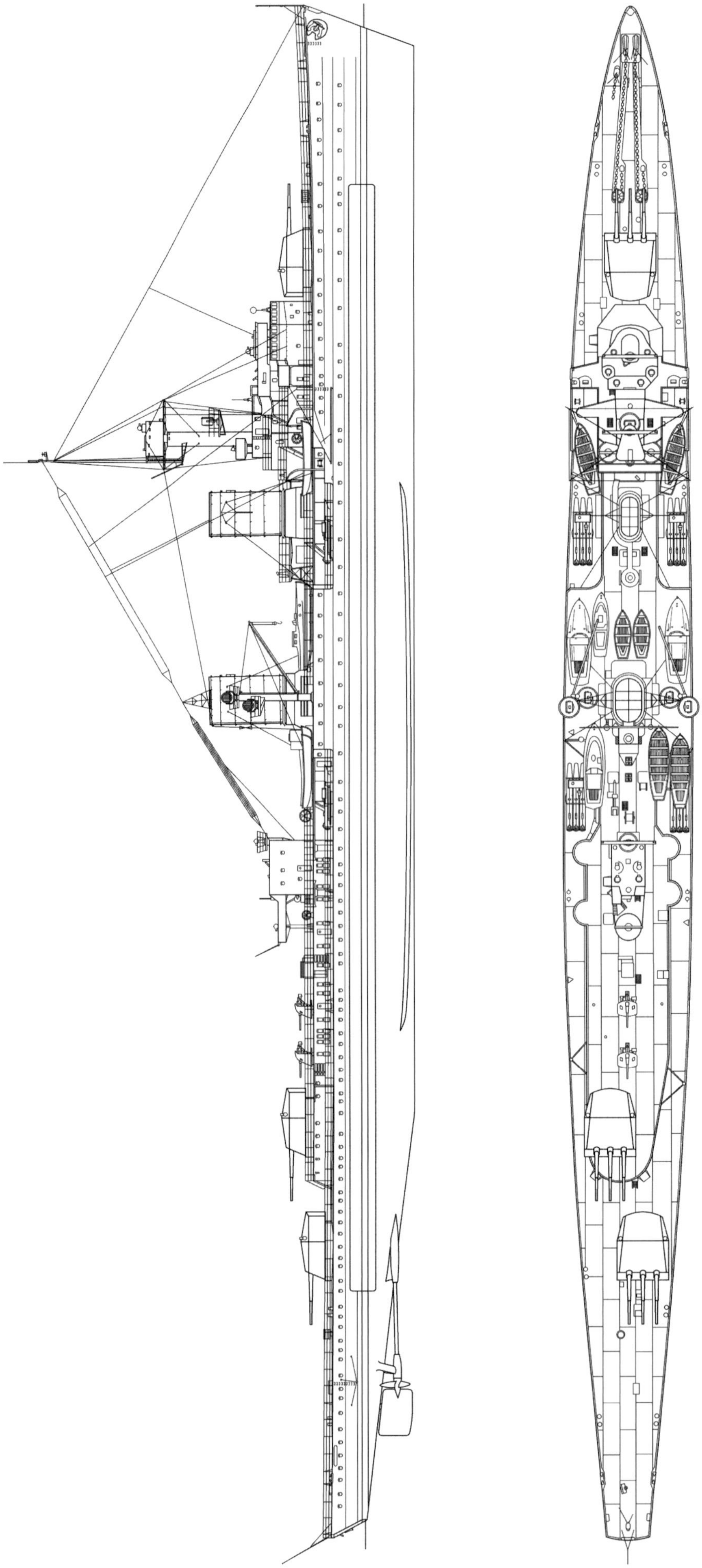

The cruiser Karlsruhe *in the initial period of her service.*

ships, although perhaps not of ideal combat value and seaworthiness, but still extremely important for the *Reichsmarine* which was reviving at that time.

It must be remembered that the days in which the K-class cruisers were built were very difficult for Germany. There was a lot going on during the assembly work on the *Karlsruhe*'s hull at the Deutsche Werke's slipway. All over Germany, despite relative economic stability, the problem of unemployment was still not dealt with, which meant that many Germans turned their attention to extreme parties, mainly communists and national socialists. Political quarrels constantly involved many high-ranking *Reichsmarine* officers, which undoubtedly had an impact on the development and functioning of the fleet.

Many political groups were still reluctant to spend money on arms, so it was noticed more than once that whenever the issue of building a new warship was raised in the *Reichstag* forum, it met with harsh criticism and opposition. The subsequent scandal known as the "Lohmann affair" was also significant, as a result of which the defence minister Otto Gessler and the aforementioned Admiral Zenker were forced to step down.

It cannot be said that all these events had no affect the development of the German fleet, including the cruisers most interesting to us at the moment, which were designed and built in these conditions.

However, this is all politics, and we are interested in the *Karlsruhe*, the construction of which, marked with the number 207, was proceeding.

Month by month, her hull was taking shape. Structural elements, drive assemblies and other equipment were installed and after a little over a year the hull of the ship was ready for launching.

The ceremony itself, which could not be missed by important guests including the head of the *Reichsmarine* Admiral Hans Zenker and *Reichswer* minister Otto Karl Gessler, took place on 20 August 1927.

Considering the symbol represented by the ship and the importance of the whole event, this day became a great festival in Kiel, during which many inhabitants of this city came to the shipyard to participate in the ceremony. Well, maybe these were not the days of the future spectacular launchings of major *Kriegsmarine* ships which the ruling Nazis turned into great spectacles, but many Germans saw in her the signs of the reviving power of their country.

A speech given on the occasion by the mayor of the city of Karlsruhe, Dr Julius Finter, was also a show of power, as he spoke in superlatives about the cruiser herself and the country under the flag of which she was supposed to sail.

It was also important that the honour of name-giving was performed by the widow of the commander of the first cruiser named *Karlsruhe* – Lt. Cmdr. Erich Köhler[1].

Name of the ship

The name given to the cruiser came from the city located in western Germany on the Upper North Rhine Plain on the rivers Alb and Pfinz. It was founded in 1715 and received city status in 1745. In 1930, its population was estimated at 182,000 inhabitants, and currently stands at about 300,000.

At the time of naming the cruiser, the city was an important industrial, machinery, food and scientific centre. Today, such well-known companies as Siemens, Bosch, L'Oreal and Pfizer have their branches located there. There are also several banks and insurance companies.

The city is also an important communication hub combining rail, road and inland waterway routes.

Throughout the period of the cruiser's service, the city was the patron of the ship.

The ship herself was not completed yet.

1 The *Karlsruhe* we are describing here was the third ship in the German Navy to bear this name.
The first was a cruiser, commissioned in 1914, built at the Germaniawerft shipyard in Kiel.
The ship had 6,190 t full displacement, 142.2 m in length, 13.7 m beam and 6.2 m draft.
The output of her machinery was 37,885 HP, and maximum speed was 28.5 knots.
She was armed with 12 x 105 mm guns, 2 x 500 mm torpedo tubes and could carry a supply of up to 120 naval mines.
She went down in history as one of the most effective German raiding ships with 17 vessels sunk of a total tonnage of over 76,600 tonnes. She sank on 4 November 1914, about 350 NM east of Trinidad as a result of an internal explosion that could not be explained.
Among the victims was the commander of the ship, Lt. Cdr. Erich Köhler.
The second *Karlsruhe* was the *Königsberg*-class cruiser built at the Kaiserliche Werft shipyard in Kiel, which was put into service in November 1916.
This ship had 5,440 tons displacement, was 151.4 m long, 14.2 beam and 6.3 m draft.
The output of the engines was estimated at 45,900 HP, and maximum speed was 27.8 knots.

Interesting view of the Karlsruhe's *stern with the name plate, as well as the coat-of-arms of the Third Reich. In the background one of the Deutschland-class battleships can be seen.*

When the echoes of champagne cork shots faded away, the cruiser's hull was moored at the fitting-out wharf, where superstructures and various types of equipment were installed over the next months, and above all the most important elements – armament and sights.

In total, it took more than two years before shipyard workers could report the completion of the work, and it was not until 15 October 1929 that the ship was officially approved by a commission appointed by the navy. Following that, a period of intensive trials and tests began.

The performance of all types of mechanisms was checked, measurements of speed and fuel consumption were made and listing tests were carried out. The ship repeatedly went out to sea, both in the Baltic and North Sea waters, with shipyard specialists on board and a gradually completed crew.

Considering the fact that, as we have already learned, the *Karlsruhe* was the sister ship of *Königsberg* whose description can be found in the previous chapter, we will not describe her construction meticulously here, focusing only on mentioning the minor differences between the two ships.

In general, the technical characteristics of the ships from their initial period of service were almost identical, all the more so as the standard displacement was given officially as 6,000 tons, which was to comply with the permissible limits.

Of course, this had nothing to do with reality because once the construction had been completed, the standard displacement of *Karlsruhe* was 6,380 tons, which of course was a clear violation of the already mentioned limits. Well, from the very beginning, the Germans, keeping the actual data secret, were breaking the peace treaty arrangements in almost every possible field, but let us be honest – could you build a relatively capable cruiser ship that would fit within those 6,000 tons? It is interesting that specialists from the British or French fleets had to be aware of this. Also interesting is the fact that when the first German battleship was launched, also built according to the treaty provisions, her displacement limit set at 10,000 tons was exceeded by 20 percent!

It is difficult to say whether the Allies did not realize this or simply did not want to, but with the irony of fate the cleverly faked statistics meant that they were actually the ones to blame for the fraud they would fall victim to themselves in the future[2].

She had eight 150 mm guns, two 88 mm guns and four 500 mm torpedo tubes.

She was scuttled in Scapa Flow on 21 June 1919.

2 Many authors claim that although officially understated technical data of the cruisers and "pocket" battleships came to light only in 1945, the Allies had really been aware that something must had be wrong, but bearing in mind the role that Germany was to fulfil at that time, in the case of Soviet Russia's

Karlsruhe *passing through the Holtenau Lock in the Kiel Canal.*

In any case, *Karlsruhe* officially entered service as a cruiser with a displacement of 6,000 tons, carrying nine 150 mm guns.

As far as external appearance was concerned, she was almost identical to her sister ship *Königsberg*, differing from her only by minor details resulting more from the fact that she was built at another shipyard rather than changes made to the design itself.

The situation was different in the ship's interior. Here, the most important difference distinguishing *Karlsruhe* from her sister ships *Königsberg* and *Köln* was the drive, which used indirect operating modes, disconnected at maximum limits of performance.

Turbines manufactured by Germania Werft from Kiel were another difference. Their total output fell slightly compared to *Königsberg* and amounted to 68,200 HP, while the maximum speed reached during tests on a measured mile was not much inferior to the said sister ship, which at 362 rpm was 32.1 knots.

Speaking of propulsion, the difference between the two ships was also significant in the case of the propellers, whose diameter in the case of *Karlsruhe* was 4.1 m while on *Königsberg* this figure dropped to 3.7 m.

The basic armament of *Karlsruhe* at the time of entering service consisted of nine 150mm guns placed in three, three-barrel turrets, two 88mm guns and four triple 500 mm torpedo tubes from the same manufacturer and with the same parameters as found on *Königsberg*. Here, an interesting difference is the names of the main battery turrets, which were named successively as: fore turret SMS *Moltke* (A) and aft turrets SMS *Derfflinger* (B)[3] and SMS *Göben*.

Raising for the first time the war flag on the ship that cost the German taxpayers 36 million marks took place on 6 November 1929, and the command of a crew consisting of over five hundred officers, non-commissioned officers and naval ratings, consisting mainly of the crew of the decommissioned cruiser *Berlin*, was taken over by Lt. Cdr. Eugen Lindau. A very experienced officer, forty-six years old at that time, whose origin with the German fleet dated back to 1903.

Under the orders of Cdr. Lindau, *Karlsruhe* performed many trial and training cruises until May 1930, during which the crew was getting acquainted with the ship as well as with each other and it was not until May that preparations for the first cruise began.

Classified similarly to *Emden* and *Königsberg* as a training ship, on 24 May 1930 *Karlsruhe* left Wilhelmshaven and set sail on her first and, more importantly, extremely long and interesting

attempts at Western Europe, they just kept a blind eye! However, it is difficult to say whether this is true without without documents confirming such speculations...

3 Actually it is uncertain whether the B turret was given this name.

In the inter-war period decks of the K-class cruisers were made available to the public many times.

training cruise around Africa and the shores of South America. The route initially led through the North Sea along the northern shores of the European continent, and later, encircling the Iberian Peninsula, entered the Mediterranean.

The ship headed for the Suez Canal, visiting Cagliari in Sicily along the way and dropped her anchors in the bay of Suda in Crete. Later she passed through the Suez Canal and after entering the waters of the Red Sea in the first days of July she called at the port of Massaua in Italian Eritrea.

Then she headed to the Indian Ocean to visit Port Victoria in the Seychelles from 7 to 21 July, and later, setting her course westward, visited Tanga in former German East Africa, and then Tanzania as well as Mombasa in Kenya.

Next on the route of the maiden voyage of the training ship *Karlsruhe* was Zanzibar, which the cruiser visited between 26 July and 4 August. She then headed south to the port of Laurenco Marques[4] in Mozambique, afterwards calling at Durban and Capetown in South Africa.

Recalling that this unusual journey for a warship, very similar to those described in the chapters about the cruisers *Emden* and *Königsberg*, was a training cruise for the German navy cadets, therefore quite interesting was an incident en route to the aforementioned Capetown, where night firing practice was carried out.

Although Cdr. Lindau informed the South African authorities about his intentions, the night-time cannonade caused a kind of panic among the port's inhabitants, which could not be controlled for a long time. Despite explaining all the circumstances, some disgust remained, so the ship's company with some sense of relief moved on to Lüderitz Bay in the former German South-West Africa, and likewise Whale Bay which was another destination on the *Karlsruhe*'s cruise route.

The last port the ship visited on the west coast of Africa was Lobito in Angola, from which the cruiser headed west to cross the South Atlantic. On 7 October she stopped her engines on the roadstead of Rio de Janeiro.

Unfortunately, despite the proverbial attractiveness of this port, because of the dangerous riots associated with the coup in which Getúlio Dornelles Vargas took power in Brazil, Cdr. Lindau decided to shorten the visit and go on a further journey, heading north to visit much calmer Pernambuco between 4 and 7 November. This port on the easternmost tip of South America was also the most convenient place from which the ship could put to sea on a return voyage to the other side of the Atlantic, hence the *Karlsruhe* sailed north-west to drop her anchor at the approach to São Vicente – Cape Verde Islands.

Here another interesting event took place, which was a rendezvous with her sister ship *Köln*, on which the flag was raised on 15 January 1930, commanded at that time by Lieutenant Commander Ludwig von Schröder. A meeting of both skippers must have taken place as well as countless greetings

4 Today Maputo – the capital of Mozambique.

Almost a propaganda image, clearly demonstrating the ship's national identity.

from the ships' crews. The next day, the two cruisers raised their anchors and put to sea for a joint exercise, then on 17 November they halted in the Santa Cruz roadstead in Tenerife.

The next port on the *Karlsruhe*'s route was the Spanish harbour of Vigo, where the ship arrived on 26 November 26, as had *Köln*, from which she separated on 22 November.

It was also the last port on the route of the first journey of the cruiser *Karlsruhe* which had commenced in May. On 12 December the cruiser returned to Kiel where the cadets disembarked, and after a short stay she was transferred to the shipyard for the necessary inspection and maintenance works after such a long voyage.

Having left the shipyard, which took place in 1931, there are not many interesting events in the ship's activities. From January to October training tasks were carried out mainly in North Sea waters. Gun and torpedo firing were practised. In April, *Karlsruhe* took part in the major navy manoeuvres.

In 1931, the first modernization took place. It is also worth mentioning that from 1931, lightweight superstructures between funnels and in front of the poop were also installed periodically, which were to provide additional accommodation for distant cruises.

Karlsruhe *seen from the starboard side. Between the funnels a Heinkel floatplane is visible.*

Karlsruhe during a naval parade in Kiel. Behind, her sister ship Königsberg can be seen.

In September, the duties of commander of the ship were taken over from Lt. Cdr. Eugene Lindau by Lt. Cdr. Erwin Wassner. Another interesting character with vast experience, perfectly suited to the function of a training ship skipper in which he could share his knowledge with the cadets.

It was under his orders that *Karlsruhe* embarked on the second distant training voyage in the cruiser's history on 30 November, whose route led to the other side of the Atlantic, first to the Caribbean, and then to the ports of Mexico and Venezuela. An interesting event, especially for the cadets, was the passage through the Panama Canal, from where the cruiser sailed further west to visit Honolulu, Hawaii.

Later, the route led along the west coast of the Americas with calls at ports in Canada and the United States, circumnavigating Cape Horn and back along the eastern coast of the Americas. Here, the visit to New York was noteworthy, from which *Karlsruhe* later sailed back to the other side of the Atlantic. In total, the cruise lasted over a year, ending on 8 December 1932 in Kiel.

It is worth adding that it went down in history as one of the longest training voyages that German training ships of that period made, reaching a distance of 38,000 NM.

On this occasion, immediately after return, the cruiser was visited by the Head of the *Reichsmarine* Board, Admiral Erich Raeder, and the Head of the Naval Training Inspectorate, Rear Admiral Otto Schultze.

Later, just as after the previous voyage, the ship went to the shipyard for inspection, and then carried out training tasks in home waters for the following months.

At that time, her new skipper was Cdr. Lt. Freiherr Wilhelm Hardsdorf von Enderndorf, who replaced Lt. Cdr. Wassner in December 1932.

Then from January to September 1933 it is difficult to find any highlights in the story of the ship's service, except the annual fleet manoeuvres or numerous visits to Baltic ports.

Mention should also be made of a minor modernization in the form of a platform enlargement at bridge level and the installation of two additional 88 mm guns, which were placed on both sides of the stern.

Contrary to the *Karlsruhe*'s activities, much more can be said about the politics, which, like in no other fleet, played such an important role in the service of its ships. In January Adolf Hitler became Chancellor to head the coalition government. In February, the *Reichstag* was burned down, which became an excuse to deal with the communists he hated so much. Many laws were introduced, including the one that banned the activities of political parties other than the NSDAP, which was in practice an easy way for Hitler to take full power.

Germany was changing, and together with it the fleet as well as the mentality of many officers and sailors serving in it. When on 14 October 1933 *Karlsruhe* left Wilhelmshaven for the third long training voyage, certainly many crew members had in mind what was happening in the country, and were mainly supporting Hitler, whose policies gave hope for improving the situation and rebuilding Germany's power. For now, not everyone was yet aware of what this would lead to, quickly forgetting about politics in a situation where the ship's route was to lead around the globe, often calling at the most beautiful places in the world.

Initially, the cruiser's route was very similar to the first cruise, on which she set off in May 1930, and led through the Mediterranean Sea, and then through the Suez Canal and the Indian Ocean. Then she visited among others Calcutta, Padang and Sorebaja.

It is worth noting that earlier, while sailing the Mediterranean waters, the ship anchored in the Bay of Suda in Crete where she met her sister ship *Köln*, which was on her way back from the Far East.

Later, she circumnavigated Australia and arrived in Brisbane, from where she would head east and visit Apia in Samoa and later Honolulu in Hawaii.

At that time, the cruiser encountered a severe storm, during which she suffered serious damage, forcing the commander to make a longer halt in San Diego between 27 March and 2 June 1934, where repairs were made. Having left San Diego, *Karlsruhe* headed south to pass through the Panama Canal, then headed back to the other side of the Atlantic.

In the initial period of service, beside the main 150 mm guns, the ship was also armed with 88 mm guns on single mounts.

Yet another photograph of an 88 mm gun.

Karlsruhe *while leaving the harbour of Swinemünde.*

After visiting the Spanish port of Caramintal, she returned home on 15 June 1934, dropping her anchor on the Schilling roadstead, and thus ending the third distant training cruise in her history. That day the ship was visited by the Head of the *Reichsmarine* Board Adm. Erich Raeder, meeting the commander and crew and conducting an inspection.

On 16 June the *Karlsruhe* arrived in Kiel, where she underwent shipyard maintenance in July, after which she carried out a series of trials and tests preparing her for further service.

An important event was the change in the position of the commander of the ship, who from 16 September was Commander Günther Lutjens – a character well known later from, among others, Operation *Rheinübung*, during which he commanded the battleship *Bismarck* on board which he died in 1941.

Karlsruhe *viewed from astern.*

The main battery turrets of the K-class cruisers inspired photographers many times.

Preparations were underway for the next training voyage, this time slightly shorter since its route led around South America, the west coast of North America, through the Panama Canal and the east coast of North America. She set sail on 22 October and once she left Kiel and passed the Skagen Peninsula, she headed into the Atlantic to continue through the Azores, Trinidad and, after sailing around Cape Horn, north along the west coast of South America.

On 5 January 1935, the ship arrived at Chilean Puerto Montt – a port city picturesquely situated at the foot of two volcanoes, which, without doubt turned such expeditions into a real adventure for many cadets. The Peruvian port of Callao was no different, in which the ship stayed between 25 January and 6 February. Here, the ship's company took part in the celebrations related to the anniversary of the establishment of this country.

Then *Karlsruhe* sailed north to the Colombian port of Buenaventura, where she was moored between 11 and 16 February, and ten days later she arrived at the US naval base of San Pedro. In that area, a series of firing practices, including night-time ones, was also carried out, which, as you can guess, was one of the elements provided for in the cruise programme.

Beautiful image of Karlsruhe *in the Kiel Canal.*

Later, the ship moved further north to visit San Francisco between 2 and 12 March, as well as Vancouver, where she called on 15 March. The last port on the route of the ship in the region of the west coast of the Americas was the Mexican city of Acapulco, where *Karlsruhe* stayed between 1 and 8 April and from which she later sailed through the Panama Canal.

On 26 April, the ship arrived at Houston, Texas and later on to Charleston, South Carolina, where she stayed between 10 and 18 May. From there, the cruiser commenced her way back, crossing to the other side of the Atlantic.

Having visited the Spanish port of Vigo between 1 and 8 June, she arrived in Kiel on 15 June, where her fourth long-distance training cruise came to an end.

It is worth adding here that the ship arrived in a completely different Germany. Adolf Hitler already had full power, causing anxiety in Europe and spreading real terror among his opponents, who were gradually eliminated in a very brutal way. The Third Reich – this name, although not official yet – would have been heard more and more often, began to become a power.

When the renovation of the *Karlsruhe* began in Kiel, a German delegation signed a maritime agreement with the British, which set the target total displacement of German warships at 450,000 tons, which was 35% compared to the Royal Navy.

The day on which this agreement was signed, Adolf Hitler called the happiest day in his life because, no matter how you look at it, it cancelled the restrictions imposed on Germany by the Treaty of Versailles. It legitimised many secretly implemented fleet expansion programmes, such as construction of the battleships *Scharnhorst* and *Gneisenau*, which had started much earlier than the aforementioned agreement was signed, or the submarines, which until then the Germans were not allowed to possess.

What did this mean for *Karlsruhe* herself? Very much, because from May 1935 the cruiser already belonged to the new branch of the German armed forces, which was the *Kriegsmarine*, brought into being to replace the *Reichsmarine*, often associated with insignificant combat capabilities.

Let us go back on board the *Karlsruhe* in Kiel, where she was undergoing renovation works. Apart from the standard work during which the ship was inspected and equipment worn out during the last long voyage was replaced, the stay in the shipyard was also used to carry out modernization.

It was then that a catapult for a floatplane was installed on board, which had already been planned at the design stage, and was set up on a special base between the funnels[5]. For lifting the

5 Pursuant to the provisions of the Versailles Treaty, the Germans were not allowed until then to have either land or naval military aviation, and it was only after the signing of the said agreement and the rejection of the Versailles restrictions on ships that they began to install aircraft equipment. It is worth adding here that, despite the bans, in this area also the Germans quickly found a way to secretly develop this matter using their merchant fleet. For example, the well-known *Bremen* and *Europa* transatlantic liners entered service with catapults and floatplanes, officially designed for faster delivery of mail to destination ports. They disappeared from them in 1935.

Karlsruhe seen from starboard.

plane, which at that time was a Heinkel He 60 reconnaissance aircraft[6], from the water a special truss crane was provided, located on the deck at the level of the second funnel on the port side.

In addition, the platforms in the area of the battle mast were enlarged again and the rod antenna from the second funnel was replaced with a mast on a yard. An interesting fact is that when the ship set out on another training voyage, the aircraft equipment was dismantled and the lightweight superstructures mentioned earlier were installed for additional training facilities.

Karlsruhe's stay at the shipyard lasted a relatively long time. For example, for the first tests with the use of a catapult, the ship did not go into the waters of Kiel Bay until 23 September. Later, standard tests of machinery and armament were conducted and crew training was carried out.

At that time, preparations were also made for embarking on another distant training cruise, which was to circumnavigate the globe. The ship left Kiel on 21 October 1935 with 606 cadets and crew members on board, commanded by Lt. Cdr. Leopold Siemens, appointed in September. The cruise route was extremely interesting and at the initial stage it was significantly different from the one for which the ship left in October 1933.

Now the cruiser, having entered Atlantic waters, headed south along the western coast of the African continent. The first of the most interesting points of the trip was Tenerife, where she arrived on 30 October.

She then sailed to the Gulf of Guinea, where on 18 November she halted near the island of Sao Thome, which was at that time a Portuguese colony, then headed south to the Angolan port

6 This was a single-engine, twin-float biplane of plywood and metal construction. Its weight was 2,730 kg, dimensions: wing span 13.5 m, length 11.5 m and height 5.3 m. The power unit was a 12-cylinder BMW VI 6.0 engine of 660 HP, allowing a maximum speed of 240 km/h and a range of 640 km. The plane was armed with one 7.92 mm machine gun and could take 12 bombs weighing 10 kg each. Crew was two men.

Another view of the cruiser's profile, this time from the port side.

Souvenir photograph taken at the fore main battery turret.

of Lobito, where she was moored between 25 and 27 November. Later, once the southern coast of Africa had been rounded, on 6 December she arrived at Durban, from which six days later she went to the Seychelles to stop at Port Victoria between 19 and 29 December.

Cdr. Siemens directed his ship further east and on 10 January 1936 she called at Batavia which was at that time the capital of the then Dutch East Indies. She stayed there until 16 January, then put to sea on 23 January, calling at Ilo-Ilo in the Philippines and on 7 February Hong Kong.

Japan was another country on the ship's route. It is worth adding, until that time Japan was relatively rarely visited by German ships. The first port was Nagasaki, where *Karlsruhe* stayed between 21 February and 2 March. Later, cruising the Japanese Sea on 4 March she arrived in Kobe, where she stayed until 12 March and from which she later headed east to visit the ports of the west coast of North America.

Karlsruhe *viewed from astern.*

It was during this voyage that on 14 March the ship entered the zone of an exceptional storm, which later turned into a hurricane with a wind force of 12 on the Beaufort scale. It was then that the structural defects of both *Karlsruhe* and other K-class cruisers manifested themselves in the worst possible way.

The hurricane wind and raging waves almost sank the ship, leading to some serious damage in the form of, among others, cracks in several frames and other structural elements, and the appearance of a crack in the boat deck.

A few days of the stormy voyage gave both ship and crew a difficult experience, eventually interrupting the training programme and forcing Cdr. Siemens to set course to the Aleutians, where after calling at Dutch Harbor on 23 March, provisional repairs were made.

The ship was in a terrible condition and it was impossible to continue the voyage, so as soon as the most important problems had been dealt with, *Karlsruhe* went to San Diego where, with the help of the Americans, the cruiser was docked and the necessary repairs were carried out to allow her to return home.

In total, *Karlsruhe* remained in this American base until 17 April, after which she set off on her way back to Germany, setting a course to the Panama Canal and passing through it. On 6 May she stopped at the roadstead of St. Thomas in the Caribbean.

Later, having crossed the Atlantic, on 29 May she called at Pontevedra in Spain, from where on 4 June she went directly back home, where she arrived on 8 June, dropping anchor in the roadstead of Schillig.

The skipper of the *Karlsruhe,* Lt. Cdr. Leopold Siemens, did not have much good news for his superiors. The ship was heavily strained and required urgent transfer to the shipyard. For this reason, shipyard specialists very quickly appeared on board to examine the damage and work out how to repair them.

Shortly afterwards, officers from the Naval Training Inspectorate made their visits to the ship and after none other than German Chancellor Adolf Hitler himself, who turned up on board on 11 June, *Karlsruhe* passed through the Kiel Canal and moored in Kiel, where her renovation began on 22 June.

This refurbishment had been partly planned, therefore apart from obvious repairs carried out in connection with the damage suffered, the vessel underwent a significant modernization in the form of, among others, modernization of her weapons.

It was then that the 88 mm guns installed in 1933 were replaced with much three more modern twin-gun sets of the same calibre, mounted on their characteristic LC/31 mounts. Moreover, the ship was additionally equipped with four twin mounts for the SK C/30 cal. 37 mm L/83 AA guns.

Such a significant increase of the armament necessitated the reconstruction of, among others, the aft superstructure with additional fire control positions. Added to this was the installation of a deckhouse between the battle mast and the front funnel, the addition of bridge wings and mounting of yet another platform on the battle mast and, interestingly, reinstalling the aircraft equipment. In total, the ship's stay at the shipyard lasted over two months and came to an end on 9 September.

It is worth adding that after this time *Karlsruhe* no longer served as a training ship. From 31 June onwards she was subordinated to the Commanding Officer of the BdA reconnaissance forces.

Having left the shipyard, the ship – still remaining under the command of Lt. Cdr. Leopold Siemens – was subjected to countless trials and tests throughout almost all of September. For a short time, between 21 and 23 October, she underwent minor maintenance works, after which she carried out tasks based in home waters, taking part in, among others, exercises related to gun and torpedo fire practice.

An important event was sending her to operate in Spanish waters, where the Civil War had already been going on for several months. For this first

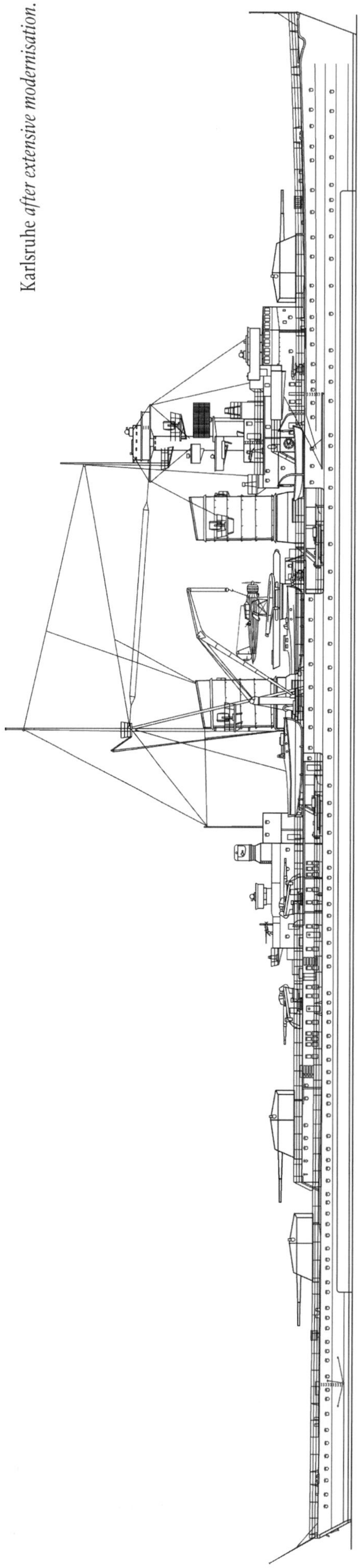

Karlsruhe *after extensive modernisation.*

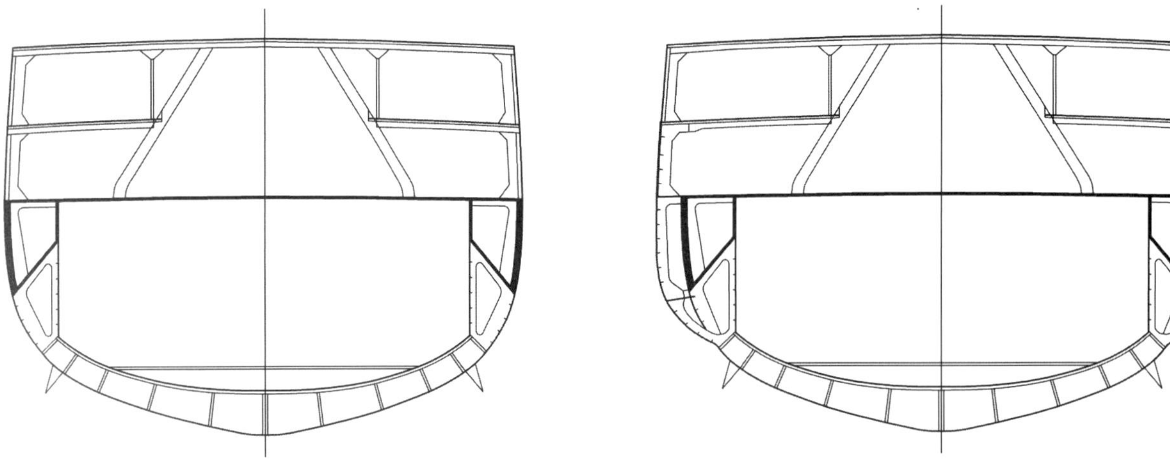

Cross-section transverse views of the Karlsruhe, *demonstrating modifications carried out during refurbishment.*

"combat mission" in *Karlsruhe*'s history, the cruiser set off on 27 December. First port of call on 1 January 1937 in the war-torn country was El Ferrol, located in north-western Spain.

We will not describe here what was happening in that area, bearing in mind that this was already mentioned in other chapters, and will focus only on the activities of the ship herself and the places where she stayed.

As part of its activity at that time, still mainly consisting of ensuring the safety and evacuation of citizens of other nationalities, including of course Germans, of whom there were quite a lot, *Karlsruhe* operated along the Spanish coast, visiting a number of ports in that region.

Between 5 and 9 January she was in the port of Melilla in Spanish Africa. On 10 January she found herself in Tangier, from which she later sailed to the Atlantic to conduct a series of exercises and to which she returned three days later.

Later she stayed in the Bay of Corcubion on 19–20 January, La Coruna on 23 January, followed by El Ferrol where she stayed until 26 January, and Passajes on 27 January. Later, she alternately operated between the ports of La Coruna and El Ferrol until 19 February, when, after she had been called back home, the ship set off on her return to Germany, thus ending her first combat mission. Once she returned to home waters, the *Karlsruhe* went to Kiel where she underwent shipyard maintenance.

Later, not much happened in her activities.

From April, she participated in a series of different types of exercises and manoeuvres of the fleet, serving, among others, as a target ship for submarines. Practically until the end of the second half of June her service consisted mainly of participation in exercises and stays at the shipyard, at which she was docked twice during this short period.

It was not until later that the time came for a more interesting event, which was returning to Spanish waters again. *Karlsruhe* set sail for the second combat mission to Spain on 17 June 1937.

This time, the stay in this inflammatory region, mainly based in El Ferrol, lasted for a relatively short time and came to an end on 30 June, when the cruiser dropped anchor in the Kiel roadstead. Actually this event can be considered the most interesting in which the ship participated in 1937.

Later there were only endless exercises and participation in manoeuvres, interspersed with stays at the shipyard or in smaller home ports on both the North Sea and Baltic Sea coasts.

More important was the change in the position of skipper, who in September became Commander Erich Förste.

Skippers of the ship

- 6 November 1929 – 25 September 1931 – Lt. Cdr. Eugen Lindau
- 26 September 1931 – 8 December 1932 – Lt. Cdr. Erwin Wassner
- 9 December 1932 – 15 September 1934 – Lt. Cdr. Freiherr Wilhelm Harsdorf von Enderndorf
- 16 September 1934 – 23 September 1935 – Cdr. Günther Lütjens
- 24 September 1935 – 28 September 1937 – Lt. Cdr. Leopold Siemens
- 29 September 1937 – 20 May 1938 – Cdr. Erich Förste
- 13 November 1939 – 10 April 1940 – Cdr. Friedrich Rieve

1938 for the *Karlsruhe* began in her home waters. Between January and May a slightly monotonous training programme was still implemented, which was interrupted on 20 May when the cruiser was withdrawn from the line and sent to the shipyard.

The ship disappeared from the list of ships available to the *Kriegsmarine* for a very long time, until autumn 1939, therefore there is not much to write about her, as opposed to what was happening around her.

In addition to the ongoing Civil War in Spain, to which Germany had already committed enormous resources, in Europe the diplomatic crisis caused by Hitler's aspirations to annex the lands inhabited by the German minority in the Sudetenland, was increasingly felt. This was followed by a plan to partition Czechoslovakia and connect the said lands to the Reich.

The seriousness of the situation may be evidenced by the fact that some of the major *Kriegsmarine* ships received orders to put to sea and proceed to the Atlantic, where they were to conduct exercises officially near the coastlines of, among others, Spain.

A sharp reaction from Western European countries to the upcoming events in Czechoslovakia was expected, and in such a case Hitler was even ready to attack if his territorial claims were not recognized.

Well, the passivity of Britain and France, which preferred a policy of concessions to the German leader at almost all cost so as to prevent the outbreak of another world war, meant that there were no turbulent events, likewise with similar actions during the capture of Klaipeda in Lithuania, which Hitler put in place after the Sudetenland, left him with no doubts whatsoever.

Let us go back to the *Karlsruhe*, which all this time stood quietly at the shipyard away from these turbulent events and where she became a part of the plan approved in November 1937 to improve the design and extend the life of all three K-class cruisers. According to this plan, *Karlsruhe* was to be the first to undergo modernization, which was undoubtedly the result of her having the most strained structure of all three of the above mentioned vessels, which suffered seriously during a hurricane in the Pacific Ocean.

According to the requirements of the re-building, once it was completed *Karlsruhe* would serve as a warship until the spring of 1940, after which she would be reclassified as an experimental ship, and from the beginning of 1942 as a gun-torpedo training ship.

Following her, *Köln*, whose commencement of reconstruction was scheduled for June 1939, was to go to the shipyard next and then *Königsberg* in September 1940. As history later demonstrated, out of these plans only the reconstruction of *Karlsuhe*, which was dealt with by the *Kriegsmarinewerft* shipyard in Wilhelmshaven, was implemented.

The scope of work alone was quite impressive. The reconstruction, costing a total of 5.7 million marks, was managed by the very experienced ship engineer Erwin Strohbusch, mainly focused on hull strengthening, which involved the construction of additional broadside panels expanding the vessel by 1.4 metres.

These were something like anti-torpedo bulges, built into the hull to improve its strength, which started in the upper part, separating from the hull proper by 50–70 cm, and then descending down gently and merged with the hull about 2 m below the waterline.

Beautiful view of Karlsruhe *during one of her many passages of the Kiel Canal.*

Karlsruhe seen from astern, in the Holtenau Lock.

Also, 14 mm thick armour belts were placed above the waterline, and the upper deck was reinforced with 16 mm thick armour steel sheets, which significantly improved the ship's protection.

In addition, the hull was equipped with a small bow bulb and the right anchor port was rebuilt.

The fore superstructure and the aft funnel were also rebuilt by reducing its height, with the simultaneous installation of caps on both funnels and setting a new tripod mast behind them. New cranes were installed. Demagnetizing devices were fitted and space for a trawl was prepared.

Changes were also introduced in the armament by replacing the existing 88 mm sets with new SK C 33 105 mm L/65 guns on the triaxially stabilized Doppel LC/31 mounts.

A lot of minor changes had been made, however, due to the lack of space, we will not describe them here, referring the interested parties to the references on K-class cruisers[7].

In total, the reconstruction of *Karlsruhe* significantly improved the strength of the ship's structure, thereby up-grading her combat value while increasing her full displacement to 8,350 t and beam up to 16.8 metres. The ship only entered service again on 13 November 1939, when the war in Europe gained momentum.

According to the Ribbentrop-Molotov Pact, Poland had already been divided between the victorious armies, and Hitler directed his attention to France and Britain, which he had hoped that after 1 September they would behave similarly to previous "quarrels" over Czechoslovakia or Klaipeda.

This time they behaved differently, but it did not help much because the German dictator dealt very quickly with France, using the *Blitzkrieg* tactics used with good effect in Poland and eventually forcing the country to surrender on 22 June 1940. This and the withdrawal of British troops resulted in the isolation of Britain.

At the same time wanting, among others, to secure the iron ore supply important for the operation of the German defence industry, Hitler prepared an invasion of Scandinavia known as Operation *Weserübung*, or the attack on Denmark and Norway.

For this reason, the newly re-built *Karlsruhe*, under the command of her new and as it would later turn out, last commander Cdr. Friedrich Rieve, had little time to carry out the necessary tests and trials of equipment, and above all to train a crew mostly from scratch.

Commander Rieve faced a difficult task. Having completed all the shipyard tests at a rapid pace in a situation where you had to reckon on the attacks of enemy aircraft and ships was not easy, since everything was seriously hindered by the ongoing winter, during which frost and general icing of communication routes prevented the task from being finished quickly.

---

7 Some references claim that during the refurbishment the diesel engines were dismantled, which however, is not confirmed by the sources.

Yet another starboard view of the ship.

But there was no way out when the invasion plan was ready and *Karlsruhe* was part of it. Finally, by shortening the entire trial and training programme, in March preparations for the invasion began aboard the ship.

Karlsruhe stayed at that time in Bremerhaven, where the necessary supplies were taken on board.

Other *Kriegsmarine* ships, such as the battleships *Scharnhorst* and *Gneisenau*, *Lützow* (ex – *Deutschland*) now "re-classified" as cruisers and the cruisers *Blücher*, *Admiral Hipper*, *Königsberg*, *Köln* and *Emden*, were divided into separate task forces (groups).

Karlsruhe herself became the flagship of the Fourth Group, which in addition included torpedo ships from the 5th Flotilla, *Greif*, *Seeadler* and *Luchs*, under the command of Cdr. Hans Bütow, and seven torpedo boats with their base ship *Tsingtau*, whose target was to be Kristiansand, to which all vessels were to deliver 1,100 troops.

Time went by.

On 7 April 1940, *Karlsruhe* was ready to set sail, taking onboard on that day Rear Admiral Otto Schenk, who was designated as Admiral of the southern coast of Norway, as well as embarking the troops and their equipment.

At last, on 8 April at about 0500 hrs the cruiser left Bremerhaven and moved towards her destiny.

Initially, the weather was fine and after a rendezvous with other vessels at Jütland, the force headed north. At this point, it should be mentioned that the transports *August*, *Kreta*, *Leonhardt*, *Westsee* and *Wiegand* were also assigned to the force, and much earlier on 6 April they left Stettin and sailed to the area north of Hantsholm, designated as the meeting point of the group.

Over time, the weather deteriorated, making navigation difficult. Fog gradually rose, limiting visibility to just 50 metres at times. This was a problem, but also an advantage, given the fact that it gave the Germans the important element of surprise for such kind of operations. The group of ships sailing in the fog was very difficult to track, which made them imperceptible as close as possible to the Norwegian coast.

However, *Karlsruhe* was not very lucky. On the morning of 9 April the fog lifted, and the entire force found itself at the entrance to the fjord leading to Kristiansand. Shortly after 0600 hrs the German ships were detected by a Norwegian aircraft. This meant the loss of surprise and action stations at the coastal batteries Odderøy[8] and Gleodden[9] which defended Kristiansand.

Earlier, due to the prevailing weather conditions, the transfer of troops to the small torpedo boats, planned for 0415–0500 hrs, failed.

8 Consisting of four 240 mm howitzers, two 210 mm guns, six 150 mm guns 65 mm guns.

9 Three 150 mm guns and two 65 mm guns.

An interesting photograph of Karlsruhe *approaching a wharf.*

After 0500 the fog began to slowly disappear – it hindered navigation, but also perfectly concealed the entire action.

Karlsruhe's captain, Commander Rieve, was in a tricky situation. Passing through a narrow fjord where manoeuvrability was very limited, as well as guarded by the aforementioned batteries, was extremely dangerous. For this reason, the first attempt to approach Kristansand was unsuccessful.

Near *Karlsruhe* – it is worth remembering, the largest ship of the whole group, and thus attracting attention first – 210 mm rounds fired from the Odderøy battery began to fall, the operation had to be temporarily abandoned and the force withdrew.

It was equally dangerous during the fourth approach, when *Karlsruhe* almost ran into underwater rocks which could have caused serious complications. Careful manoeuvres allowed her to avoid danger and save the ship almost at the very last moment, but the task was still not achieved. Only after *Luftwaffe* aircraft had arrived and attacked the Norwegian batteries at 1000 hrs could the final assault be carried out.

Having transferred part of the troops onto torpedo boats, the ships started moving and an hour later the *Karlsruhe* entered Kristansand, where the disembarkation of the troops began. After reports had begun to arrive about the seizure of Arendal port, which was also the target of the force, and the elimination of dangerous coastal batteries, it seemed that everything was going well and the ship could safely return to Germany.

However, luck still did not favour the cruiser.

After the ship left the harbour of Kristansand at 1900 hrs and headed back home, messages streamed in with warnings about British submarines that had been detected. At 1951 hrs, accompanied by the torpedo ships *Greif*, *Seeadler* and *Luchs*, *Karlsruhe* left the fjord and, setting a course of 147° and increasing speed to 21 knots, began zigzagging. In addition, to ensure the safety of the cruiser, the torpedo ships took up positions at a distance of 600 and 800 metres in front of the cruiser. This accomplished nothing.

Soon the German vessels were spotted by the British submarine HMS *Truant* (N 68), commanded by Lt. Cdr. Christoper Haynes Hutchinson[10]. It did not take much time before the British skipper gave the order to fire. Four torpedoes were launched towards the German group, the track marks of which were seen by the crew of the torpedo ship *Luchs*[11].

Despite the alarm, speed increase and evasive manoeuvres, at 1958 hrs one of the torpedoes hit *Karlsruhe* in the vicinity of compartments V and VI, immobilizing the engines and power generators. Despite undertaking an immediate damage control operation, it quickly became apparent that the ship could not be saved.

Water pouring into the hull resulted in a list of 12 degrees. The engines, rudder and most importantly the pumps were not working, which meant more and more water flooding the adjacent

10 Built in 1939 at the Vickers-Armstrong shipyard in Barrow, the T-class submarine (Trident) had a surface displacement of 1,090 t and an underwater displacement of 1,575 t. The ship was 83.8 m long, 8.1 wide and had 4.4 m draft. Diesel-electric drive with an output of 2,500 HP-1,450 HP. 13.7 knots surface speed, 10 knots underwater speed. She had one 102 mm gun, two machine guns and ten (6 + 4) 533 mm torpedo tubes. The crew was 53 men.

11 Some authors claim that the submarine fired as many as ten torpedoes in total.

Two images of Karlsruhe *depicting the ship's profile after she had been re-built in 1939/40 .*

compartments of the hull. The fate of *Karlsruhe* was a foregone conclusion and not much could be done.

Realizing this, Cdr. Rive ordered the skippers of *Luchs* and *Seeadler* to approach *Karlsruhe* and take off the surviving crewmen. In less than half an hour the torpedo ships embarked the sailors from the cruiser, then at 2245 hrs Cdr. Rieve gave the order to "finish off" the damaged ship.

Five minutes later, an accurate salvo fired from the torpedo ship *Greif* sealed the fate of the cruiser. The first of the torpedoes hit the bow and the second one the midships area, and shortly afterwards *Karlsruhe* began to sink with a list to the starboard. After a few minutes she disappeared under the surface of the water at position 58°04'N, 08°04'E.

Only eleven crew members perished.

The loss of *Karlsruhe* was a severe blow to the Germans, given the fact that the ship was newly modernized and this had significant combat potential, and even worse she was one of three cruisers that the *Kriegsmarine* lost as a result of operations in Norway.

After *Königsberg* had been lost in Bergen and now with the loss of *Karlsruhe*, only the third of the K-class cruisers remained in the service of the *Kriegsmarine* – *Köln*, for whom fate proved to be more favourable.

Characteristics of the cruiser *Karlsruhe* (*Kreuzer* "C")[12]

Type K

- Shipyard Deutsche Werke, Kilonia
- No. of construction 207
- Keel laid 27 July 1926
- Launched 20 August 1927
- Commissioned 6 November 1929
- Standard displacement (official) 6,000 t
- Standard displacement (actual) 6,380 t
- Constructional displacement (official) 6,750 t
- Constructional displacement (actual) 7,700 t
- Full displacement after re-building 8,350 t
- Overall length 174.0 m
- Length on waterline 169.0 m
- Beam 15.2 m
- Beam after re-building 16.8 m
- Draft (full) 5.4 m
- Propulsion 6 x Marine Schuls-Thornycroft boilers, 4 x steam turbine sets, 2 x diesel engines with a total output of 68,200 HP
- Max. speed 32.1 knots
- Fuel supply 1,100 t for boilers and 139 for diesel engines
- Range 5,700 NM at 19 knots: 7,300 NM at 17 knots, 8,000 NM at 10 knots (with diesel engines)
- Crew 514–614 officers, NCOs and naval ratings
- Armament (1929) 9 (3x3) 150 mm guns: 2 (2x1) 88 mm guns, 12 (4x3) 500 mm torpedo tubes
- Armament (1936) 9 (3x3) 150 mm guns: 6 (3x2) 88 mm guns, 8 (4x2) 37 mm guns, 8 (8x1) 20 mm cannons, 12 (4x3) 533 mm torpedo tubes
- Armament (1938/39) 9 (9x3) 150 mm guns: 6 (3x2) 105 mm guns, 8 (4x2) 37 mm guns, 10 (10x1) 20 mm cannons, 12 (4x3) 533 mm torpedo tubes
- Armour 50 mm broadsides (later + 14 mm): 70 mm transverse bulkheads, 20–40 mm decks (later + 16 mm), 30–100 mm command post, 20–30 mm main battery turrets
- Aircraft equipment 1 x pneumatic catapult FL22 type, 1–2 x Heinkel He 60 floatplane, later Arado Ar 196

12 In the sources and references from which the data come, there are many discrepancies in the parameters of the ship, which makes determining them with absolute certainty extremely difficult and one should take into account the fact that they may not coincide with the data from other studies.

Köln
A Pocket Cruiser?

This ship actually ended the series of the first three modern cruisers constructed and put into service in the German Navy after the end of World War One.

As we have already learned, not including the controversial *Emden*, *Köln*, along with her sister ships *Königsberg* and *Karlsruhe*, was a tangible example of the significant progress that German shipbuilders made from the design and construction of the former. Despite the weakness of the hull and subsequent problems with stability increasing with the modernization of these ships, they were extremely interesting vessels.

Paying attention to the treaty restrictions here, which resulted in the creation of, among others, the commonly known battleships, or more specifically *Deutschland* armoured ships, which the British press mockingly called "pocket battleships" and which in fact turned out to be ships quite well suited to raiding missions, in some sense also in the case of K-class cruisers due to the unrealistic limit of 6,000 tons, one might be tempted to call these "pocket cruisers" as well.

After all, these ships had quite good armament and reached considerable speed, and although due to the weakness of the hull structure they were not suitable for anti-warship operations, it should be remembered that no other German cruisers did so many training voyages. During these the cadets aboard had the opportunity to reach the farthest corners of the globe and get acquainted with the lands and ports from which, during the war, they attacked Allied transports in all those areas when commanding their own ships.

The second modern cruiser of the Weimar Republic – Köln in her full glory.

The hull of the Köln *slipped into the water on 23 May 1928. The ceremony attracted much attention among the citizens of Wilhelmshaven. Note a mainmast which has been prepared for installation and is provisionally stored against a wall.*

To answer the opinions of many specialists who strongly criticize these ships, one should ask the question whether they really were that bad. Theoretically, various pros and cons can be put forward, but the real value of any ship can be seen in actual combat in wartime. After all, what is even the most modern ship, if, for example, it is commanded by an inept skipper. History provides many examples of such cases often ending with the loss of a great ship, which – in theory – should have never occurred.

One could say that it was similar in the case of the K-class cruisers, because in fact none of them had the opportunity to show their true capabilities in an engagement with an enemy warship.

The *Königsberg* and *Karlsruhe* which were lost in the first months of the war simply had bad luck, although one could argue, of course, that they went down due to the fact that their structures could not withstand the explosion of torpedoes and shells when the tasks they were faced with had been met without major problems.

Köln *in an interesting image seen from her bow.*

Köln *depicted on one of the postcards published in the inter-war period.*

Reading this chapter, also in the case of the cruiser *Köln*, it is easy to see that, despite the shortcomings which have been already pointed out, the ship proved many times that she was a capable vessel that could carry out her tasks without major problems. Anyway, the times when she was built were slightly different from those we know from the wartime period.

When in 1926 at the *Reichsmarinewerft* shipyard in Wilhelmshaven – in which by the way the construction of the prototype *Königsberg* was already underway in April of the same year – the construction of *Köln* commenced, and in a country struggling with various tensions and conflicts, it was quite difficult.

Some political parties, which prioritized the reconstruction of the war-ruined economy, were reluctant and did what they could to block the programme of building a large and expensive ship, but supporters of the expansion of the fleet had a lot to say, thanks to which slowly but surely the Germans successfully managed to push through the construction of new ships. These K-class cruisers, which at that time were ships that were not to be expensive, were also extremely important considering the fact that they were the first large and modern ships to take up service in the *Reichsmarine.*

We will not write here again what the design work looked like and how the cruiser was built, referring interested parties to the chapter on the prototype *Königsberg* ship, and we will focus on the ship herself, whose construction, as we have already learned, had started at the *Reichsmarinewerft* shipyard in Wilhelmshaven.

The keel of cruiser D, because that was the name of the future *Köln* at that time, was officially laid on 7 August 1926, and the construction was given the number 116. According to the plans, the ship was to replace the badly worn out cruiser *Arcona*, hence the initial designation of the ship, often known as *Ersatz Arcona*, which, as you can easily guess, meant that ship was to be replaced by the newly built vessel.

The assembly work on the hull took over twenty-one months, which means that the construction of *Köln* was one of the longest among all K-class cruisers. Launching took place only on 23 May 1928, and as you can guess there was a huge celebration both at the shipyard and in Wilhelmshaven itself.

In the ceremony during which the widow of the commander of the first ship sporting this name, Lt. Cdr. Hans Meidinger, by the traditional breaking of a bottle of champagne gave the ship the name after one of the largest German cities[1]. Commander-in-Chief of the *Reichsmarine* Adm. Hans Zenker, Head of the North Sea force base, Vice-Adm. Herman Bauer, General Manager of the shipyard Rear Adm. Franz and many honoured guests were present.

---

1 The cruiser was the third ship of that name in the German fleet. The first *Köln* was built at the Germaniawerft shipyard in Kiel and entered service in June 1911. This vessel had 4,362 t standard displacement and 4,864 t full displacement. Hull length was 130.5 m, beam 14.0 m and draft 5.7 m. The engines gave a total output of 29,030 HP, due to which it reached the speed of 26.8 kts. She had twelve 105 mm guns, four 52 mm guns and two 450 mm torpedo tubes. The crew was 367 men. The ship sank on 28 August 1914 in the Battle of Helgoland Bay. The second *Köln* was built in 1916 at the Blohm & Voss shipyard in Hamburg. It was 155.5 m long, 14.2 m wide and had 6.4 m draft, the displacement was determined at 5,620 t standard and 7,486 t full. The power of the machinery was estimated at 48,700 HP, and speed reached 29.3 knots. It was armed with eight 150 mm, three 88 mm guns and four 600 mm torpedo tubes. Crew was 560 men. The ship was sunk on 21 June 1919 at the British Scapa Flow naval base.

Köln *accompanied by the pocket battleship* Admiral Scheer, *seen on the left.*

An appropriate speech on the occasion of the launch of the newest ship of the *Reichsmarine* was made by the then Mayor of Cologne, Dr. Konrad Adenauer. He later became the first Chancellor of the Federal Republic of Germany.

Name of the ship

The name of the cruiser was given in honour of the city of Cologne (German: Köln) located in western Germany on the River Rhine. In the mid-1930s it had a population of 1,530,000 and is currently about a million. It is one of the oldest cities in Germany with its origins in a small Germanic settlement transformed in 50 A.D. into a Roman colony.

The city is an important industrial and scientific centre. Companies producing car engines, railway wagons, plastics, cosmetics, clothing etc. have their branches there. Throughout its existence, the city was famous for its numerous monuments, that suffered severely during Allied air raids during the war. Currently, Cologne is considered the fourth largest city in Germany.

When the celebrations, during which the cruiser's fine-looking hull slid off the shipyard's slipway into the water, came to an end, *Köln* was moored at the quay where the fitting out work continued.

Over the next dozen or so months, the ship took shape, so that finally on 15 January 1930, Cdr. Ludwig von Schöder was designated as her first commander, and accompanied by the crew gathered on board, he could issue the order to raise the colours for the first time. It is worth noting that the crew was composed mainly of officers and seamen of the decommissioned cruiser *Amazone*.

At the time, *Köln* was the newest and most modern vessel of the *Reichsmarine*, but not much different from the previously described *Königsberg* and *Karlsruhe*.

It is difficult to find any significant differences between these ships in the initial period of their service. Their armament and characteristics were practically the same, which is why we will not quote them here, mentioning only such curiosities as the names of the main battery turrets, which, unlike earlier cruisers where they referred to the names of *Kaiserliche Marine* ships, in this case referred to famous naval battles involving the German Navy in World War One.

And so the fore turret A was called Helgoland, which, as we know, was a reference to the events in the waters of the North Sea. The aft turrets were called Doggerbank (B turret), i.e. the naval battle fought in 1915 known as the Battle of Dogger Bank, and Skagerrak (C turret), was named after the battle which in German histography is known as the Battle of Skagerrak, while to us it is better known as the Battle of Jutland.

Köln had the same propulsion as the other cruisers, with the turbine manufacturer in her case being the Blohm & Voss shipyard in Hamburg. The total output of the engines reached during tests was 68,485 HP at 378 rpm, and the speed was 32.2 knots. It is worth noting here that, according to design requirements, the power of the engines for K-class cruisers was estimated at 65,000 HP, which can only testify to the excellent results achieved by German engineers.

It is also worth adding that the construction of the ship cost the German taxpayer 36 million *Reichsmarks* at that time.

Let us now return to the description of the history of the ship's service. The ship was undoubtedly the *Reichsmarine*'s pride at that time and no one was critical of her, though it never occurred to anyone that in a few years she would become part of the Nazi war machine.

A poor quality photograph, nevertheless interesting as it depicts Köln *in the initial period of her service.*

Over the next few months, the cruiser set sail several times, the machinery and equipment were tested and trials were carried out. The first sea trials were carried out on 4–7 February at the mouth of the Jade River. Later, the ship was putting to sea almost regularly, sailing both in the waters of the North Sea and Baltic Sea.

The most important events of that period include, for example, 23 and 24 April, when the first firing practices of the 150 mm main battery guns as well as the heavy 88 mm anti-aircraft guns were carried out in the waters of the German Bay. It was not until 19 July, after almost half a year, that the trials and training of the crew ended, after which the cruiser became a part the reconnaissance force.

Starting from 4 August she was subordinated to the command of the Naval Artillery Experimental Section (AVK) almost regularly. The crew conducted intensive training combined with, among others, gun and torpedo launch firing practices. The first foreign cruise took place from 29 August to 1 September and its destination was Copenhagen.

An interesting event was hosted on board of the ship on 14–15 October, when the above-mentioned Mayor of Cologne, Dr. Konrad Adenauer, paid a visit.

Köln *during a visit to Copenhagen in 1930.*

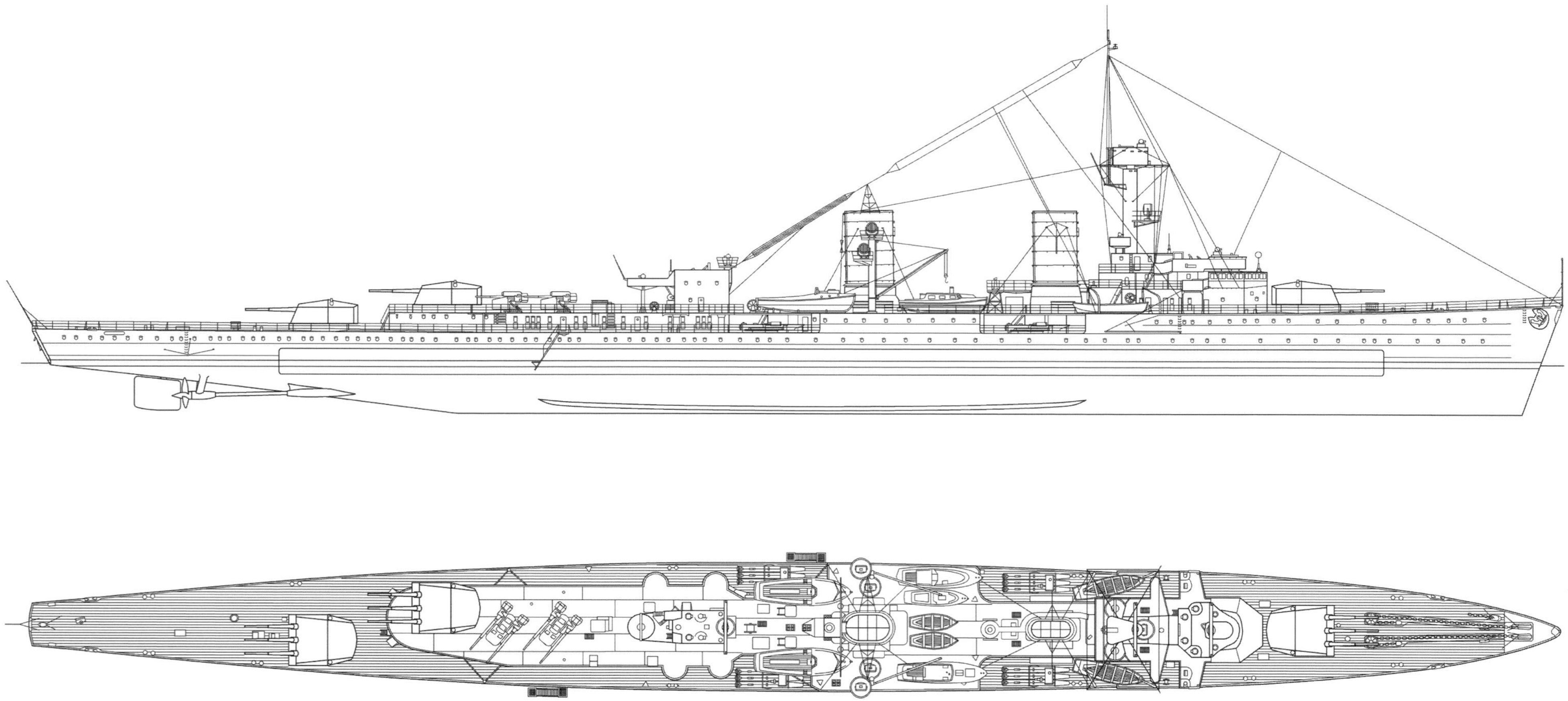

The Köln's *profile from the initial period of service.*

Köln seen from the port side.

Undoubtedly, one of the most important voyages of the first months of the *Köln*'s service was the one into Atlantic waters for exercises and trials, on which she set out on 28 October. Her route led to the Cape Verde area via the port of La Luz in the Canary Islands from 4 to 7 November, and crossing the Tropic of Cancer on 8 November. On 10 November, *Köln* arrived in the area of these islands by dropping anchor on the Mindello roadstead of São Vicente.

Here on 12 November an interesting event took place, which was the encounter with her sister ship *Karlsruhe*, which under the command of Lt. Cdr. Eugen Lindau was returning home from her first distant training trip. The next day, the two cruisers raised their anchors and went out to sea in a joint exercise, after which on 17 November they stopped at the Santa Cruz roadstead in Tenerife. The ships split up only on 22 November, to meet again four days later on the roadstead of the Spanish harbour of Vigo.

Köln returned to Wilhelmshaven on 2 December, and actually it was the last main event in the story of the ship for 1930. It should be mentioned here that this year she also underwent her

Interesting view of the midship superstructure. The port side crane can clearly be seen together with searchlight platforms.

Poor quality but fine image of Köln *with a Heinkel floatplane seen in the foreground.*

first modernization, consisting of the extension of the aft superstructure, and also adding a small superstructure between the funnels, installing additional fire control devices and, most importantly, replacing the single 88 mm L/45 Flak gun mounts with two sets of experimental twin 88 mm L/75 Flak guns on C/25 mountings, which were fitted on the aft superstructure just in front of the main battery turret.

1931 for *Köln* began with a stay in the shipyard, which lasted until 15 February. Later, she returned to the training programme including, among others, gun and torpedo firing practice in the waters of Kiel Bay or the mouth of the Jade River.

An interruption of these monotonous activities was her participation on 13–23 April in the spring fleet manoeuvres, in which most of the major *Reichsmarine* ships usually participated.

On 20 May the cruiser took part in the fleet review organized to honour President von Hindenburg, and between 2 and 11 September she took part in the navy's autumn manoeuvres. That would be it for the more interesting events in the ship's story this year, adding only that she underwent a minor modernization at the time, consisting of shortening the high topmast and adding broad signal yardarms.

It is easy to see that the cruiser's service looked a bit different compared to her sister ships, which after their trial and training period set off on distant training voyages almost at once. *Köln* remained in home waters for a long time, being subordinated to the reconnaissance force, carrying out training tasks and also serving as an experimental platform for gunnery tests.

A brief interruption from this was a short trip to the Balearic Islands between 15 and 21 January 1932, and also performing a series of further tests in the Atlantic.

Later, there is little to write about.

The ship continued to carry out training tasks confined to the waters of the North Sea and Baltic Sea. On 30 March she was removed from the reconnaissance force, and on 2 April the vessel was subordinated to the Naval Training Inspectorate.

An interesting event was the visit made on board of the ship on 26 May by Adolf Hitler, then just one of the leaders of the NSDAP, but already enjoying great support.

It is worth mentioning here that two days later the flag was dropped to half mast on the ship, which was related to the death on 25 May of Adm. Franz von Hipper, the German hero of the Great War.

A similar event took place on 13 September but this time *Köln* played a much more important role, due to the fact that from her deck the urn with the ashes of Hans Zenker, who died on 18 August, was committed in the sea[2].

2 56°58'3"N i 06°16'5"E

Two photographs taken during night time firing practice.

Earlier, on 6–10 September, the ship had participated in the autumn fleet manoeuvres, and on 28 September her new skipper became Lt. Cdr. Otto Schniewind.

In November, the ship went to the shipyard where, among other actions, she was docked and prepared for the first long voyage, the same as we are already familiar with from previous chapters.

For the sake of historical necessity it should be mentioned here that this year the ship also underwent modernization consisting of the removal of one set of 88 mm guns, dismantling of the superstructure located between the funnels and the addition of wings to the navigation bridge.

In connection with the planned long journey in the first days of December, intensive preparations were carried out on the ship. Larger than usual food and fuel supplies were taken aboard. Finally, on 8 December the cruiser, under command of Lt. Cdr. Schniewind and with a crew of over six hundred men consisting mainly of naval cadets, left home waters and headed west to drop anchor in Spain two days later in the harbour of Pueblo del Caraminal.

On 27 December, the ship proceeded south, then after passing through the Straits of Gibraltar and entering the Mediterranean Sea between 2 and 14 January 1933, she paid a visit to Messina, Italy. The next port on the *Köln*'s route was Alexandria, where the ship arrived on 17 January. The stay in the second-largest city of Egypt was interesting because Lt. Cdr. Schniewind was received in an audience by the king of that country, Fu'ad I.

Further on, the route led through the Suez Canal, which was passed on 25–26 January, and across the Red Sea, Gulf of Aden and Arabian Sea, and finally after rounding the Indian Peninsula on 8 February she reached Madras, known today as Chennai.

Next the route led to Sabang (Dutch East Indies) where she visited between 20 February and 1 March, Tandjong in Sumatra on 5 March, later Australia with the ports of Freemantle (11–17 March), Adelaide (22–30 March), Mornington (1–10 April), Melbourne (10–19 April), Hobart in Tasmania (21–24 April and 28 April– 4 May) – here the ship called twice, between going out to sea for gunnery exercises – and finally Sydney (6–16 May), which was also the last port in Australia where the cruiser moored at that time.

The aft main battery turrets of the Köln *cruiser. Their location in relation to the plane of symmetry of the hull was the peculiar feature of the K-class cruisers.*

Further on, *Köln* headed for Fiji to drop anchor on 23 May in the roadstead of the port of Suva on the island of Viti Levu. She stayed there until 29 May, then headed to the Bismarck Archipelago to visit Rabaul between 7 and 16 June, then north to Apra on the island of Guam where she stayed from 20 to 24 June.

There was a cruise in Japanese waters between 29 June and 11 July, during which the ship performed a series of different types of exercises, and between 3 and 5 July was docked at the shipyard in Kobe. Between 15 and 20 July, the cruiser paid a visit to Dairen (Dalian), a former Japanese enclave in north-eastern China on the Yellow Sea, then on 20 July, a delegation from the *Köln* crew laid a wreath in the Shanting Hills to commemorate the gunboat *Iltis* which sank during a typhoon in the Yellow Sea on 23 July 1896.[3] Next, she visited China, Tsingtau between 21 and 31 July 21 and Shanghai between 2 and 14 August.

On 21 August she crossed the equator and headed back, from 23 August-5 September she visited Makasar on the Celebes in Dutch East Indies, and later, after crossing the Singapore and Malacca Straits, she called at Belawan in Sumatra (September 20–26) and Colombo in what was then Ceylon between 2 and 10 October.

On 22 October the cruiser passed through the Suez Canal and stopped at Port Said, from which she continued her journey on 25 October, heading for Crete. The stay on this largest Greek island was interesting because during anchoring in the Bay of Suda (October 27 – November 6), *Köln* met with her sister ship *Karlsruhe*, which had just started her third distant training trip, whose route led around the world.

Lt. Cdr. Schniewind then directed his ship north-west to visit Corfu between November 8 and 11, and the Italian port of Taranto between November 15 and 24.

Having headed for the Strait of Gibraltar and entered the North Atlantic, on 30 November the cruiser called at Vigo, from which on 7 December she set off on her way back home, and on 10 December she anchored near the Weser lighthouse at Wesermünde, thus finishing the first and – as later it would turn out only – distant training trip.

A lot was going on in the country to which the ship returned. In January while the ship was sailing in the Mediterranean, Adolf Hitler became Chancellor of Germany, thus slowly starting to implement his ruthless policies.

It must have been a great surprise for the crew, but also an honour, when during the ship's voyage to Wilhelmshaven and crossing the Grosser Bahnhof lock, he paid an unexpected visit on board the vessel together with the Minister of War, General Werner von Blomberg[4]. This event was

3 This was a former colonial gunboat built in 1878 at the *Kaiserliche Werft* shipyard in Danzig serving with the *Kaiserliche Marine*. The vessel had a displacement of 561 tons and was 44.5 m in length, 7.6 m beam and 3.4 m draft. Her armament consisted of two 125 mm, two 87 mm guns and two 37 mm cannons. The boat sank during a typhoon raging in the Yellow Sea near Qingdao. From the crew of 85 men only 10 survived.

4 In 1938, Werner von Blomberg, who was at the time the Minister of War and the Commander-in-Chief of the *Wehrmacht*, in the rank of Field Marshal, was unexpectedly removed from his position as a result of an intrigue conceived by Herman Göring and Heinrich Himmler.

Köln *approaching a wharf.*

remarkable because at the same time the Commander-in-Chief, Adm. Erich Raeder, was also on board the cruiser together with the Officer Commanding of fleet training, which in turn meant that aboard the cruiser at one time there were the most important men who later had the greatest impact on the further history of *Köln* and other cruisers described in this book.

On 18 December the cruiser arrived in Flensburg, where the cadets were disembarked, and it was actually the last major event in the story of the ship in 1933, not counting 30 December when the worn out ship moved to the shipyard where her renovation began.

On 1 January 1934, the cruiser returned under the command of the reconnaissance force, but at that time it did not change much for the ship herself, since the shipyard works were carried out until 22 March. It is important that the day before – on 21 March – Lt. Cdr. Werner Fuchs became her new commander.

Later, a series of trials and tests began, but it is impossible not to mention here the collision that occurred during mooring manoeuvres on 20 April with the battleship *Deutschland*, which by the way just a few days before had returned from a cruise to Norway, which was important for Adolf Hitler as during it he asked Adm. Erich Raeder and Generals Werner von Blomberg and Werner von Fritsch, who were also on board, for support in his efforts to obtain the position of the President of the Reich. It cannot be hidden that politics more and more often "visited" the German ships and began to influence their fate. Anyway, this was not the only "encounter" of *Köln* with this most important *Reichsmarine* ship of that time.

After the cruiser took part in fleet manoeuvres in May, both ships set off on a long training voyage on 9 June, the route of which led all the way to Madeira. The vessel then underwent a series

Köln *in Swinemünde.*

Köln *passing through the Kiel Canal. Details of the superstructure as well as deck equipment are clearly visible.*

of exercises, testing, among others, the fire control systems. The return to Wilhelmshaven took place on 28 June and the list of places visited included Porto Santo, Funchal, Bay of Cascais and Lisbon.

On 2 August, during a stop in Kiel, there was also the sad event of lowering the colours to half mast, having received a message about the death of German President Paul von Hindenburg. This event was all the more sad because it gave Hitler full power and was the beginning of the tragic events of the following years.

It is worth adding that Hindenburg's death was just a formality after the high-ranking officers on board the battleship *Deutschland*, mentioned earlier, had offered Hitler full authority, especially since he was sure of his future after he had ruthlessly dealt with the internal opposition mainly in the SA as well other political opponents during the so-called "Night of the Long Knives".

Let us leave politics and get back on board *Köln*. Over the following months, the ship carried out a training programme, visiting both the North Sea and the Baltic. Between 14 and 17 September she stayed in Swinemünde and between 26 and 30 October in Stettin. The last major event in 1934 was her move on 2 November to the shipyard, where another modernization began which lasted until the following year.

A lot changed on the ship then. First of all, the old 88 mm guns were removed and in their place three twin 88 mm SK C 32 gun mounts were installed. A catapult was fitted and the left side boom was replaced with a crane with a folding arm for floatplane operations. At the rear of the battle mast, additional platforms were added at the level of the searchlights and the control deck was extended beyond the battle mast column. Changes were also made to the stern superstructure by transferring, among others, the rangefinder farther aft, and an anti-aircraft fire control station was built in the space thus freed.

Köln began 1935 with a series of test cruises, during which mechanisms were tested, new equipment was tried and the crew had to be exercised after a long break. The most interesting events of the first half of this year include the participation of the vessel in the spring fleet manoeuvres, and later the celebration of the *Marinevolkswoche* navy festival during which the ship was made available to the public.

At this point, it is impossible not to add that at the time of the wave of ever more sound rejections of the Versailles Treaty, *Köln* already belonged to the *Kriegsmarine* which had been formed in May – a new military formation built on the ruins of the *Reichsmarine* and intensively expanded.

An interesting event was also the transition on 8 July to the waters of the Baltic Sea, where until 30 August the ship took part in various types of exercises, visiting among others the coastal towns of Göhren, Niendorf and Boltenhagen. Then on 26 and 27 July she was once again visited by none other than Adolf Hitler himself who was the most important person in the state at that time.

In September, the ship stayed in the dock of the shipyard in Wilhelmshaven, and on 1 October her new skipper became Lt. Cdr. Otto Backenköhler. It was also the last major event of 1935.

The crew of the ship greeted the new year in Wilhelmshaven.

After that, the *Köln* story was also becoming more and more interesting considering the fact that the sister ships *Königsberg* and *Karlsruhe* had already performed several distant cruises, during which they visited many unusual corners of the world. On 6 January the ship put to sea, where she took part in a series of exercises with the cruiser *Leipzig*.

On 28 January the flag was once again dropped to half mast after the news of the death of King George V.

Later, between 20 February and 4 March the cruiser performed the task of fishery protection in Norwegian waters. At the turn of April and May, she also travelled with the cruisers *Leipzig* and *Nürnberg* to North Atlantic waters, once again visiting Funchal in Madeira between 23 and 27 April and the Portuguese port of Lagos between 29 April and 3 May.

On 29–31 May *Köln* took part in a very solemn naval parade on the occasion of the anniversary of the Battle of Jutland and the unveiling of a monument in honour of the German sailors killed in 1914–1918 in Laboe, 10 km north-east of Kiel. Of course, this was the time when such celebrations were organized with great spectacle, which could not fail to include Adolf Hitler along with the most important government dignitaries and the diplomatic corps. He personally unveiled the almost 85-metre monument which, interestingly, is one of the few surviving to this day which has become a tangible reminder of those events.

It is interesting that even then the German leader did not fail to visit the cruiser, and meet with her commanding officer, Lt. Cdr. Backenköhler.

Later, *Köln* put to sea several times to undergo crew training until July, when disturbing news came from Spain, in which an anti-republican military coup broke out. For this reason, orders were sent to the cruiser which was then in the Baltic to immediately move to Wilhelmshaven and collect fuel, ammunition and food supplies. On 27 July *Köln* left Wilhelmshaven and headed west towards the Bay of Biscay.

At the same time, the battleships *Deutschland* and *Admiral Scheer* were also entering the inflamed region, and were to provide protection and support the operation of large torpedo ships from the 2nd Flotilla. Thus began the first combat tour of the cruiser *Köln* in the waters of war-torn Spain.

With the task of ensuring the security of German nationals remaining in this country at that time, *Köln* operated on the Spanish coast for nearly a month, including calls at the ports of Musel, Santander, Bilbao, Gijon and Portu. In total, she stayed there until 23 August, when she left Spanish waters and arrived at Wilhelmshaven three days later.

On 3 September the cruiser moved to her home shipyard for renovation, after which she underwent a series of tests lasting until the first days of October.

Köln left Wilhelmshaven on 5 October and, setting a course for Spanish waters, began her second combat tour. This time the ship's stay in the inflamed area lasted much longer. Similarly to before, the cruiser guarded German interests by calling at ports, among others La Coruna, Pueblo del Carmanial, Guetaria, Beermeo, Santona, Santander, El Ferrol, San Sebastian and Portugalete.

As a curiosity, she encountered many other German ships operating there, such as the cruisers *Nürnberg* which she met on 13 November and *Leipzig* two days later, and the battleships *Deutschland* on 16 November and *Admiral Scheer* on 25 November. The seemingly most important event occurred on 28 November, when near the El Ferol while staying in the roadstead, *Köln* was replaced by her sister ship *Königsberg* which arrived to exchange with her at this station.

This marked the end of the second tour and she returned home heading for Kiel, which she reached on 1 December and where she underwent the necessary inspection. *Köln* however did not stay in the motherland for very long. A few days after greeting the new year – 1937 – she was ready to set sail, with the task of travelling for the third consecutive tour to war-torn Spain.

For this reason, as early as on 5 January, having passed the Kiel Canal, she left home waters and headed west to soon find herself in the inflamed area. On 9 January

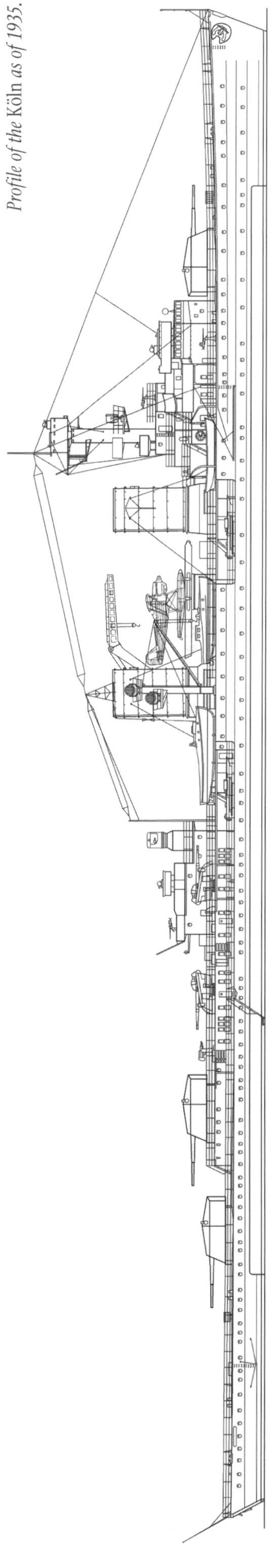

Profile of the Köln *as of 1935.*

Köln *in one of many postcards published in the 1930s.*

the cruiser found herself in El Ferrol, where the next day she met with the *Königsberg* which she was scheduled to replace, and the following day there was also an encounter with the third of the trio – *Karlsruhe* – which operated in that area as part of her first tour.

Köln's third combat tour lasted the longest and ended on 13 March, when the ship set out on her way back home, having been replaced at that time by the cruiser *Leipzig.* During this time, as on the previous tour, the ship visited a number of ports on the Spanish coast while meeting many German ships.

A more interesting, but also very controversial event, can be considered that of 5 February, when the cruiser along with the battleship *Admiral Graf Spee* supported the ships belonging to Nationalist forces in shelling Republican positions during operations in the region of Malaga. Both vessels then provided protection for the Spanish force against possible attack by Republican ships, which was one of many proofs that at that time Germany was already fully involved in the ongoing war.

On 15 March *Köln* returned to Kiel and, as before, after a short break, moved to the shipyard for renovation. This time the works took a bit longer because the renovation was only completed on 12 May. The necessary trials later lasted until the end of May, after which on 6 June the cruiser left Kiel and once again set course for Spanish waters, and thus began the fourth combat tour in her history.

Unfortunately, at that time the situation was already very serious. After the battleship *Deutschland*, while staying in Ibiza, had on 29 May been bombed by Republican aircraft and as a result as many as 31 crew members of this ship were killed, an enraged Hitler almost declared open war on the Republicans. It was not until later that he calmed down, contented with retaliation by the battleship *Admiral Scheer* shelling the actually defenceless city of Almeria, as a result of which 24 civilians died, about 100 were wounded and more than 8,000 were made homeless.

What did this mean for *Köln* herself? Certainly, by then many Spaniards looked on German ships with particular hatred. On 24 June in Gibraltar a group of injured crew members from *Deutschland*, hospitalized there, were embarked, with whom she later would sail home.

Besides that during this combat tour of the ship, despite the very complicated situation, nothing serious happened that deserved to be noted, and on 29 June she returned to Wilhelmshaven, having brought the wounded from *Deutschland*, of whom German propaganda would make real heroes. Several high-ranking state dignitaries then came aboard the ship, including Rear Admiral Herman von Fischel.

The ship herself moved to Kiel the next day to undertake a brief inspection at that shipyard. Later, several trials were conducted and on 30 July she was already at sea heading for Spain, the fifth such tour of the cruiser.

This time it lasted until October, and the most interesting events include a cruise on the waters of the Mediterranean between 11 and 14 August and joint shelling alongside the battleship *Admiral Scheer*, which was carried out on 21 – 22 September.

The ship returned home on 8 October when she dropped anchor in the Kiel roadstead, thus ending the last combat tour and a particular stage in her story. Compared to what had happened with the ship so far, there is really nothing to write about until the end of that year except for another stay

One of the changes to everyday routine were rowing regattas, organised frequently.

at the shipyard, or more significantly a change in the post of commander, who from 15 October was Cdr. Theodor Burchardi.

At the turn of January and February, *Köln* stayed at the dock of the shipyard in Kiel, where she underwent renovation, and later, from 21 February, she operated in the North Sea. On 25 February she carried out exercises together with the 406th Coastal Aviation Group. From 26 February to 13 March, she was subordinated to a group of vessels designated for fisheries protection in the waters of Norway and the North Atlantic. She then paid a short visit between 7 and 9 March to the Norwegian port of Kristansand.

The rest of March, April and May were alternated with exercises and stays at the shipyard.

Noteworthy was the visit to Latvian Riga between 28 May and 3 June. She made a similar visit to Pilau in East Prussia at the beginning of July, at Swedish Udevalla on 2–5 August and Swinemünde between 12 and 15 August.

Throughout this time, the ship also participated in countless exercises, which from time to time were distinguished by the fact that important guests visited the ship, such as Vice Admiral Herman Densch – the BdA Commander – who turned up on board on 18 – 19 July during torpedo firing practice, or as repeatedly mentioned here Admiral Erich Raeder on 15 August.

An interesting event was the participation of the ship on 22 August in a solemn naval review organized in Kiel Bay to celebrate the launch of the heavy cruiser *Prinz Eugen* and the visit to Germany of the Regent of Hungary, Admiral Miklos Horthy von Nagybanya.

The battleship *Gneisenau* opened the huge parade of ships organized on this occasion; then sailed *Deutschland*, *Admiral Scheer*, *Admiral Graf Spee*, the cruisers *Nurnberg*, *Leipzig* and *Köln* – the most interesting to us – followed by the destroyers *Richard Beitzen*, *Georg Thiel*, *Max Schultz*, *Theodor Ihn*, *Erich Steinbrinck*, *Friedrich Eckold*, *Bruno Heinemann*, *Wolfgang Zenker* and *Lebrecht Maass*. At the end came the vessels from the 1st Torpedo Ship Flotilla, 2nd Escort Flotilla, 2nd Minesweeper Flotilla and 1st Torpedo Boat Flotilla.

Later, until almost the end of the year, it is difficult to find interesting events in the ship's service, and it should be mentioned here that in 1938 the catapult was dismantled, which was never to be installed again. A kind of curiosity is also the fact that in the summer of this year a series of tests were carried out aboard the ship with an American Vought V 85 Corsair floatplane!

Köln welcomed 1939 at the Deutsche Werke shipyard in Kiel, where it underwent another renovation at the time, which ended on 3 January.

Köln *moored to a barrel.*

Considering that this was already the time of unrest obvious in almost every state in Europe, the *Köln*'s service began to look a bit different. After Hitler "cracked down" on the Czech Republic, next he turned his eyes to Klaipeda. For this reason, *Köln* was included in the force of *Kriegsmarine* vessels selected to seize the Lithuanian port.

The occupation of Klaipeda was another triumph of the leader of the Third Reich, whom no one would seem to be able to oppose at that time. Anyway, Hitler was probably well aware of this, because in this case he personally participated in the entire operation, embarked on board the battleship *Deutschland*, from where he and his fleet sailed to the target.

His presence was probably a very clear message for everyone, and the same applied to the composition of the aforementioned force, which at that time was sent to Klaipeda because, apart from *Deutschland*, it included the battleships *Admiral Scheer* and *Admiral Graf Spee*, "our" *Köln* as well as the cruisers *Leipzig* and *Nürnberg*, together with the destroyers *Leberecht Maas*, *Georg Thiele*, *Max Schultz*, *Richard Beitzen*, *Friedrich Ihn*, *Friedrich Eckoldt*, *Dieter von Roeder* and *Hermann Künne*, and a dozen or so torpedo ships, minesweepers and auxiliary vessels.

As you can guess, no one would dare to oppose such a force, making the right impression not only on the Lithuanians, but also on the Poles. The Polish fleet was put in a state of readiness at the time, taking into account that immediately after the capture of Klaipeda, Hitler "on the way back" might do the same with Danzig, which, as we know, was the main spark of the conflict between Poland and Germany. Fortunately this did not happen, although it was only a matter of months.

Hitler's actions were a clear signal of the impending conflict, but for the crew and commanding officer of *Köln*, Theodor Burchardi, there was the next task. When on 11 April Hitler issued a directive under the codename "*Fall Weiss*" (Code White), i.e. the attack on Poland scheduled later on 1 September 1939, it became obvious to German commanders against whom the exercises conducted since that time were to be used[5].

This was also the case with the training cruise on which *Köln* set off on 17 April together with the battleships *Deutschland* and *Admiral Graf Spee*, light cruisers *Leipzig* and *Nürnberg*, eight destroyers from the 1st and 3rd Squadrons, fifteen submarines from the *Salzwedel*, *Hundius* and *Wegener* flotillas and the base ship *Erwin Wassner*. The goal was to conduct further exercises in the Atlantic, but this time preparing the crews of the ships for combat operations, including attacking shipping and cooperation with submarines and supply auxiliaries.

For almost a month, the cruiser operated from Spanish ports, and the crew practised everything needed to meet the requirements of difficult and dangerous warfare. It was clear that the outbreak of

5 Fall Weiss was a consequence of signing the Polish-British agreement of 6 April 1939 providing mutual guarantees for military assistance in the event of a German attack on one of these countries. As everyone knows, it came into force on 1 September 1939 at exactly 0445 and became the first military operation of World War Two.

A common situation aboard the cruiser.

war was only a matter of time. In the ship's everyday life this could be seen at every turn. Numerous gunnery and torpedo firing practices, sailing in groups, alarms raised etc. were conspicuous signals of what she was heading for.

Unlike most major *Kriegsmarine* ships, *Köln* took a more honourable place in history by getting into the group of ships designated to blockade the approaches to the Gulf of Gdańsk, after salvos from the battleship *Schleswig-Holstein* were to wake up Europe.

As a result, on 25 August *Köln* left her base having collected supplies and went to the island of Bornholm, in the area where all the ships assigned to the task were to concentrate, including the cruisers *Leipzig* and *Nurnberg*. The latter also served as the flagship of the entire group, included in the reconnaissance force commanded by Vice Admiral Herman Densch, and subordinated to the Commander of the *Gruppenkommando "Ost"*, General-Admiral Conrad Albrecht.

An interesting thread here is about the sighting on 31 August by the lookouts on *Köln*, whilst sailing toward Bornholm, of a group of Polish destroyers composed of ORP *Burza*, ORP *Grom* and ORP *Błyskawica*, which at that time were leaving their home waters and were en route to Britain, where they later formed the embryo of the Polish Navy fighting in the West[6]. Germany could not afford any incident considering what was to happen in a few hours, although opinions here are divided, because many authors believe that the task of cruisers was to stop the Polish ships?

Anyway, when 1 September came, *Köln* was commencing her mission and after she was recalled to Kiel, she was directed to the waters of the North Sea. Together with the cruisers *Königsberg*, *Emden* and *Leipzig* she participated in mine laying, ranging from the coast of the Netherlands to Skagerrak.

The war had started for real, which meant that there was no shortage of tasks. On 7 October *Köln* in fairly good company, which undoubtedly was the battleship *Gneisenau*[7] and the destroyers *Bernd von Arnim*, *Dieter von Roeder*, *Erich Steinbrinck*, *Friedrich Ihn*, *Friedrich Eckold*, *Paul Jacobi*, *Karl Galster*, *Wilhelm Heidkamp* and *Mac Schultz*, left Kiel and headed north.

The target of such a powerful force was the region to the south of Norway where, along with other ships, the cruiser was to attack Allied shipping, but this mission also had one more goal. The German High Command hoped that the putting to sea of such a force, in which we should not forget was the eye-catching newest and most powerful *Kriegsmarine* ship and, no matter how dangerous, the cruiser would entice the Royal Navy into a trap set there.

These plans did not work out because the British did not miss the fact of the German setting sail, but they took it for an attempt to break into the Atlantic, so Royal Navy ships were sent onto the high seas. Instead of chasing the German group south of Norway they headed for the area between Iceland and the Shetland Islands, where *Köln* and *Gneisenau* were to be intercepted. Eventually, the mission was aborted, and then on 9 October the cruiser returned to Kiel.

6 The entire operation was codenamed "Peking" (Bejing) and had been planned before the war broke out.

7 Some references claim that *Scharnhorst* took part in this operation too, but this has not been confirmed.

Bird's eye view of the Köln. *Deck layout can be clearly seen.*

Another notable action took place in November, more precisely on 21 November, when *Köln* and the cruiser *Leipzig* put to sea to provide cover for the battleships *Scharnhorst* and *Gneisenau* and to take action against enemy shipping in the waters of Skagerrak.

On the night of November 24–25, *Köln* also became part of a powerful naval force consisting of the cruisers *Lützow*[8] and *Leipzig* and destroyers *Bernd von Arnim, Karl Galster, Friedrich Ihn* and *Bruno Heinemann*, as well as torpedo ships from the 6th Flotilla, commanded by Rear Admiral Gunter Lütjens.

On 12 December *Köln*, together with the cruisers *Leipzig* and *Nürnberg*, set sail with the task of providing cover to destroyers returning from a mine-laying action, and it can be said that this action was a form of tempting the enemy, given the fact that the units sailed without any cover! The next day the crews of *Leipzig* and *Nürnberg* became convinced of this after these ships were torpedoed by the British submarine HMS *Salmon*. It was due to this event *Köln* that was the only survivor to take over the role of the flagship of the reconnaissance force, first of Rear Admiral Gunter Lütjens and then Rear Admiral Hubert Schmundt. Considering the cruisers *Leipzig* and *Nürnberg* were excluded from action, *Köln* did not participate in major operations until the end of the year, performing the role of the flagship until May 1940.

As a curiosity, it can be mentioned that on the occasion of Christmas, Rudolf Hess – one of Adolf Hitler's closest associates and one of the main leaders of the Third Reich – paid a visit to the ship.

During virtually almost the entire period of acting as flagship, not much happened. The harsh winter of the turn of 1939–1940, during which heavy snowfalls and severe frosts effectively immobilized the *Kriegsmarine* in its ports, was sharply felt, so one had to wait patiently.

At that time, Hitler would not rest and prepared a plan of attack on Denmark and Norway for which he needed almost all ships of the German fleet.

At that time, the ship's commander also changed – from 15 January the skipper was Cdr. Ernst Kratzenberg.

Commanders of the ship

- 15 January 1930 – 27 September 1932 – Cdr. Ludwig von Schröder
- 28 September 1932 – 20 March 1934 – Lt. Cdr. Otto Schniewind
- 21 March 1934 – 30 September 1935 – Lt. Cdr. Werner Fuchs
- 1 October 1935 – 15 October 1937 – Lt. Cdr. Otto Backenöhler
- 15 October 1937 – 14 January 1940 – Cdr. Theodor Burchardi
- 15 January 1940 – 29 May 1941 – Cdr. Ernst Kratzenberg
- 29 May 1941 – 28 March, 1942 – Cdr. Friedrich Hüffmeier
- 29 March 1942 – 24 May 1942 – Cdr. Hellmuth Strobel
- 25 May 1942 – 12 December 1942 – Cdr. Martin Baltzer
- 13 December 1942 – 17 February 1943 – Cdr. Hans Meyer
- 1 April 1944 – January 1945 – Lt. Cdr. Hellmuth Strobel
- January 1945 – 5 April 1945 – Cdr. Fritz Henning

8 She was the ex-battleship *Deutschland* re-classfied to a cruiser.

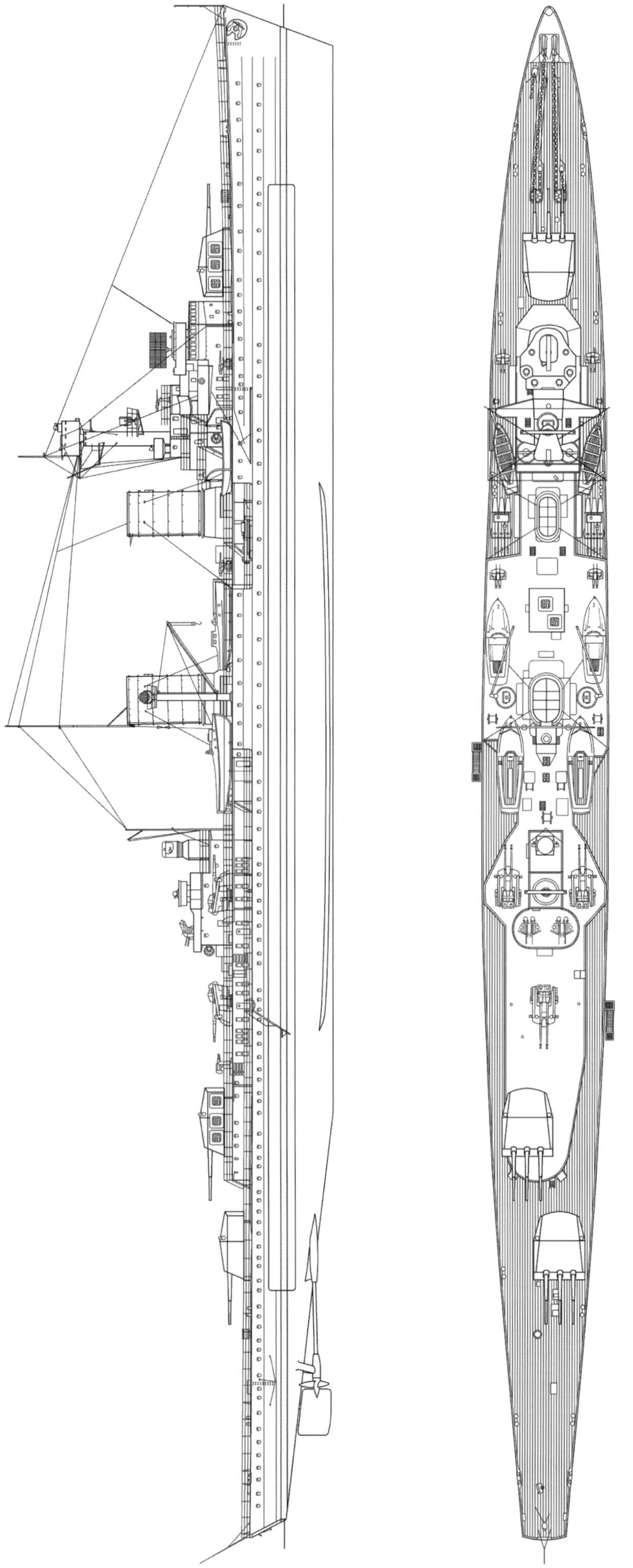

The Köln's profile as of 1941.

Köln on the roadstead. Note the crane which was for floatplane operations.

Bearing in mind that these events have already been mentioned, we will limit ourselves only to information as part of this operation bearing the code name *Weserübung*, *Köln* was in the third group, which as we learned in a previous chapter also included her sister ship *Königsberg*, and the gun training ship *Bremse*, torpedo ships *Leopard* and *Wolf*, the 1st Torpedo Boat Flotilla (S19, S21, S22, S23, S24) along with the depot ship *Carl Peters* and auxiliary vessels *Schiff* 9 and *Schiff* 18, and the force's target was Bergen.

In contrast to the aforementioned *Königsberg*, for *Köln* the entire operation was successful and the ship carried out the task without major incidents. After the entire group had halted at the entrance of Karsfjord on 9 April at about 0200 hrs, the leading *Köln* was quickly detected by the Norwegians, however, when asked for her identity, they were told that they were dealing with the British cruiser *Cairo*, which was obviously a trick planned long ago.

Analyzing the previous course of the cruiser's service, it is easy to see that she was enjoying proverbial luck, which is why the unsuspecting Norwegians believed the answer and without raising the alarm they let the German ship in. The whole action proceeded as planned.

Moving further along their course at dawn, the force found itself in Byifjord, where *Köln* and the torpedo ships mentioned above stopped to disembark the troops carried aboard, who were to eliminate the Kvarven coastal battery which was denying access to Bergen.

As we know from the previous chapter, this plan was not fully implemented and before the German troops neutralized the battery, it managed to open fire on the *Königsberg* which was now leading the formation and the *Bremse* and *Carl Peters* following her.

Köln herself was more fortunate, and once she disembarked the troops brought to Bergen and having avoided the British aircraft attacking the port, she set off on her way back to her home waters.

The Norwegian campaign, excluding two mine laying operations in the North Sea on 16 and 18 May, was actually the only major event in the history of the ship in 1940. From 26 June to 10 August, the cruiser stayed at the shipyard and again from 19 November until early 1941. During these stays, among others two torpedo tubes were removed from the ship and demagnetizing devices were installed. In total, renovation works lasted until 28 March 1941.

A curiosity here is the fact that on top of the aft main battery turret, a special platform was temporarily fitted for testing the Flettner FI 282 *Kolibri* helicopter[9], at the time of its prototype trials. Afterwards, between April and August, based in Gdynia (now renamed Gotenhafen) *Köln*

9 This was a light multi-purpose helicopter designed and built at the Anton Flettner plant.The machine had basic weight of 760 km and 1,000 kg take-off weight. The rotor diameter was 11.9 m, fuselage length was 6.6 m and height 2.2 m. The drive unit was an engine with 160 HP output, and its maximum speed was determined at 150 km/h. It is widely recognized as the first helicopter in the world to be mass-produced in versions including a one-seat naval reconnaissance aircraft, two-seat reconnaissance-liaison machine and one-seat reconnaissance helicopter operating from submarines.

Köln *while entering the port of Swinemünde. Again, the floatplane crane is clearly visible as well as the catapult.*

performed many tests with this unusual machine, sailing among others in the waters of the Gulf of Gdańsk and the southern Baltic. At the same time, her commander changed once again, Cdr. Friedrich Hüffmeier became the skipper on 29 May.

At that time, the cruiser's service seemed rather monotonous, however, the moment for the "*Barbarossa*" plan, in other words Germany's attack on the USSR, was approaching. As a result, *Köln* ended up in the *Baltenflotte*'s composition, the force led by Vice Admiral Otto Ciliax, whose task was to take action in the event of attempts to break westwards by the ships of the Soviet Baltic Fleet. Apart from *Köln*, it consisted of the battleships *Admiral Scheer* and *Tirpitz* – the latter of course was the largest, hence she became the flagship of Vice Adm. Ciliax – as well as the cruisers *Emden*, *Leipzig* and *Nürnberg*, three destroyers, five torpedo ships and a *schnellboot* flotilla.

After the *Luftwaffe* had dealt with the main threat posed by the Soviet battleships *Oktyabrskaya Revolutsya* and *Marat*, the *Admiral Scheer* and *Tirpitz* were both withdrawn, while the remaining ships, including *Köln*, began to carry out tasks related to providing support to the ground forces. And so, between 12 and 13 October the cruiser supported the troops with her gunfire, during fighting on the Island of Dagö firing 285 rounds on the first day and 256 on the next, receiving one harmless hit. On 14 October she also shelled Soviet batteries at Cape Ristna.

An important event here was the failed attack on the cruiser carried out by the Soviet submarine ShTch-323 which occurred on 13 October 13[10].

The remainder of the year was not so abundant in interesting events. In view of the limited use of major ships which Hitler undoubtedly wanted, it is difficult to find more interesting events in *Köln*'s service, mentioning only her numerous stays at various ports of the West Baltic related to training, and in December her transition to the North Sea took place.

For the ship 1942 commenced with a stay at the shipyard in Wilhelmshaven, which lasted until 23 May. At that time, modernization was carried out on her, consisting of removing the fore rangefinder and installing a FuMO 21 radar antenna in its place. In addition, two sets of 37 mm anti-aircraft guns were removed, together with two single 20 mm cannons, and instead two quadruple 20 mm *Flakvierling* mounts were fitted.

Once again the commander of the ship changed, which on 29 March became Cdr. Hellmuth Strobel, however, not for long because on 25 May his duties were taken over by Cdr. Martin Baltzer. Later, the cruiser underwent a series of tests, after which between 9 and 13 July she was transferred to Norway, laying mines along the west coast of Denmark on her way. Initially, the ship was stationed in Oslo, and then on 6 August she moved to Narvik. And not much happened after that.

Along with Hitler's growing reluctance to use major surface ships in combat operations, which, in his understanding, consumed huge amounts of fuel and other materials as well as engaging their

10 Some references claim that the ShTch-323 sighted the cruiser but did not manage to fire torpedoes.

Köln *seen from the starboard.*

numerous crews, *Köln* practically ceased to be necessary, becoming just a part of the powerful system defending Norway against a possible Allied invasion.

The deepening fuel crisis was not without significance here, which in many cases effectively prevented the implementation of plans for attacks on Allied convoys with deliveries to Murmansk which after all were passing so close.

In this situation, the story of the cruiser's service began to be very much deprived of more interesting events. In total, until the end of July and throughout almost all of August not much was happening and only between 20 and 29 August we can note an interesting event, which was the participation of the ship in joint exercises with the battleship *Tirpitz* and cruiser *Admiral Hipper* as well as destroyers Z 23, Z 27, Z 28, Z 29 and Z 30.

Time passed, and despite the idleness negatively affecting the crew's morale, Hitler refused to take any action. After all, *Köln* was part of the powerful system defending Norway against the Allies, which for Hitler sometimes became a real obsession pushing other, sometimes more important, needs out of the way. In his understanding, undertaking combat operations was only an unnecessary exposure of the ship just as much as an attempt to use, among others, *Köln* against the PQ-18 convoy, which the Allies sent to the USSR on 2 September.

After the spectacular defeat of the PQ-17 convoy, when the Allies suffered severe losses, Adm. Raeder had already developed a plan to attack PQ-18, thinking that Hitler could be persuaded in this situation to send larger ships out to sea. Under the code name "*Doppelschlag*", the plan provided for the involvement in the attack of other ships which were in a similar situation to *Köln*, i.e. the battleship *Tirpitz* and cruisers *Admiral Scheer, Admiral Hipper* and of course *Köln* herself. Eventually, Raeder's plans did not work out and due to the lack of proper reconnaissance the action had been abandoned before it properly began.

Actually that would be it as far as the noteworthy events in the ship's history of that period are concerned, not counting another change in the position of commander, who on 13 December became Cdr. Hans Karl Mayer.

After Hitler had enacted his frantic directive, having ordered the disarmament and scrapping of all the major ships, the activities of the *Kriegsmarine*'s surface vessels virtually stopped, and so it happened with *Köln*.

It was not until February 1943 that the ship, together with the cruiser *Admiral Hipper*, left Norway and returned to Kiel, but this was not related to new combat tasks. On 17 February the ship was withdrawn from service, and for almost a year stayed idle at the Blücherbücke quay, acting only as a floating anti-aircraft battery.

It was not until March 1944 that something began to happen aboard the cruiser. Having embarked a small party of sailors, the vessel was towed to Königsberg, where the ship was refurbished at the local shipyard and her combat capabilities were restored[11]. The ship was re-incorporated into service on 1 April as a training ship, operating mainly in the Baltic Sea.

At that time, her new commander, or rather the old one because he was appointed for the second time, became Cdr. Lieutenant Hellmuth Strobel, who took over his duties on 1 April.

Despite being restored to active service, throughout the summer of 1944 it is difficult to find more interesting events related to the ship. Having left the shipyard, which took place on 1 September,

11 According to some references, the AA weapons of the ship were also strengthened but today it is hard to determine whether this actually took place, or remained only an intention.

only in October is there information about the ship being directed to Norwegian waters, where she was subordinated to the battle group.

The ship set out from Swinemünde on 11 October escorted by the destroyers *Richard Beitzen* and *Friedrich Ihn*, with 90 mines on board which were laid on minelaying operations. The cruiser operated in the Oslofjord waters covering transports. In mid-November she also took part in joint exercises in the waters of the aforementioned fjord alongside the cruiser *Emden*.

At that time, Germany's situation was getting more and more complicated. The *Wehrmacht* was retreating on all fronts, and Allied air raids were almost commonplace. Despite the fact that *Köln* was stationed in Oslo, this area also drew attention from RAF aircraft.

The first major raid took place on 13 December, when approximately 80 Beaufighter aircraft flew over the Norwegian port. It was similar on 31 December, when a formation of Avro Lancaster heavy bombers came over Oslo. The ship then suffered serious damage in the area of, among others, her drive shafts, thus limiting the maximum speed to only 15 knots[12]. The damage did not make it possible to continue operations, which resulted in orders to return to home waters in January 1945.

The last commander of the ship was Cdr. Fritz Henning, who took over the position in January 1945.

The ship arrived at Kiel, and was transferred to Wilhelmshaven not long after, where the damage was scheduled to be repaired at the local shipyard. This was not easy because during the transition to Wilhelmshaven, the cruiser once again became the target of an air attack, almost miraculously avoiding direct hits.

Fore view of the Köln. *Note the anchors as well as the ship's emblem.*

The cruiser arrived at the shipyard on 14 January. However, due to the hopeless situation at the front and the growing problems with supply, the work progressed very slowly until it was finally stopped. The fate of the ship was sealed on 30 March[13], when another formation of Allied bombers arrived over Wilhelmshaven.

The cruiser, standing at the shipyard's basin, received a direct hit from a heavy bomb, which caused serious damage and finally sank the ship. *Köln* settled at the bottom on an even keel, which left the superstructures and main battery turrets above the surface of the water. For the following days, the heavily damaged ship was used as an anti-aircraft battery.

Ultimately, *Köln* was de-commissioned on 5 April 1945, and on 6 May shortly before the Polish 1st Armoured Division entered Wilhelmshaven, the wreckage was blown up. Scrapping of the wreck began in 1946, with the last fragments of the vessel raised from the bottom only in 1956, during the reconstruction of the area of today's arsenal in Wilhelmshaven.

Characteristics of the cruiser *Köln* (*Kreuzer* "D")[14]

Type K

- Shipyard Reichsmarinewerft, Wilhmshaven
- Construction No. 116
- Keel laid 7 August 1926
- Launching 23 May 1928
- Commissioning 15 January 1930
- Standard displacement (official) 6,000 t
- Standard displacement (actual) 6,380 t
- Constructional displacement (official) 6,750 t

12 Some authors claim the ship's AA guns shot down five British aircraft during the raid.

13 According to some references it was on 31 March.

14 In the sources from which the quoted data come, there are many discrepancies as to the given parameters of the ship, which makes determining them with absolute certainty extremely difficult and one should be aware of the fact that they may not coincide with data from other studies.

Köln *at anchor.*

- Constructional displacement (actual) 7,700 t
- Overall length 174.0 m
- Length on waterline 169.0 m
- Beam 15.2 m
- Draft (full) 5.4 m
- Propulsion 6 x Marine Schuls-Thornycroft boilers, 4 x steam turbine sets, 2 x diesel engines with total output of 68,485 HP
- Max. speed 32.2 knots
- Fuel supply 1,239 t of boiler fuel, 139 t for diesel engines
- Range 5,700 NM at 19 knots: 7,300 NM at 17 knots, 8,000 NM at 10 knots (with diesel engines)
- Crew 514–614 officers, NCOs and naval ratings. Later 820–850 men
- Armament (1930) 9 (3x3) 150 mm guns: 2 (2x1) 88 mm guns, Later 4 (2x2) 88 mm guns, 12 (4x3) 500 mm torpedo tubes
- Armament (1936) 9 (3x3) 150 mm guns: 6 (3x2) 88 mm guns, 8 (4x2) 37 mm guns, 8 (8x1) 20 mm cannons, 12 (4x3) 533 mm torpedo tubes
- Armament (1944) 9 (3x3) 150 mm guns: 6 (3x2) 88 mm guns, 8 (4x2) 37 mm guns, 18 (9x2) 20 mm cannons, 6 (2x3) 533 mm torpedo tubes
- Armour 50 mm broadsides: 70 mm transverse bulkheads, 20–40 mm decks, 30–100 mm command post, 20–30 mm main battery turrets
- Aircraft equipment 1 x FL22 type pneumatic catapult, 1–2 x Heinkel He 60 floatplanes, later Arado Ar 196 floatplanes

Köln *in 1940.*

Leipzig
A Different Sister Ship

Having worked on the *Königsberg*, *Karlsruhe* and *Köln* K-class cruisers at the Reichsmarinewerft shipyards in Wilhelmshaven and Deutsche Werke in Kiel, in accordance with the implementation plan for the construction of the first modern *Reichsmarine* cruisers the team of German engineers began work on the design of a new cruiser ship, in which they tried to eliminate all the disadvantages and faults of the K-class. It is no secret that already at that time many deficiencies in the construction of the above-mentioned vessels were recognised, which became apparent during their operations.

Anyway, Albrecht Ehrenberg, who was responsible for the entire project, had himself to admit that not all the solutions adopted in their design and construction proved to be correct, so now when work on a new ship was about to begin he had to do everything to eliminate them. Remembering that treaty limits were still in force when designing the future *Leipzig* cruiser, the task turned out to be extremely difficult to accomplish, but German engineers like no others had mastered the art of "stuffing" modern and capable ships into the imposed limits.

It should be remembered that this was a time when, along with the work on the new cruiser, the team of engineers of the *Reichsmarine*'s design department, headed by Ministerial Director Dr. Eng. Paul Presse, also faced a much more difficult task, which was to design a battleship within the limit of 10,000 tons. All this allowed for the development of many innovative solutions, such as the wide-scale application of the method of joining structural elements by electric welding, which would result in huge weight savings.

The Leipzig *cruiser was slightly different compared to the K-class ships. The ship was longer and wider, and she had a different shape of bow and a cruiser stern. As a result of a different arrangement of smoke ducts discharging exhaust fumes, she featured only one funnel, which visually modernized her silhouette.*

Of course, as we have already learned, the Germans could not practically fit any of the ships built into the limited values without exceeding them many times, but in fact no one was worried about it and cleverly falsified statistics which made it possible to "lose" a few unwanted tons. Almost from the very beginning, the Germans had been mocking the Versailles provisions, not only in the navy but also in other arms, having secretly implemented various programmes leading to the reconstruction of the state's military power.

A similar situation was also with *Leipzig*, whose unofficial displacement significantly exceeded even those achieved by the K-class cruisers, but it was clear that it would end up this way.

Leipzig, when compared to the earlier cruisers, differed from them by locating the main battery turrets on the axis of symmetry while maintaining their layout at the same time, i.e. one on the bow and two on the stern. The ship was slightly longer and wider. It also had a different bow shape, the transom stern peculiar to the K-class ships was abandoned and would be replaced with the traditional cruiser one.

As a result of a different arrangement of the funnel shafts discharging the fumes, in this case despite six boilers just one funnel was designed, which modernized the ship's silhouette. It is worth noting here that thus the ship became the first single-smokestack cruiser in the German fleet.

The proverbial "thorn in the flesh" of the K-class was poor stability and insufficient strength of the hull structure, which it was now decided to improve with even more widespread use of electric welding. This now exceeded over 90% of joints for all components.

The changes also included the propulsion unit, which was almost completely redesigned and a third drive shaft was added. The mixed drive system was preserved.

An important change was the modification of the armour protection, in which it was decided to give up the slopes of the armoured deck while covering the broadsides with an armoured belt with characteristic side bulges.

Overall, despite the fact that the *Leipzig* project was a kind of development of the K-class cruisers produced according to only slightly modified assumptions adopted in the construction of the earlier cruisers, she was significantly different from them and definitely better, although also in her case problems of hull strength could not be completely eliminated. Either way, it was a good ship, although the weight of the armament in relation to the relatively low displacement still severely limited her buoyancy and seaworthiness.

Even so, in a situation where the core of the *Reichsmarine* warships still consisted of old vessels of limited combat capabilities and put into service at the beginning of the century, *Leipzig* when compared to them presented a huge leap in quality, hence significantly increasing the combat potential of the navy.

At the time the ship, designated as the E cruiser, was ordered as part of the expenditure for the 1927 financial year at the Reichsmarinewerft shipyard in Wilhelmshaven. The same one at which at the same time the fitting out works were in progress on the *Königsberg* and *Köln*. The keel was laid on 18 April 1928 on slipway No. 1, and the construction itself was given the number 117.

According to the schedule, the newly built ship was to replace the old cruiser *Amazone* which had entered service in 1901, hence also another designation – "*Ersatz Amazone*".

The assembly work on the hull lasted a year and a half and came to an end in October 1929, when it was launched. The ceremony itself, which took place on 18 October, was a great festival at the shipyard, which gathered many important state dignitaries and invited guests as well as those wanting to see the whole "spectacle" – the residents of Wilhelmshaven.

Among the most important guests were the newly appointed head of the Navy Admiral Erich Raeder, Commander-in-Chief of the *Reichswehr* Dr. Wilhelm Groener and Vice-Admiral W. Franz. The mayor of Leipzig, Dr. Karl Rothe, made a speech while the honour of godmother was given to Mrs. Susanne Haun, widow of the last commander of the cruiser of the same name of the World War One era, Lt. Cdr. Johannes Haun[1]. After the traditional bottle of champagne had been smashed on the bow, to the sounds of the national anthem and cheering crowds, the hull slid from the slipway onto the water and at the end of the official part of the ceremony it moored at the fitting out wharf.

It is worth adding here that the launching date was not accidental and took place on the anniversary of the Battle of Leipzig fought from 16 to 19 October 1813 between the forces of Napoleon Bonaparte and those of the anti-French coalition of Austria, Russia, Sweden and of course Prussia.

1 Earlier this name was carried by the *Bremen*-class cruiser introduced into service in 1906. This vessel was built at the AG Weser shipyard in Bremen and had 3,278 t standard displacement and 3,816 t full displacement. Hull dimensions were 111.0 m overall length, 13.3 m beam and 5.6 m draft. Her armament consisted of ten 105 mm guns, ten 53 mm guns and two 450 mm torpedo tubes. The ship sank during the Falklands battle on 8 December 1914. A second ship which was to be given this name at that time was never completed.

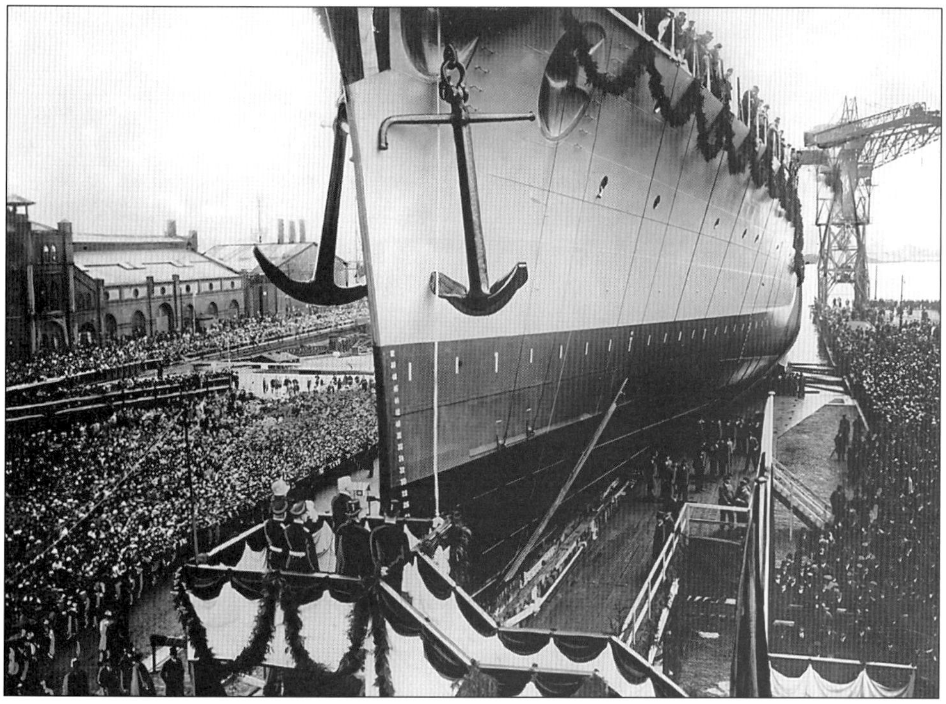

A series of interesting images taken during the launching ceremony of Leipzig *on 18 October 1929.*

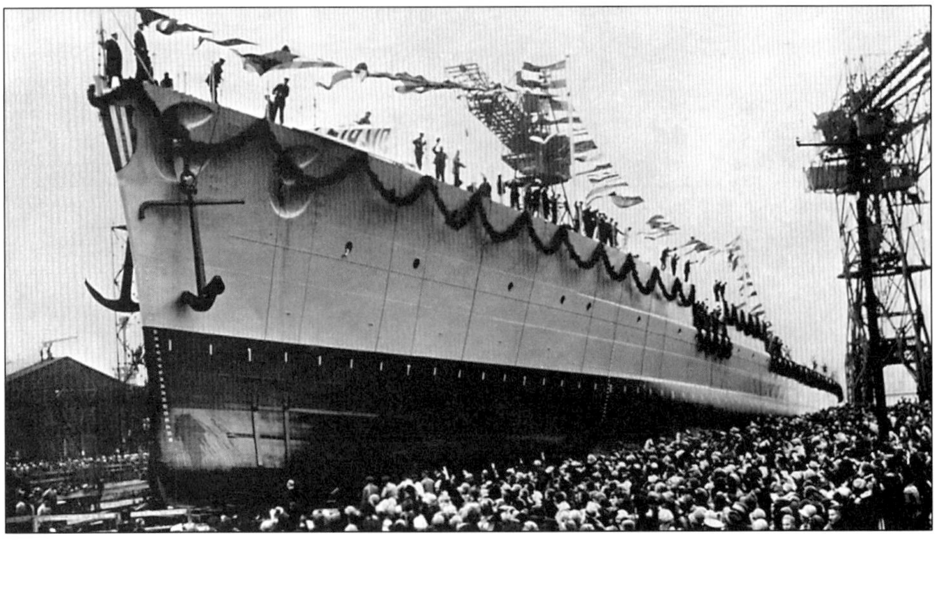

Name of the ship

The name of the ship was given in honour of the city of Leipzig in eastern Germany. Its foundation dates back to the 7th century, and it received city rights in 1165. The city is one of the largest German metropolises. During World War Two it was one of the few which avoided serious damage, thanks to which a number of unique global scale relics of architecture have been preserved to date.

Leipzig, both at the time when it took patronage over the latest German cruiser as well as nowadays, is an important industrial centre. Well-known brands such as Porsche and BMW and many others have their factories there. Today it is known for the exhibition and conference centre where the so-called Leipzig Trade Fair is held.

Further work, during which the superstructures were built, armament installed together with all kinds of equipment necessary for operating the ship, lasted almost two years and came to an end in autumn 1931. The official ceremony of raising the colours for the first time took place on 8 October 1931, and from then *Leipzig* began her service as the fifth consecutive – after *Emden*, *Königsberg*, *Karlsruhe* and *Köln* – cruiser of the *Reichsmarine* and eventually the *Kriegsmarine* of the Third Reich.

Commander Hans-Hubert Stobwasser took over command of the crew of over five hundred and thirty men, and under his orders she began a period of intense tests and trials. At this time, having been the latest acquisition of *Reichsmarine* and imposing a burden of 38 million Reichsmarks on German taxpayers, she looked magnificent. The long and slender hull with a bow stem sloped forward and cruiser stern gave her silhouette a kind of lightness, which in combination with quite extensive superstructures, gun turrets and a single funnel gave her the look of a fast and dangerous ship.

Her hull was 177 metres long overall, with its structure based on the longitudinal sections system and was divided by fifteen watertight bulkheads into sixteen compartments in which there were, in order from the stern: compartment I – rudder equipment and torpedo warhead magazines, II – ammunition magazines for C turret and 88 mm guns, III – ammunition magazines for B turret, IV – diesel engines, auxiliary equipment and a set of power generators, V – engine room No. 1 for port side turbines, VI – turbine gears, VII – engine room No. 2 for turbines driving the starboard propeller, VII – fuel tanks, magazines and ammunition magazines for 88 mm guns, IX – boiler room No. 1, X – boiler room No. 2, XI – boiler room No. 3, XII – anti-listing equipment, XIII – main command post, fire control room, converter compartments and aggregate set, XIV – ammunition magazines for the A turret, XV – magazines and XVI – magazines and echo-sounder rooms.

As in the case of the K-class vessels, the ship had a double bottom running 75% of the length of the hull. The relatively good armour protection, which had been developed along the same lines as the pattern characteristic for the Germans from the Great War period, was based on a 50 mm thick armoured belt running on the broadsides and inclined at an angle of 12°[2], the thickness of which decreased towards the bottom to 25 mm, towards the bow down to 18 mm and towards the stern to 35 mm.

2 Some references claim it was 18 degrees.

It was clear at first glance that Leipzig *was significantly different from the K-class cruisers.*

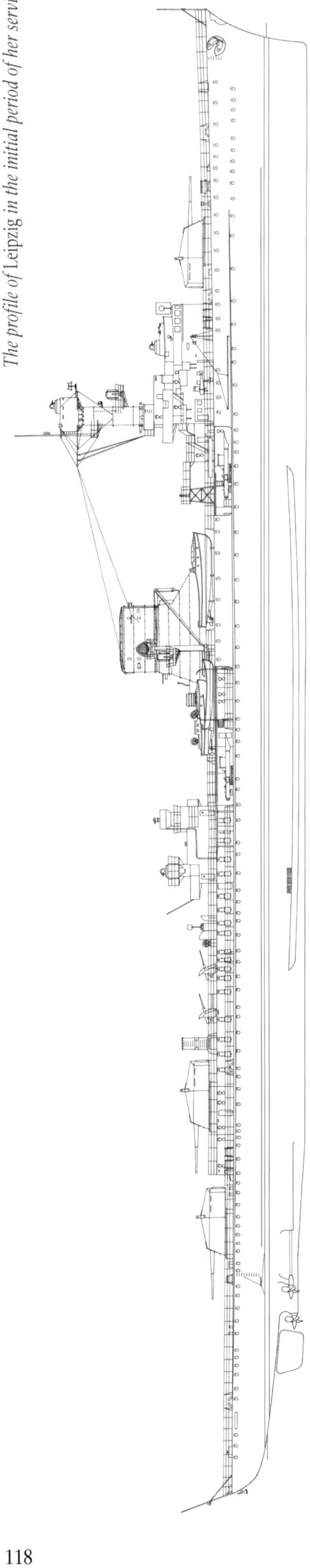

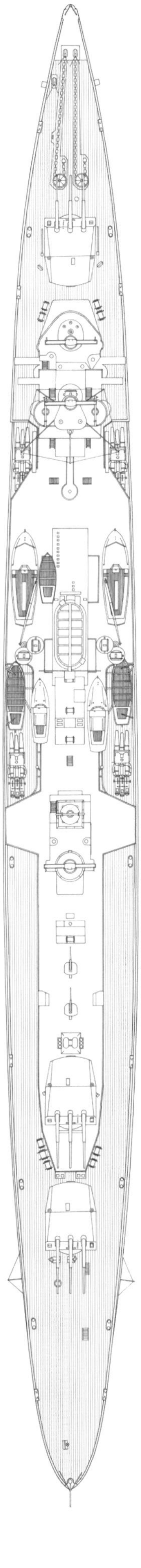

The profile of Leipzig *in the initial period of her service.*

The armoured deck had a thickness in the range of 20 to 25 mm, while in the area of the ammunition magazines its thickness increased to 40 mm. The two-level command post was covered with armour of the following thicknesses: top 100 mm, front wall 50 mm, the remaining parts 30 mm and armour protection of the shaft connecting it with the control room was 50 mm thick. The main battery turrets in this ship's case had 80 mm armour on the front plates, 20 mm on the side walls, 32 mm at the rear, 20–33 mm on the tops and the barbettes supporting them were covered with 60 mm thick armour.

As in the case of the earlier cruisers, it was decided to keep a combined drive on *Leipzig*, based on both steam turbines and diesel engines. The ship had two Parsons system steam turbine assemblies, manufactured at the Germaniawerft shipyard in Kiel, with toothed gears and consisting of one high pressure and two low pressure stages, with a reverse turbine built into one of the low pressure stages. They worked on the two outside propellers, turbine No. 1 for the port side one and turbine No. 2 for the starboard. Steam was supplied to them by six double-sided Marine boilers, which produced steam at a pressure of 17 kg/cm^2 and a temperature of 206° Celsius, and their heating area was 5,500 m^2.

In addition, there were four seven-cylinder, two-stroke diesel engines from the MAN company of the M 7Z 30/44 type, designed for economical speed. They drove the third propeller, which was new compared to previous cruisers. It greatly facilitated the process of switching from one drive to another, very complicated and hindering in the earlier ships.

As a curiosity, it is worth adding that, in order to reduce hydrodynamic drag while sailing with the turbine drive, the middle propeller blades were feathered, while in the opposite situation both outer propellers were rotated using an electric motor, which according to the design assumptions, was to save up to 2,500 HP. The total output of the power unit of the ship was 78,400 HP, of which 12,400 HP was for diesel propulsion.

The basic armament of the ship was the same as in the case of the K-class cruisers and consisted of nine SK C/25 150 mm L/60 guns, manufactured at the Rheinmetall-Borsig plant, placed in three triple turrets of the LC/25 type[3]. In this case, the names of the turrets were noteworthy as they referred to German cruisers from the World War One period that were part of the Squadron led by Vice Admiral Maximilian von Spee. And so the fore A turret was called SMS *Dresden*, B turret on the aft superstructure was called SMS *Leipzig*, and C turret on the aft deck was called SMS *Nürnberg*.

In the initial period of service, the heavy anti-aircraft defence consisted of two Krupp SK C/13 88 mm L/45 guns placed on single MPL C/13 mounts, which, as in the case of the K-class cruisers, were located on the aft deck of the superstructure, between the command post and main battery turret. It is worth adding here that according to the original intentions, instead of them it was planned to install twin sets of the SK C/25 88 mm L/75 guns, i.e. the same ones that were tested in the initial period of service on the cruiser *Köln*. However, the poor opinions about this weapon meant that eventually it was decided to equip the new ship with the quite outdated but proven SK C/13 guns.

3 The actual calibre of the main battery guns was 149.1 mm.

Leipzig *seen in a perfect perspective to demonstrate her superstructure.*

The 88 mm guns were complemented by two single SK C/30 37 mm L/83 guns on MPL C/30 mounts located on the boat deck, as well as two SK C/30 20 mm L/65 cannons on MPL C/30 mounts installed in the area of the Admiral's bridge. In addition, the ship was armed with four triple 500 mm torpedo tubes spaced in pairs on each side of the midships. Here, as a curiosity, it is worth adding that each of these launchers, according to the tradition of the German Navy, had its ownname: *Cameroon, Samoa, Tanga and Togo.*

For fire control, three rangefinders with an optical base of six metres were provided, installed on top of the command post, a battle mast and aft superstructure, two sets of SL-1 systems, two portable rangefinders with an optical base of one metre and two rangefinders with a base of three metres, in this case provided for the torpedo tubes.

At this point we will leave the technical description of the ship and focus on her operational story, which – we recall – commenced on 8 October 1931, when the war colours were raised for the first time. From that time, *Leipzig* was subjected to countless trials and tests.

Leipzig *in a beautifully issued postcard showing her in the company of cruiser* Emden.

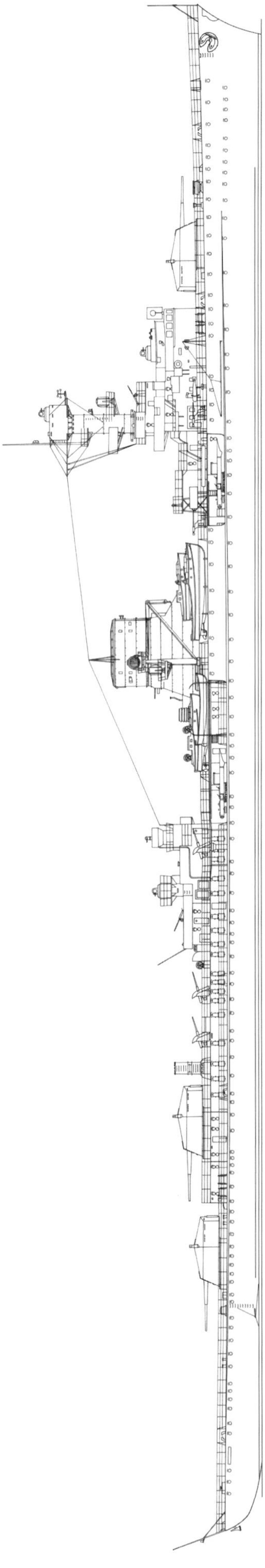

The silhouette of Leipzig *after the first modernisation, as of 1934.*

Listing tests and all kinds of mechanism trials were carried out, as well as deviation and compass compensation measurements. The ship put to sea for the first time on 1 November, and then a period of intensive speed tests, fuel consumption measurements etc. began. It is worth adding that a little earlier, on 31 October, an inspection of the ship was carried out by the BdF fleet commander, Vice Admiral Walter Gladisch. A similar event occurred on 30 November, when the BdA reconnaissance commander, Rear Admiral Conrad Albrecht, turned up on board.

Almost until the end of the year, the ship regularly set sail both to the Baltic and North Sea waters and was subjected to continual tests together with the most important ones, i.e. firing practice. It was not until December that there was a break caused by heavy ice, making it impossible to navigate safely, and *Leipzig* spent the winter of 1931/32 in Wilhelmshaven.

The first major event in 1932 was the passage of the ship on 12–13 February through the Kiel Canal to the Baltic Sea, where the testing program was resumed. The speed of the vessel on a measured mile was further checked, the fuel consumption measured and the circulation determined.

On 26 February, the cruiser moored in Swinemünde, where she "scored" the first collision after the *Sturm* tug damaged her port side propeller during manoeuvres. Consequently, Cdr. Strobwasser was forced to abandon testing and directed the ship to Kiel, where she was docked at the Deutsche Werke shipyard and repairs were made.

The months of March, April and May followed with further trials and training of the crew, and it was not until 16 June that the ship was officially taken over by the navy. For the ship herself, however, this did not change much, as in the following months further tests were carried out, differing only by their location. For example, between 7 and 10 July, the ship was subjected to an uninterrupted 72-hour propulsion unit test, sailing from Kiel through the Great Belt, around Skagen to Wilhelmshaven.

An interesting event was the ship's participation in a series of exercises in the waters of the North Sea and Baltic Sea in cooperation with the cruisers *Köln*, *Königsberg* and *Emden*, as well as the target ship *Zähringen* and battleships *Schleswig-Holstein* and *Schlesien*, which lasted from 2 to 12 August.

An important date for *Leipzig* was 18 August, when the ship was officially incorporated into the reconnaissance force subordinated to *Befelshaber der Aufklarunskräfte* (BdA).

A few days later, a delegation from the ship's crew took part in the funeral ceremony of sailors from the sailing training ship *Niobe*, aboard which 69 cadets and crew members perished[4].

An interesting event was also a visit aboard the ship on 24 August of Vice-Admiral Walter Gladich and Vice-Admiral von Troth. A similar visit took place on 3–5 September, paid by the new Mayor of Leipzig Dr. Carl Friedrich Goerdeler, and between 18 and 22 September, when the Commander-in-Chief of the Navy, Adm. Erich Raeder, turned up with his staff. At that time, the ship took part in the autumn fleet manoeuvres, being subordinated to the so-called "Blue Forces".

A kind of "stepping stone" from the seaman's routine was a visit by some crew members to *Leipzig*'s patron city between September 24 and 27, in which, as a curiosity, it is worth mentioning that apart from the obvious reception during such events by the city authorities, the local zoo offered the crew a young Berber tiger named Simba, which, as you can easily guess, later would become one of the most important crew members.

The rest of the year did not abound in such interesting events and, apart from the next series of tests and training, in December the ship was docked at the Wilhelmshaven shipyard. Finally, it is worth adding that in 1932, during numerous

4 This was a four-masted gaff schooner built in 1913 in Denmark. Initially, she sailed under the Danish flag and the name *Morten Jensen*, and later flying the Norwegian flag under the name *Tyholm*. In 1916, the vessel was taken over as a prize by the Germans. In 1922–1923, she underwent rebuilding which converted her into a three-masted barque with regal sails and from 1924 she served in the *Reichsmarine* as a training vessel with accommodation for 75 cadets and 32 cadre crewmen.

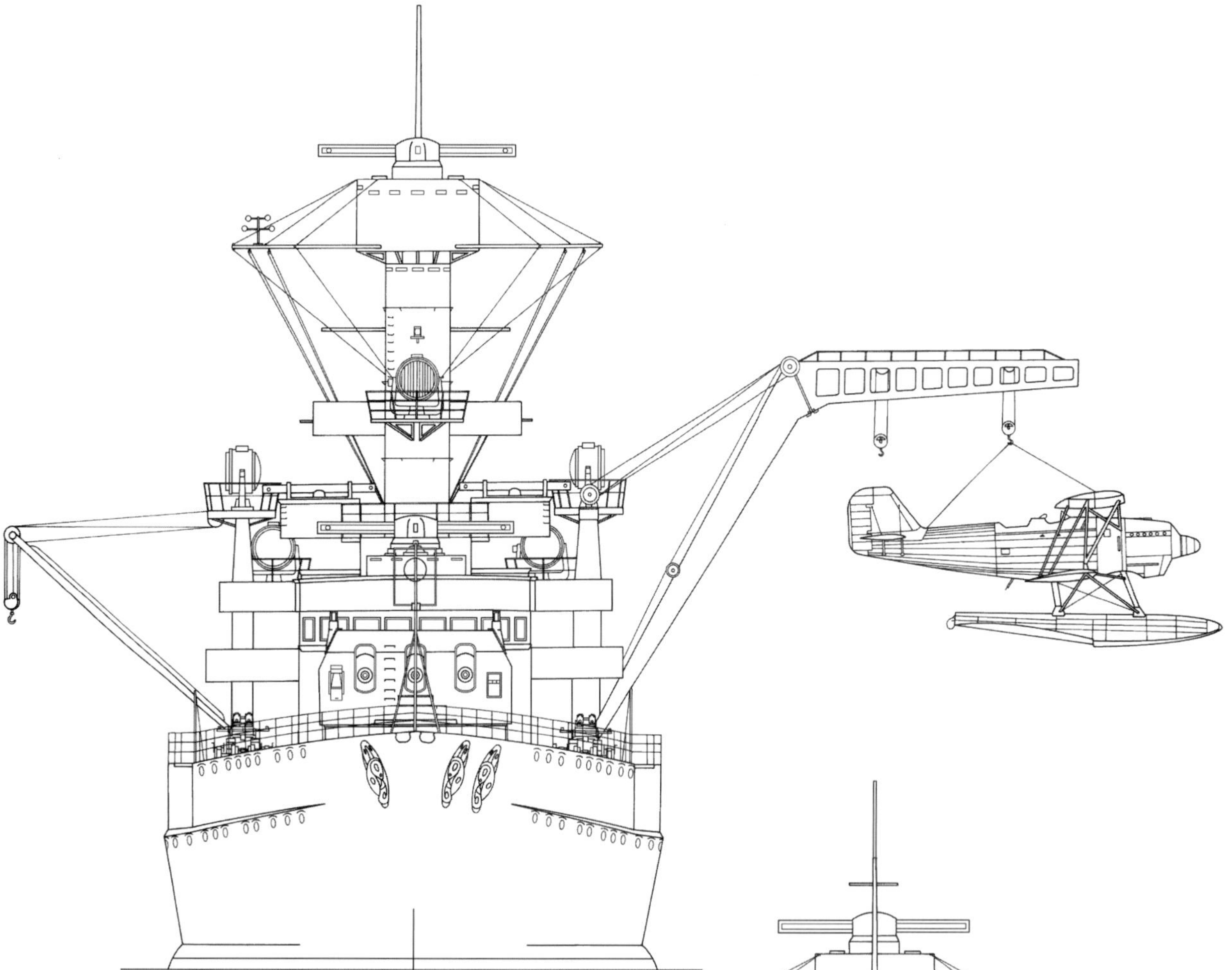

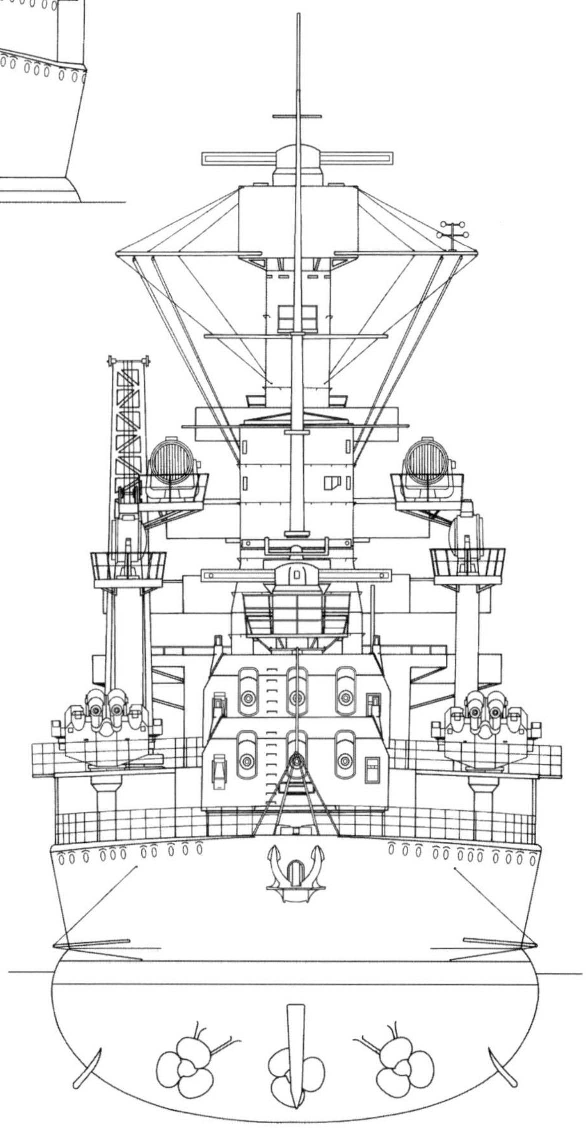

Leipzig *viewed from the bow and stern.*

Leipzig in an interesting view from the bow. The ship's emblem is clearly visible.

visits to the shipyards, there were several minor changes made to the cruiser in the form of, among others, the aft rangefinder installation and anti-aircraft gun fire control sets SL-1, which have already been mentioned above and which had not been yet fitted when the flag was raised for the first time[5].

In 1933 *Leipzig*'s service, similarly to the previous year, began with a move to the Baltic Sea where she implemented a training programme, while the first noteworthy event was the transfer of the ship to North Atlantic waters, where she stayed between 21 February and 15 March, conducting a series of armament and fire control systems tests. The vessel was then accompanied by the cruiser *Emden*, with which she visited Funchal and Las Palmas, with specialists from the Aero and Zeiss factories on board. After she had returned home, the ship stayed briefly at the shipyard, and then returned to training tasks.

On 30 March, an inspection of the cruiser was carried out by Adm. Raeder, who came to Wilhelmshaven to take part in the launching of the battleship *Admiral Scheer*, to be held two days later. On *Leipzig*, full dress was displayed, and the ship herself took part in a naval review organized for the occasion.

It is worth adding at this point that this was a time when the German fleet was beginning to expand and demonstrate combat potential. Five modern cruisers were already in service, and on the day of the launch of the aforementioned *Admiral Scheer* the colours were raised on the pocket battleship *Deutschland*, which was a huge event for Germans at that time and a clear signal that their navy was slowly and surely beginning to revive.

Considering that this was already the time when Adolf Hitler held the post of Chancellor and his takeover of full power was also only a matter of time, *Leipzig* became part of the capabilities which he would later use to implement his mad plans to dominate Europe. For now, this was still a long way off, although it was already clear then what Hitler's policy was leading to.

Meanwhile, after the ceremony *Leipzig* returned to her everyday service, during which in the second half of April she took part in the spring manoeuvres of the fleet in the Baltic Sea, calling at Swinemünde several times.

An interesting event was also the "show" manoeuvres in May, in which *Leipzig* took part, hosting on board none other than German Chancellor Adolf Hitler himself, accompanied by Vice Chancellor Franz von Papen, Prime Minister of Prussia Herman Göring, Admiral Erich Raeder and Minister Joseph Goebbels. This was a great event during which Adolf Hitler, while at the same time also visiting the most powerful ship of the *Reichsmarine* of this era – the battleship *Deutschland* – actually for the first time had the opportunity to see the ships of the German Navy, whose powerful guns would undoubtedly make a huge impression on him.

5 *Leipzig* was the first ship on which this equipment was installed.

Leipzig *during a stop in Swinemünde in 1934.*

Noteworthy also were joint exercises with the battleships *Schleswig-Holstein*, *Schlesien* and *Hessen*, which were carried out between 12 and 18 June, and later embarking on a training cruise on the Baltic Sea, to which the ship set off on 19 June. The cruise in its initial stage was interesting because two days later the cruiser encountered at sea the Polish gunboat ORP *Generał Haller*, with which honours were exchanged.

Later *Leipzig* on 23–26 June was moored in the Finnish port of Hangö, between 1 and 3 July in Königsberg, and then on 21 July in the area of Hälsingborg she encountered the British cruiser HMS *Exeter.*

Between 5 and 9 July *Leipzig* anchored in the Danish harbour of Aarhus, where on 7 July, after the flag gala had been raised, she was visited by an unusual guest, the King of Denmark and Iceland Christian X.

She returned to Kiel on 15 July, having performed a series of exercises along the way including, among others, firing practice as well as exchanging honours with the US ships USS *Cayuga* and USS *Sebago* that she met en route. Another more interesting event was the participation of the ship in the autumn fleet manoeuvres, during which Adm. Raeder paid a visit.

Later, on 24 September, the cruiser arrived at the Wilhelmshaven shipyard, where the first stage of the introduction of changes to her armament and equipment commenced, which, with a break for a short training cruise in October, lasted until February of the following year. Around the same time, more precisely on 25 September, the skipper of the ship changed, and Cdr. Otto Hormel took over this post.

During the refurbishment, the single 37 mm guns were dismantled and replaced by four twin-barrel SK C/30 37 mm L83 sets on C/30 mounts. In addition, two twin-barrel SK C/30 20 mm sets and two SK C/13 88 mm L/45 guns were installed, which were positioned on the superstructure deck amidships. Changes also took place in the funnel, where additional diagonal brackets were installed, and the torpedo tubes were replaced with new ones of 533 mm calibre.

Summarising, the ship had gained significantly in her combat potential, and was now armed with nine 150 mm, four 88 mm, eight 37 mm, six 20 mm guns and twelve 533mm torpedo tubes in total.

In total, the period of these shipbuilding works combined with all necessary tests and training of the crew, lasted until the second half of March 1934 and it is only in April that we can note the next more interesting event, which was paying an official visit to Kristansand in Norway on 26 April. An honorary salute of 21 shots was fired from the ship and the German consul paid a visit.

Later, as usual, various types of training cruises took place, mainly based in the Baltic region, during which, among others, in May she cooperated with the battleships *Schleswig-Holstein*, *Schlesien* and *Hessen*.

An interesting event was the participation between 21 June and 3 July in the rescue operation after the merchantman *Dresden*, belonging to the *Kraft durch Freude* organization, hit the rocks in the Stavanger area.

Another interesting event began on 9 July, when *Leipzig* set off on a cruise that led to Portsmouth. More importantly, *Leipzig* was not alone because she was also accompanied by the cruiser *Königsberg*,

Leipzig *in an interesting view from the bow.*

with which she visited Portsmouth from 11 to 15 July and later together they sailed further through the Irish Sea, then around Ireland and into the North Sea. On 20 July she returned to Kiel.

Equally interesting was the cruise for which she put to sea on 26 July. This time her route led through the North Sea to the Atlantic, where later she would head far north to pay a visit to the capital of Iceland, Reykjavik. She returned home on 30 July, and there soon bad news arrived aboard.

On 2 August, German President Paul von Hindenburg passed away, which caused the commander to lower the flag to half mast, and the next day an oath of loyalty was sworn to the new head of the armed forces, Adolf Hitler. For this reason, we can assume that from then *Leipzig* began a new chapter of her service story, which was to lose its peacetime features rather quickly and focus on actions leading to war.

For now, however, the planned tasks were carried out. In August, the cruiser participated in team exercises together with other *Reichsmarine* ships, for which an interesting interruption was on 29 August when some crewmen took part in the annual rowing competition. Later, exercises continued until the second half of September.

Leipzig *during the Kieler-Woche festival in Kiel in 1934.*

This event can also be considered the last noteworthy one of that period, though mention should also be made of the ship being directed to the shipyard where she underwent a number of significant changes.

A catapult was installed, which was located on the superstructure deck just in front of the funnel, together with two Heinkel He 60C floatplanes. In addition, the single 88 mm gun mounts were removed and replaced with much more modern twin-barrel SK C/32 88 mm L/76 sets. In connection with the installation of the catapult, the ship was also equipped with a powerful crane with a folding arm, designed for lifting floatplanes from the water. The gaffs on the funnel were dismantled and a jib-boom with a small grommet mounted on it.

1935 *Leipzig* began with the aforementioned stay at the shipyard, which came to an end on 18 February, and while analysing the available documents, we can consider it extremely sparse in interesting events except, of course, countless training cruises in the waters of the North Sea and the Baltic Sea and more important participation in fleet manoeuvres.

Highlights of this period may include: detachment to the Experimental Gunnery Command on 19–20 March, visit of Adm. Raeder on 14 June 14, and another visit by Adolf Hitler on 19 August, assistance given to the torpedo ship T 151 on 18 September and a change in the ship's commander post when on 30 September Lt. Cdr. Otto Schenk was appointed.

Leipzig *photographed from one of the K-class cruisers.*

Commanders of the ship

- 8 October 1931 – 24 September 1933 – Cdr. Hans Herbert Strobwasser
- 25 September 1933 – 29 September 1935 – Cdr. Otto Hormel
- 30 September 1935 – October 1937 – Cdr. Otto Schenk
- October 1937 – April 1939 – Cdr. Werner Löwisch
- April 1939 – February 1940 – Cdr. Heinz Nordmann
- December 1, 1940 – August 1942 – Cdr. Werner Stichling
- August 1942 – September 1942 – Cdr. Friedrich-Traugott Schmidt
- 25 September 1942 – 18 February 1943 – Cdr. Waldemar Winther
- February 1943 – March 1943 – Lt. Cdr. Joachim Asmus
- 1 August 1943 – 25 August 1944 – Cdr. Walter Hülsemann
- 26 August 1944 – November 1944 – Cdr. Heinrich Spörel
- November 1944 – December 1944 – Cdr. Hagen Küster
- December 1944 – January 1945 – Cdr. Joachim Hinckeldeyn
- January 1945 – December 1945 – Cdr. Walter Bach

This year also brought another very important change, which was lowering the flag of the Weimar Republic and raising the colours of the *Kriegsmarine*.

1936 for *Leipzig* began with the assignment to the Baltic Sea force with its base port in Kiel and then began less monotonous and more active service. On 6 January, the ship set sail with the task of conducting joint exercises with the cruiser *Köln*, first in the waters of the North Sea and then the Baltic. Later, she carried out a series of exercises including torpedo firing, after which on 17 February she arrived at the shipyard for renovation combined with another modernization.

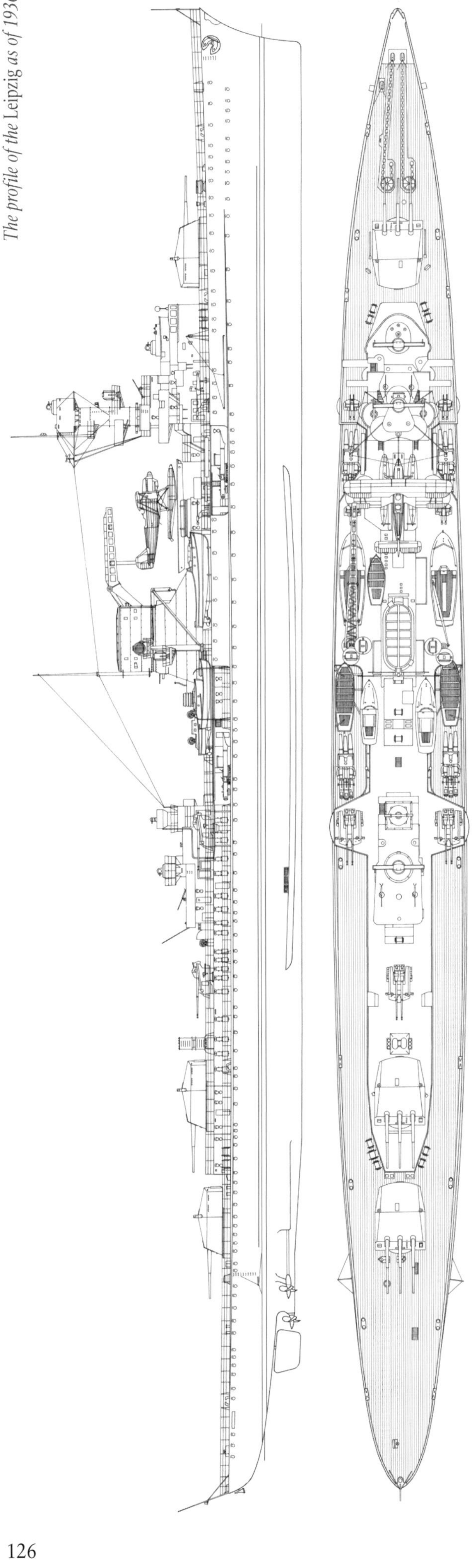

The profile of the Leipzig *as of 1936.*

The scope of this work included the reconstruction of the deckhouse, installation of training cannon and replacement of the generating sets for much more efficient ones with an output of 540 kW. In total, the work lasted two months and came to an end only on 14 April.

The next day, the ship put to sea and, along with the accompanying cruisers *Nürnberg* and *Köln*, went on a cruise in the waters of the North Atlantic, visiting Funchal in Madeira between 23 and 27 April, and Portuguese Lagos between 29 April and 3 May. At that time, the ships carried out joint exercises, including sailing at variable speed, firing practices and catapulting off and picking up the floatplanes.

Having returned to her home waters, on 29–31 May *Leipzig* took part in an extraordinary event, which was the solemn maritime parade organized on the occasion of the anniversary of the Battle of Jutland and the unveiling a monument honouring German sailors killed in 1914–1918 in Laboe, approximately 10 km north-east from Kiel. As we have already learned, this was a great event, in which almost all major *Kriegsmarine* ships took part, including of course *Leipzig.*

The months of July and August were spent in the planned implementation of the training programme, but 1936 was also marked by tragic events in Spain, to which Hitler quickly turned his attention. In connection with this, once fuel, ammunition and food supplies had been replenished, on 20 August *Leipzig* left home waters and headed for Spain, thus starting her first combat tour in that region.

She started her operations in Portugalete, where she met with the cruiser *Köln* just completing her first tour, from which she took over the current tasks consisting mainly of patrolling from Cape Gata to Cape Oropesa. The ship operated on the Spanish coast until October, calling at ports including San Sebastian, Gijon, La Coruna, Caraminal and El Ferrol.

In total, *Leipzig* operated in the inflamed area until 8 October, when her duties were taken over by the aforementioned *Köln.* Two days later she arrived at Wilhelmshaven, where soon afterwards she transferred to the shipyard for renovation.

The works lasted quite a long time, and their scope covered, among other things, maintenance and modifications to the engines, so the entire refurbishment lasted until 3 February 1937. Added to this was a period of necessary tests and crew training lasting over a month, i.e. from 4 February to 9 March.

Since the war in Spain had flared up, it was clear that sooner or later *Leipzig* would be directed again to conduct operations in that region, so as soon as the aforementioned period of testing and training came to an end, and with all supplies loaded, on 9 March she set off, thus giving rise to her second combat tour. Similarly to the previous one, she started her operations by exchanging with the cruiser *Köln* on 12 March, but it is impossible not to mention here that during the voyage to the war-torn region, while sailing in the waters of the Bay of Biscay, on 11 March she found herself in a zone of severe storm, which caused much damage.

Among others, there was damage to the floatplane crane mountings as well as cracks on the deck in the area of compartments VI and VII. It is worth adding, this type of damage was well known to crews of the K-class cruisers, resulting from poor hull structure. For this reason, *Leipzig* began her operations by dealing with the damage and only later put to sea for her first patrol. The second combat tour lasted until the second half of May and the most important ports which

Leipzig *at anchor.*

the ship visited at that time include Algeciras, Ceuta, Malaga, Mellili, Algiers, Valencia and Palma de Mallorca.

In May *Leipzig* was back home, and from the 19th of this month was in Kiel, where at the local shipyard she underwent an inspection of her propulsion systems and a minor renovation, this time very brief because on 1 June she put to sea heading for the third time to Spanish waters.

A few days later, the ship was already operating as part of her third combat tour, and based in the ports of, among others, Algeciras, Cadiz, Tange, Cadiz and Caraminal. The more interesting events of that period include frequent courtesy visits aboard foreign ships.

And so, for example, on 11 June the commanding officer of *Leipzig*, Commander Otto Schenk, visited the pride of the Royal Navy, the battlecruiser HMS *Hood*. A German officer later made similar visits aboard the French cruiser *Duquesne*, the Italian destroyer *Emanuele Pessagno* and the Spanish cruiser *Baleares*.

A rather interesting but also important event was a probable torpedo attack on *Leipzig* in the area of Cape Tres Forcas, most likely performed by an unidentified submarine. It is difficult to locate any documents telling what actually happened, but there is no doubt that the operator of the sound direction-finder reported receiving the noise of an approaching torpedo, which most likely hit the ship without exploding, and on 18 June a torpedo attack report was sent to headquarters and it mentioned the position 36°06'N and 00°23'W.

These assumptions were confirmed by later inspection of the hull, which showed that there was a slight dent in the hull plating on the port side, with a diameter of about 15 cm that could have been result of the impact of a torpedo. All this suggests that *Leipzig* was close to sharing the fate of the battleship *Deutschland*, which was mistakenly bombed in Ibiza in the last days of May.

It is worth noting here that this was the time when Germany was explicitly on the side of General Franco's forces, which resulted in armed incidents on which very often a blind eye was turned. But above all, due to the fact that many rebel ships used the same bases in which German and Italian vessels were stationed and in which they undoubtedly received support, sooner or later all this had to be reflected in the actions of the Republican forces. The events associated with the battleship *Deutschland* that took place on 24 May in Palma were a perfect example.

Then Republican aircraft carried out an air raid on the rebel ships based in the port, damaging several Italian vessels, and several of the bombs fell very close to the German torpedo ship *Albatros*, slightly damaging her. *Deutschland* herself did not suffer any damage, although it was close as four bombs fell at distances from 50 to 200 metres from the ship, which as you can easily guess, at that time could have ended tragically for her. Interestingly, it was at that time that the commander of the German forces was on board

Adm. Fischel issued a rather controversial order in which he demanded opening fire on any Republican vessel should they only approach one of the German ships. Thus, the *Kriegsmarine* warships including *Leipzig* were without any doubt involved in the war as a warring party. The worst was yet to come.

When on 28 May *Deutschland* moved to Ibiza, which was supposed to provide her with greater security, on the next day she became the target of an attack by the Republican forces when a formation of two SB bombers, commanded by the Soviet volunteer G.K. Livinski according to some sources, mistakenly launched an attack on *Deutschland*, mistaking her for the heavy cruiser *Canarias* – also with one smokestack – which can be considered a feature making the two ships similar to each other. However, this seems quite strange considering that both the battleship's turrets had bright stripes – very clearly visible – showing her neutrality.

It is not entirely certain whether the attack on *Deutschland*, resulting in the death of 31 members of her crew, was indeed the result of a mistake or rather intentional action, but it does not change the fact that it had actually taken place and having learned about it, Adolf Hitler almost started a world war then. Later he would become satisfied with the shelling of Almeria.

It is difficult to speculate nowadays what would have happened if the aforementioned torpedo attack on *Leipzig* had resulted in the sinking of the ship or even in serious damage, both certainly causing a substantial death toll. Considering that both events were only two weeks apart, one can safely assume that an enraged Hitler would not have limited his reprisals only to Almeria, but he would certainly unleash hell in Spain by throwing in a much larger contingent of troops than those who actually participated in hostilities there.

Fortunately, *Leipzig*'s attack ended with a slight indentation in the hull and after she had completed the mission, together with the cruiser *Köln*, she returned to home waters, thus finishing the third and – as it was to turn out later – the final combat tour.

The rest of the year did not abound in such interesting events.

Having returned from Spain, the ship moved to Kiel where she underwent renovation at the local Deutsche Werke shipyard, which lasted until 4 August. Later, throughout almost all of August, the cruiser performed various types of tests and exercises in gunnery and torpedo firing.

In September she took part in the autumn fleet manoeuvres. During this time, on board her came, among others, Admiral Raeder and then later Rear Admiral Densch. In October she performed a series of training cruises on the Baltic Sea.

Then her commander changed again – the position was taken over by Commander Werner Löwisch.

Until the end of the year *Leipzig* implemented the training programme scheduled for her, several times participating in joint exercises with the cruisers *Köln*, *Karlsruhe* and *Nürnberg*. Noteworthy was the visit to Tallinn that the ship made between 19 and 23 November. It is worth adding that the commander of the Estonian Navy came on board and the crew laid a wreath at the local war heroes' cemetery.

At the start of 1938 *Leipzig* arrived in Kiel and despite the ongoing winter from 4 to 8 January she took part in the exercises as a target ship for torpedo firing practice in Kiel Bay. This is what the whole year in her service looked like. Almost all this time she took part in countless exercises, both on her own and in a group, alternating between the waters of the Baltic Sea and North Sea.

For lack of space, we will not describe them all here, focusing only on the most important and interesting ones. For example, the March training cruise route led from Kiel through the Danish Straits, during which firing practice was carried out in the waters of Kattegat and Skagerrak. Later, in that area, she met with the cruiser *Köln*, with whom she returned to base.

Poor-quality but interesting image depicting the 150 mm fore main battery turret and the main superstructure.

A slight change from everyday routine.

Leipzig spent the period between 30 March and 7 May in Kiel, where she underwent renovation at the Deutsche Werke shipyard. The following months were marked by countless exercises and only on 22 August we can note an interesting event, which was the participation in the great naval review organized in Kiel on the occasion of the launch of the heavy cruiser *Prinz Eugen*, which was graced by the Regent of Hungary, Admiral Miklos Horthy von Nagybanya, who had been invited to Germany for this occasion.

Later *Leipzig* took part in the autumn fleet manoeuvres, cooperating with the battleships *Gneisenau*, *Admiral Scheer* and *Admiral Graf Spee*, as well as the cruisers *Köln* and *Nürnberg*.

An interesting event was also the review on the occasion of the launching of the aircraft carrier *Graf Zeppelin* on December 8th. This ship, which by the way was never to to enter active service, was to have been the first-ever aircraft carrier in the *Kriegsmarine*'s history[6].

And actually that would be all for the noteworthy events of the cruiser's service in 1938, not counting the transition on 17 December to the Deutsche Werke shipyard, where her renovation began, combined with another modernization.

1939 was welcomed by *Leipzig* at the shipyard where she remained until 15 March, when the works were officially completed. It is worth noting that in addition to typical repair work on the ship, the crane was replaced and the platforms on the battle mast were dismantled, which was reflected in the silhouette of the vessel.

As we know, 1939 was marked by many turbulent events in Europe, which is why, shortly after she had left the shipyard, *Leipzig* found herself in the group of ships designated to seize Klaipeda. For this reason, on 21 March the cruiser together with the battleships *Admiral Graf Spee, Deutschland* and *Admiral Scheer*, cruisers *Köln* and *Nürnberg* as well as a group of destroyers, torpedo ships, minesweepers and auxiliary vessels, put to sea heading for Klaipeda, which was another destination on the long list of the "Versailles wrongs" by Adolf Hitler. Fortunately for the Lithuanians, directing such a powerful force to the city and port remaining in their hands was to be only a demonstration of force aimed at capturing it without bloodshed, therefore it was without turbulent events, and on 24 March *Leipzig* made her way back to Swinemünde.

Actually, only then was it possible to carry out post-shipyard tests, but they did not last too long. On 17 April *Leipzig* together with the battleships *Deutschland* and *Admiral Graf Spee*, cruisers *Köln* and *Nürnberg*, eight destroyers from the 1st and 3rd Destroyer Squadron, fifteen submarines of the "*Salzwedel*", "*Hundius*" and "*Wegener*" groups and the depot ship *Erwin Wassner*, set off for the

6 The keel was laid on 28 December 1936 at the Deutsche Werke shipyard in Kiel and she was launched on 8 December 1938. Her standard displacement was estimated at 23,200 tons, and full at 33,500 tons. Overall length 262.5 m, width 36.2 m, draft 8.5 m. Drive was four turbine sets with a total output of 200,000 HP, which was to allow sailing at almost 34 knots. The armament was 16 150 mm guns, twelve 105 mm guns and 37 x cal. 37 mm and 28 x cal. 20 mm cannons. The ship was never completed and after having been taken over by the Red Army in 1947, she was sunk in the Baltic Sea 55 km north of Władysławowo.

Leipzig *seen from the stern.*

Atlantic, where for almost a month she participated in various exercises preparing the crews of ships for wartime operations. This included combat navigation and cooperation with submarines and supply ships, which, as we have already learned, was related to Hitler's directive codenamed "*Fall Weiss*" issued on 11 April. It is easy to see here that the cruiser's service quickly changed its character and became each day more and more focused on conducting wartime operations, as evidenced by increasingly frequent exercises of this nature. At that time, the crew practised team and night-time cruises, mine detection and crossing minefields, repelling air attacks, etc.

An important event was that in April the duties of commander were taken over by Cdr. Heinz Nordmann from Cdr. Werner Löwisch, who later took responsibility for the the ship for the following year.

Time passed, and finally Cdr. Nordmann received the order to direct his ship to a group of vessels blockading the approach to the Polish coast, which was part of the plan that was the introduction to the outbreak of World War Two. On 25 August 25, *Leipzig* put to sea and sailed to the island of Bornholm, designated as a rendezvous point for all ships which had been given this task, including the cruisers *Köln* and *Nurnberg*, as well as three destroyers as part of the reconnaissance forces of Vice Admiral Herman Densch and subordinated to the commander of *Gruppenkommando "Ost"*, General-Admiral Conrad Albrecht.

Although it would seem otherwise, when on the morning of 1 September 1939 the battleship *Schleswig-Holstein* began shelling the Polish military outpost at Westerplatte, *Leipzig* had other orders and moored in Kiel where she was preparing for the next task, which was to lay mines off the coast of the Netherlands up to Skagerrak. Therefore, the ship, like the other cruisers, was subordinated to the disposal of *Marinegruppe West* and, having passed through the Kiel Canal, began the implementation of her tasks.

On the first mission with the task of laying the Westwall mine barier, the ship left Wilhelmshaven on 3 September, and on the same day between 2100 a 2215 completed the task. Later she made a series of missions of this type, but quite an interesting event took place on 4 September, when five British Blenheim bombers from 107 RAF Squadron came over the port while the ship was loading the next supply of mines. In the ensuing fight, *Leipzig*'s anti-aircraft gunners were most likely able to shoot down one of the enemy machines, but it should be remembered that this fact proved to be quite difficult to confirm. In total, actions related to laying minefields lasted throughout September.

Later, between 5 and 11 October, the ship stayed in the dock of the Deutsche Werke shipyard, and between 12 and 19 October underwent shipbuilding tests combined with gunnery and torpedo firing.

Another noteworthy event took place on 7 November when the ship passed through the Kiel Canal. That day in the Holtenau area in the evening the cruiser collided with the training ship *Bremse*, as a result of which *Leipzig* suffered serious damage to the starboard plating in her stern[7].

7 *Bremse* was a gunnery training ship put into service on 14 July 1932. The ship had 1,435 t standard displacement, 103.6 m length, 9.5 m beam and 2.8 m draft. The drive was eight diesel engines with a total

Because of the damage suffered, the cruiser had to abort the mission and found herself again in the dock of the Deutsche Werke shipyard where the damage was repaired.

In total, the stay at the shipyard lasted until 16 November, after which on the next day the ship was sent to participate in the action in the area of the Terschelling Shoals where, among others her task was to provide cover to destroyers returning from mine-laying operations.

The operation on which *Leipzig* embarked on 21 November was much more interesting. Its purpose was to carry out a patrol and assist in taking action against British shipping between Iceland and the Faroe Islands by the battleships *Scharnhorst* and *Gneisenau*. The entire operation was commanded by Admiral Wilhem Marschal, and cover was provided by destroyers from the 4th Flotilla: *Bernd von Arnim*, *Erich Giese* and *Karl Galster*, torpedo ships *Leopard*, *Seeadler*, *Iltis* and *Wolf*, as well as the cruiser *Köln* and *Leipzig*.

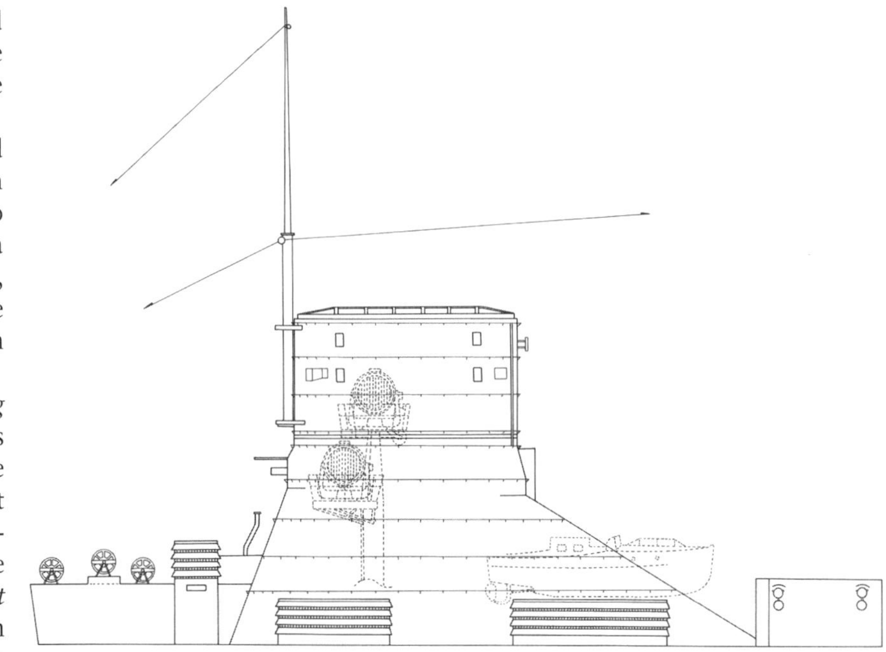

A drawing of the cruiser's funnel.

For *Leipzig* herself, whose task, besides securing the passage of the *Kriegsmarine*'s most important ships at that time, was to conduct an anti-shipping campaign in the waters of Skagerrak and Kattegat, which however would end without any spectacular events. This could not be said of the battleships' activities, which after the escorts had been sent back, on 23 November in the designated area, sank the British auxiliary cruiser *Rawalpindi*[8].

On the night of 24–25 November, *Leipzig* also acted in a similar group formed to continue the aforementioned activities and to provide cover for the returning battleships. At that time, the force consisted of the cruisers *Lützow* and *Köln* and the destroyers *Bernd von Arnim*, *Karl Galster*, *Friedrich Ihn* and *Bruno Heinemann*, as well as torpedo ships from the 6th Flotilla.

In early December, the ship stayed again for a few days at the shipyard, after which on the 12th of that month together with the cruisers *Köln* and *Nürnberg* once again put to sea with the task of providing cover to the destroyers returning from mine-laying action. This task turned out to be tragic for *Leipzig*.

After the next day the cruiser disengaged from the team to shadow the Soviet merchantman *Kharkov*, and the track of a torpedo approaching the ship was sighted from her deck. Despite the immediate raising of the alarm and the commencement of evasive manoeuvres, at 1127 hrs a huge explosion shook the cruiser.

The results of the torpedo, launched by the British submarine HMS *Salmon*,[9] commanded at that time by Captain E. O. Bickford, proved to be devastating. The torpedo hit the ship in the port side midships, tearing a huge breach in the hull plating through which water began to enter the hull, flooding boiler rooms Nos. 1 and 2. The turbines were immobilized and the steering gear was damaged. The ship stopped and only after the internal combustion engines had been started did

output of 26,800 HP, so that the ship managed a speed of 27 knots. Armament was four 127 mm guns and eight 20 mm cannons. It was sunk by Royal Navy ships on 6 September 1941.

8 She was built in 1925 for the British shipowner Peninsular & Oriental Line (P&O) as a medium-sized passenger ship with a displacement of 16,697 BRT. In 1939 she was taken over by the British government and rebuilt into an auxiliary cruiser armed with 8 x 152 mm and 2 x 76 mm guns. During this engagement she was commanded by Cdr. Edward Coverley Kennedy, for which he was posthumously honoured with a Mention in Despatches.

9 This was a British submarine belonging to the S-class built in 1935 at Cammell Laird & Co. Ltd at Birkenhead. The ship had 670 tons displacement on the surface and 960 under water, and dimensions were 62.0 m long, 7.3 m wide and 3.2 m draft. Propulsion was by 2 diesel engines and 2 electric motors allowing for sailing at 14 knots on the surface and 10 when submerged. Armament was one 76 mm gun and six 533 mm torpedo tubes.

The cruiser at anchor.

she regain the ability to move, control however could only be done manually. As a result of the explosion, 16 crew members were killed and another dozen wounded.

Despite the quick management of the situation, *Leipzig* could move at a speed of no more than 12 knots, so as soon as the machinery was started Cdr. Nordmann gave the order to go back to base, taking the shortest route and calling for help from other ships. Even worse, her return to base was not the most peaceful.

Despite the protection of the damaged ship by the other cruisers and the destroyers *Richard Beitzen* and *Bruno Heinemann*, on the same day the cruiser *Nürnberg* also fell victim to HMS *Salmon*, and the next day after the escort was strengthened by the destroyers *Friedrich Ihn* and *Hermann Schoemann* and the F 7 and F 9 patrol vessels, F 9 was struck by two torpedoes launched by the submarine HMS *Ursula*.

It was not until 14 December at 1728 hrs that the damaged *Leipzig* reached the Brunsbüttel roadstead, where the crew could breathe a sigh of relief. However, the ship was seriously damaged, which caused shipyard experts to come on board very quickly to assess the damage and develop a repair plan.

On 16 December, the cruiser arrived at the dock of the Blohm & Voss shipyard in Hamburg, where the initial work began, and four days later, at the Ohlsdorf/Hamburg cemetery, a ceremonial funeral for the fallen crew members took place, in the presence of the commander of the ship and representatives of the naval High Command.

Time for change was coming for *Leipzig* herself. Practically the whole of 1940 was spent at the shipyards, first at Blohm & Voss in Hamburg, then at Deutsche Werke in Kiel and at Danziger Werft in Danzig. At the first two shipyards the necessary repairs were performed as a start, however, in Danzig, in connection with the decision to convert *Leipzig* into a training cruiser, the ship underwent extensive refurbishment. Some areas were adapted to the new role.

Boiler rooms No. 1 and 2, destroyed during the torpedo attack, were rebuilt into lecture rooms and quarters for cadets. The number of accommodation places was increased, allowing more men to be taken aboard. In addition, the catapult was dismantled with all aviation equipment and demagnetizing devices were installed.

Much had changed in *Leipzig*'s service.

After she had been temporarily decommissioned, which took place on 27 February, she was not restored to service until 1 December 1940, as a training ship for weapon systems. Her commander also changed, which from 1 December it became Cdr. Werner Stichling.

Despite her significant combat capabilities, the ship was downgraded, becoming a training ship from now on and her further service was to be in that capacity. After the end of the shipbuilding trials and tests, in the period from 5 February to 1 April 1941, *Leipzig* was withdrawn from the combat ships' listing and subordinated to the cruiser commander BdK, Vice Admiral H. Schmundtt.

At that time, the ship made training cruises on the central and eastern Baltic, not forgetting that there was a war going on around. A kind of curiosity is the fact that in March the aft torpedo tubes were removed, which were later installed on the battleship *Gneiseanu*.

The most interesting event can be noticed in June, when Cdr. Stichling, commanding the ship, received an order to move with the cruiser *Emden* to Norwegian waters, where *Leipzig* operated for the next two months based in the ports of Oslo and Horten.

One interesting fact is that at that time the ship sported a very unusual camouflage pattern, the so-called "beam scheme" consisting of white and black stripes, known to almost everyone who had the opportunity to experience the fate of battleship *Bismarck* and her famous operation *Rheinübung*.

Having returned home *Leipzig* was included in a naval force consisting of the battleships *Schleswig-Holstein* and *Schlesien*, cruisers *Nürnberg* and *Köln*, 1st and 2nd Torpedo Flotilla, 5th Mine-Sweeper Flotilla as well as the submarines U 140, U 142, U 144, U145 and U 146, assigned to tasks related to the start of Operation *Barbarossa*, i.e. the German attack on the USSR.

On 5 August *Leipzig* arrived at the shipyard in Travemünde, where a catapult was installed again, and soon the demagnetization belt was replaced.

In September, she was included in the previously mentioned *Baltenflotte*, whose task was to take action in the event of attempts by the Soviet Baltic Fleet ships to break out westward as well as to support land forces. As part of the tasks set before the ships, from 25 September *Leipzig* supported *Wehrmacht* troops fighting inland with her gunfire. And so on 26 September, along with cruiser *Emden*, she took part in the operation codenamed *Weststurm* I, during which she shelled Soviet positions on the Sworbe peninsula.

The intensity of ongoing activities can be demonstrated by the fact that by 2000 hrs *Leipzig*'s gunners had fired a total of 327 150 mm shells and, together with *Emden*, a total of 582 150 mm and 48 88mm rounds.

The next day, both cruisers continued to fire on hostile positions as part of Operation *Weststurm* II.

This time, things did not go smoothly – at 0919 hrs in the bay of Lyu the group was attacked by a group of Soviet torpedo boats, commanded by Captain Lieutenant V.P. Gumenko. Wanting to repel the attack Cdr. Stichling gave the order to open fire, as a result of which one of the boats sporting the designation TKA-83 received a direct hit and exploded. After this event, the remaining boats retired, and *Leipzig* returned to bombarding the designated enemy positions.

Leipzig *viewed from the bow.*

In the afternoon, the cruisers completed this task and took a course to Libau/Liepaja, however, even then it was not without a nervous moment when, about 20 NM from Windau, from the deck of *Leipzig* once again the track of a torpedo could be seen in the water. Knowing the effects of the previous event it is easy to imagine what this meant, but this time a turn was made almost at the last minute and the torpedo passed just ahead of the cruiser's bow[10]. These were also the last major events of *Leipzig*'s activities while with the *Baltenflotte*.

After the disbandment of the force on 29 September, the ship arrived in Kiel where between 9 and 16 October she underwent renovation at the Deutsche Werke shipyard. Up to the end of the year, the cruiser's service was not very interesting.

In November, she took part in joint exercises with the cruiser *Admiral Scheer* several times, including preparing this ship for transfer to Norway. *Leipzig* herself remained in the Baltic Sea as a training ship, implementing a training programme during which, among others, she took part in gunnery and torpedo firing practice, and served as a target ship for destroyers and torpedo boats.

This is how 1942 began for her.

On 15 January *Leipzig* began the next stage of training cadets and was based in the waters of the Baltic Sea. Between 11 April and 8 May she was staying at the Oderwerke shipyard in Stettin in which the main battery gun barrels were changed, which as a curiosity it can be stated that they came from stocks intended for the cruiser *Karlsruhe*, lost as we know in 1940 during the Norwegian campaign.

Later in connection with the transfer of the cruiser *Lützow* to Norway, from 11 May *Leipzig* took part in joint exercises of the force consisting of the cruiser *Lützow*, destroyers Z 27, Z 29, *Richard Beitzen*, *Hans Lody* and *Karl Galster*, and torpedo ships T 14 and T 18.

10 The reference books do not agree upon what vessel could have performed this attack. The most reliable information seems to be that the submarine Shtch-317 commanded by Captain n.I. Mokhov could have been responsible for this, however in specialist literature quite often information is repeated that it was Shtch-319 commanded by Captain-Lieutenant N. S. Agashin.

The silhouette of Leipzig as of 1944.

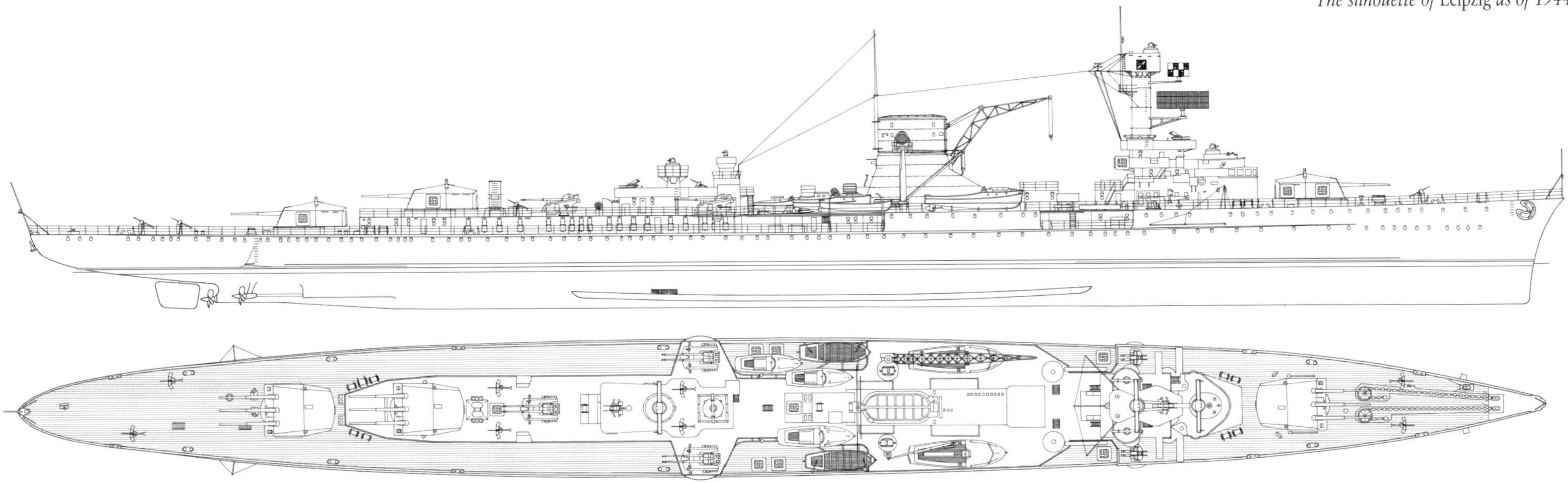

Drawing demonstrating the changes that took place on Leipzig's main mast during her service.

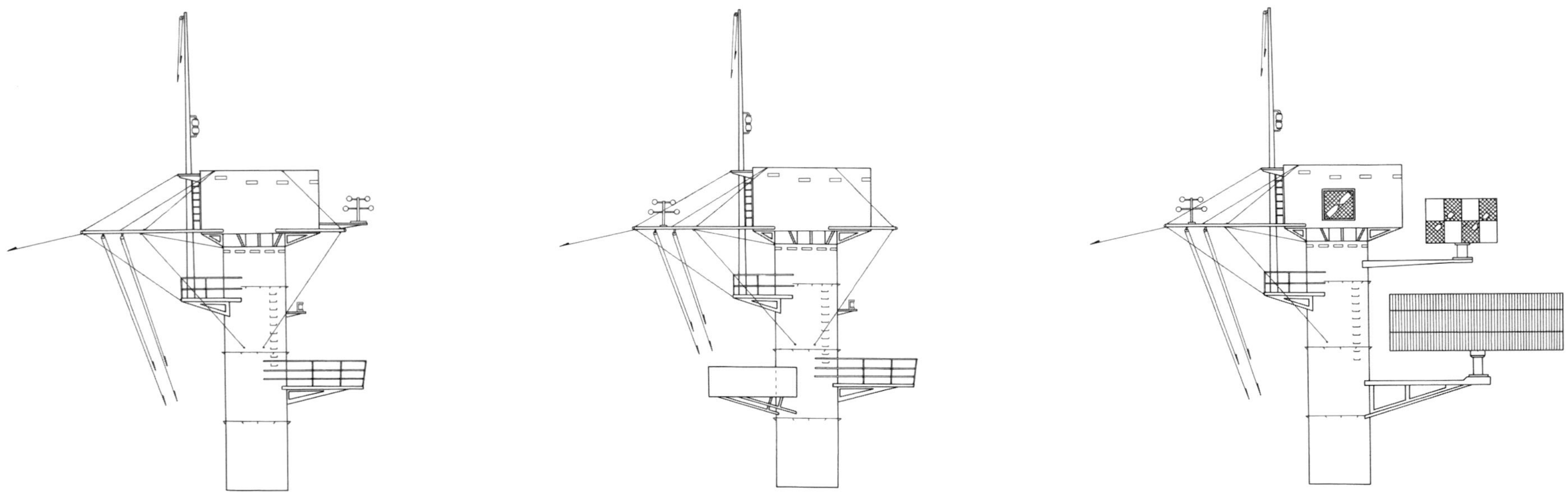

The stern of the cruiser, photographed probably during the Kieler-Woche festival in Kiel.

Practically all the period from May to November was spent on training tasks based in the Baltic Sea. Of the more interesting events of that period, we can only mention the June inspection by the Head of Naval Training, Rear Admiral August Thiele, and the double change in the position of the ship's commander, who was firstly in August-September (as a substitute) Cdr. Friedrich-Traugott Schmidt, and later from 25 September Cdr. Waldemar Winther.

Up to the end of the year, it is difficult to find noteworthy events.

Between 29 September and 20 October, the ship underwent another renovation, and between 27 November and 2 December, she hosted the Head of Naval Training, Rear Admiral Joachim Litzmann, with whom the ship put to sea for the purpose of training cadets.

The cruiser ended the year with a move on 31 December to the shipyard in Libau, where until 15 February 1943 she underwent refurbishment combined with modernization, including removal of the remaining two torpedo tube assemblies. 1943 was also marked by extremely controversial decisions, behind which was none other than Adolf Hitler himself.

After a series of failures involving the major *Kriegsmarine* ships, the effect of which was, among others, the dismissal of Admiral Erich Raeder and his replacement as fleet commander by Admiral Karl Dönitz, Adolf Hitler ordered that all large *Kriegsmarine* ships be taken out of service. For this reason, according to the plan developed by the Naval War Directorate approved by Hitler on 8 February, *Leipzig* was decommissioned on 4 March.

Well, it is hard to know what to think about such a decision, given that after all there was a war in full swing and, despite all the failures, every ship was needed. Either way, it is certain that this was more evidence of the madness of Adolf Hitler, many of whose decisions contributed to his later fall.

A fleet without major ships? Certainly this was unimaginable for Admiral Raeder, who learned of such plans on 30 January and resigned.

At that time, it meant a real tragedy for *Leipzig*, considering that after her withdrawal she was later to be scrapped due to her insufficient combat capabilities. Fortunately for the ship the situation would develop differently and on 1 August she was restored to service for the purpose of fulfilling further tasks as a training ship. *Leipzig* was saved, interestingly from an enemy that no one would expect, but such were those times.

Cdr. Walter Hülsmann became the new skipper of the cruiser, under whose orders she returned to implementing a training programme for seamen of various specialities. It is difficult to find more interesting events in the service of the ship until the end of 1943, thus we are mentioning here only the renovation carried out after she had been re-commissioned, combined with modernization or increasingly frequent air raids on the ports in which she stayed.

Here, noteworthy was 9 October when the Allies launched a heavy raid on the port and shipyard in Gdynia for the first time. At that time, *Leipzig* was in close proximity to the battleship *Gneisenau*, or rather what was left of her, but it did not change the fact that she was one of the main targets for

Leipzig *sporting the extremely interesting beam pattern camouflage as of 1941.*

the Allied aircraft[11]. *Leipzig*'s anti-aircraft gunners took part in repelling the attack, during which no damage was noted on board the ship except for one of the crew members, who was injured by a bomb fragment.

Later, there is little to write about.

1944 brought further training cruises during which from time to time she co-operated with other *Kriegsmarine* ships. For example, between 28 February and 2 March she carried out a series of exercises with the cruiser *Prinz Eugen*, on 5 July with the destroyers *Richard Beitzen* and Z 43, on 15 September with the cruiser *Admiral Scheer* and on 4 October with the cruisers *Admiral Hipper* and *Köln* and battleship *Schlesien*. At that time, the ship performed several exercises in the Bornholm area, calling at Copenhagen between 6 and 12 August.

In August there was also an outbreak of meningitis aboard, resulting in the death of two crew members. The ship was then quarantined, which was not cancelled until 12 September.

The end of the year also brought a tragic event.

After the commander of the ship, Cdr. Hülsmann, was ordered to put to sea and go to Swinemünde to collect supplies, on 15 October at 2001 hrs *Leipzig* collided north of Hel with the cruiser *Prinz Eugen* which was en route from the Klaipeda region. Only by a miracle she did not go to the bottom considering the damage suffered[12].

The heavy cruiser, moving at a speed of about 20 knots, literally stuck into *Leipzig*'s port side in the midship between the funnel and the foremast, at an angle of about 35 degrees, almost cutting her in half. Nineteen crew members perished and another 31 were injured. What was worse, both ships became stuck together and only after fourteen hours of rescue operations were both ships successfully separated!

Unlike *Prinz Eugen*, *Leipzig* was in a terrible condition and she only managed to return to Gdynia due to the assistance of a tugboat. The next day she was docked to determine the damage, and this proved to be extremely severe. The ship's hull was almost cut in half on the port side from the keel to the deck of the superstructure and it was only a matter of two metres on the starboard side that the vessel would have been completely cut. Due to the poor strength of the structure, cracks appeared in many parts of the hull from the stresses resulting from the shock.

Boiler room No. 3, radio compartment, generator set No. 3, fire control post, rooms for radio converters, ammunition chambers and cadet cabins in that area were almost completely destroyed. In summary, the damage was very serious and required a long and laborious renovation, which, given the situation on the frontline, would have hardly been practical. For this reason, it was limited to restoring safe flotation and repairing basic equipment and devices.

On 16 November, the final decision was made to remove *Leipzig* from the fleet listing and give her the status of a hulk. Shortly afterwards, the ship stood alongside the aforementioned battleship *Gneisenau*, which had the same status after her shipbuilding operations had been suspended.

At that time, her new commander was Cdr. Hagen Küster, who performed his duties from November to December 1944.

11 The battleship *Gneisenau* had suffered heavy damage during the air raid on Kiel on the night of 26–27 February 1942; according to the initial plans she was to be rebuilt and rearmed, but due to the decision to withdraw the major ships from service, these plans were abandoned. From then, the ship's armament was dismantled and the hull's bow was cut off to the area of the first main battery turret.

12 The collision took place at position 54°35.3'N 18°52.2'E

It seemed that this was the end of *Leipzig*, however, at the turn of December and January 1945, the offensive of the Soviets left no illusions. The *Wehrmacht* had to retreat under the pressure of the Red Army, and was unable to do much to stop it. Every soldier and gun was at a premium, and on *Leipzig*, after all, there were nine 150 mm guns that could still do a lot. For this reason, repair works commenced on the ship to make it possible that she could move on her own, and more importantly, to fire all her guns.

At the turn of January and February 1945, a supply of 150 mm shells was loaded on board and, after conducting test firing to check the reaction of the weakened hull, *Leipzig* moored in basin No. 1 of the port of Gdynia, waiting for the Red Army units approaching the city.

The first shots from turrets B and C were fired on 10 March and were directed at an area of groupings of Soviet troops north-east of Kartuzy. That day, both turrets fired a total of 67 rounds. Later, the situation repeated itself almost every day, the ship bombarding among others Tuchomin, Zoppot and Wielki Kack.

On 20 March, *Leipzig* left the port of Gdynia and halted in the area of Orłowo, from where she continued to fire at Soviet positions, including also A turret from which 58 shells were fired that day. The next day, the cruiser shifted position again, now moving closer to the port entrance, continuing to fire, and on 22 March again shifted position by dropping anchor in the Hel Peninsula area.

In total, *Leipzig* shelled the Soviet positions until 24 March, firing dozens of 150 mm rounds and only when the barrels were worn to their limit and the supply of ammunition almost reduced to zero, operations were stopped and the ship was directed to evacuate wounded soldiers and refugees.

Leipzig *seen from the bow. In the foreground the emblem of the ship is clearly visible.*

On 25 March, *Leipzig* was given her final task to be evacuated westward.

The incredible chaos prevailing at that time, additionally compounded by the panic escape of civilians, does not allow for accurate account of all events. What we know is that the ship left the battle area on 25 March at about 1930 hrs, having embarked about five hundred wounded troops on board and an unknown number of civilians who – as would be guessed – as many as possible were "stuffed" onto the ship. The journey itself, during which the cruiser sailed as part of a small convoy, was a series of constant alarms and endless attacks.

On 26 March at about 0400 hrs the first alarm was announced, after the periscope belonging to an unidentified submarine was seen on the surface by one of the ships. Later similar alarms were announced almost regularly. Even worse, this was not the only worry.

A few minutes after 1500 hrs the convoy was also attacked by ten Douglas A-20 Boston aircraft, which, regardless of the presence of civilians aboard, did their best to inflict as much damage on the Germans as possible. During the ensuing fight, *Leipzig*'s gunners managed to shoot down one of the machines. It was not the only such attack of that day.

After the first one had been dealt with and one of the anti-submarine alarms announced, another formation of enemy aircraft appeared over the convoy, this time of thirteen A-20s, which, as before, began to attack all the ships with ferocity. Also then, thanks to effective anti-aircraft defence, it was possible to shoot down one of the machines that was credited to *Leipzig*'s gunners.

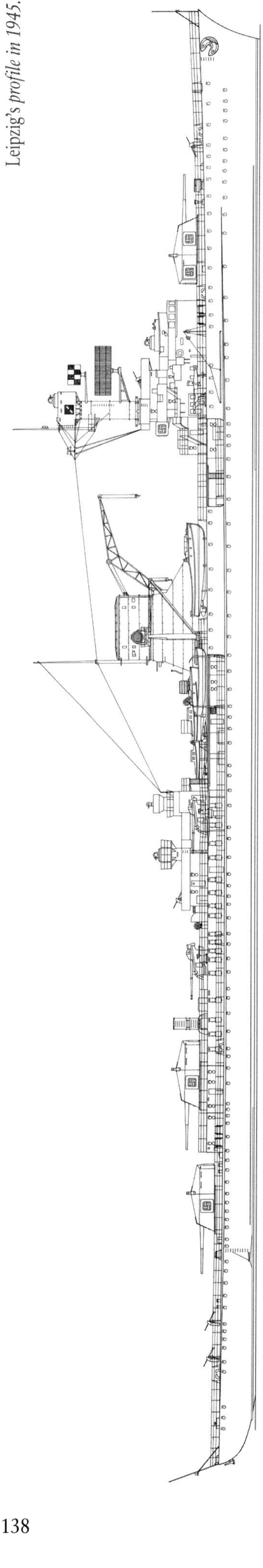

Leipzig's profile in 1945.

An interesting event was the alleged sinking that day of an unidentified submarine, which was detected at 1547 hrs. Three torpedo tracks were sighted in the water, and the escorts launched an attack after which an oil stain was observed on the surface of the water[13].

The situation did not look much better on 27 March though, and that day was not without nervous events, when around 0100 hrs after an alarm was announced and another torpedo passed behind the cruiser's stern at a distance of about thirty metres. As a curiosity, it can be stated here that in order to deceive the attacking ships, given the low speed *Leipzig* could achieve, on her bow right next to the waterline was painted a white wave that was supposed to give the impression of sailing at high speed. Of course, it is difficult to assess whether this had helped to avoid hits, but one thing is certain that despite noticing torpedo tracks in the water several times, the cruiser safely reached her destination.

On 27 March, in the morning, the entire group was in the area of Cape Arcona and soon dispersed. Due to the prevailing fog, for some time *Leipzig* anchored in the waters of Cape Arcona-Warnemünde, finally two days later headed for the Little Belt and moored in Apenrade[14]. There, she survived the last events related to the fall of the Third Reich and awaited the end of the war.

The ship remained at Apenrade for almost two months and only on 30 June put to sea heading for Wilhelmshaven. Neither the colours of the *Kriegsmarine* or any other banners flew on her masts, but only signal code flags informing about her status.

Even more explicit was the fact that on 3 July at 1338 hrs the British flag was raised on her, which was undoubtedly a great humiliation for many crew members and the ship's commander. The "Union Jack" was abandoned only four days later after she had entered Wilhelmshaven and replaced with a double flag of the international code "C", meaning the ship had surrendered.

They were also one of the last major events in the ship's history. On 23 July, an entry was made for the last time in the ship's log, and two days later most of the crew left.

The vessel was later used, among others, as a depot ship for the crews of the 14th Mine-Sweeper Flotilla, which consisted of mobilized fishing boats, and finally in mid-1946 a final decision was made to scuttle her.

On 6 July 1946, *Leipzig* left Wilhelmshaven for the last time, towed by tugboats, and went to the region south-west of Farsund and the port of Lister where, on 11 July after the previously installed explosives had been detonated, she was scuttled at position 57°53'N 06°13'E.

Finally, it is worth adding that there is a lot of divergence in the literature on the events of the last days of the cruiser. Many authors give information that chemical weapons were loaded onto her deck when she was sunk which were intended to be disposed off in this way, but this information is very difficult to confirm, however it could not be ruled out.

There are also many discrepancies as to the dates of the sinking itself, mentioning, in addition to the July 11th mentioned above, the dates of July 20th and even December 16th with the position of her sinking 57°52.01'N 06°15.75'E.

Either way, it does not change the fact that the story of the fifth cruiser in the Third Reich, which was once the pride of the *Reichsmarine* and later *Kriegsmarine*, came to an end at the bottom of the sea.

Characteristics of the cruiser *Leipzig* (Kreuzer "E")[15]

Type *Leipzig*

- Shipyard Reichsmarinewerft, Wilhelmshaven
- Construction Number 117

13 Little is known about this event. In German accounts you can find information about such an attack and the effects mentioned in the text, but it is impossible to find out more. Russian sources, which seems to be the most reliable here, are practically silent on this subject, not confirming that a submarine was lost that day.

14 At that time Apenrade belonged to the Third Reich and it was only in 1945 that it was returned to Denmark and the name Aabenraa was changed in turn in 1948 to Abenra.

15 In the sources from which the data come, there are many discrepancies as to the given parameters of the ship, which makes determining them with absolute certainty extremely difficult, and one should be aware of the fact that they may not coincide with data from other studies.

One of the most tragic events in the history of the ship was her collision with the heavy cruiser Prinz Eugen, *which occurred in October 1944.*

- Keel laid 18 April 1928
- Launched 18 October 1929
- Commissioned 8 October 1931
- Standard (official) displacement 6,000 t
- Standard (actual) displacement 6,619 t
- Full (actual) displacement 8,382 t
- Overall length 177.1 m
- Length on the waterline 165.8 m
- Beam 16.2 m
- Draft (full) 5.7 m
- Propulsion 6 x Marine water-tube boilers, 2 x Parsons steam turbine sets, 4 x diesel engines with a total output of 78,400 HP
- Maximum speed 32.0 knots
- Crew 534–850 officers, naval ratings and cadets
- Armament (1931) 9 (3x3) 150 mm guns: 2 (2x1) 88mm guns, 2 (2x1) 37mm guns, 2 (2x1) 20mm cannons, 12 (4x3) 500 mm torpedo tubes
- Armament (1934) 9 (3x3) 150 mm guns: 4 (4x1) 88mm guns, 8 (4x2) 37mm guns, 2 (2x1) 20mm cannons, 12 (4x3) 533 mm torpedo tubes
- Armament (1945) 9 (3x3) 150 mm guns: 6 (6x2) 88mm guns, 4 (2x2) 37mm guns, 8 (8x1) 20mm cannons
- Armour 18–50 mm broadsides: 70 mm transverse bulkheads, 20–25 mm decks, 30–100 mm command post, 20–30 mm main battery turrets
- Aviation equipment 1 x pneumatic catapult, 1–2 Heinkel He 60 floatplanes, later Arado Ar 196

Leipzig *seen from the starboard.*

A *profile of* Emden *in the camouflage pattern of 1938.*

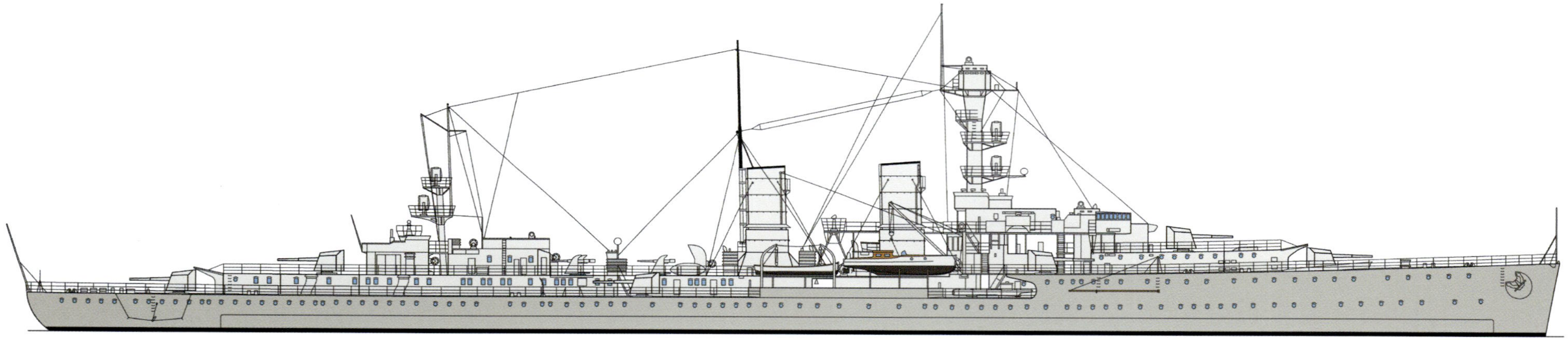

Emden *sporting colours as of initial period of her service.*

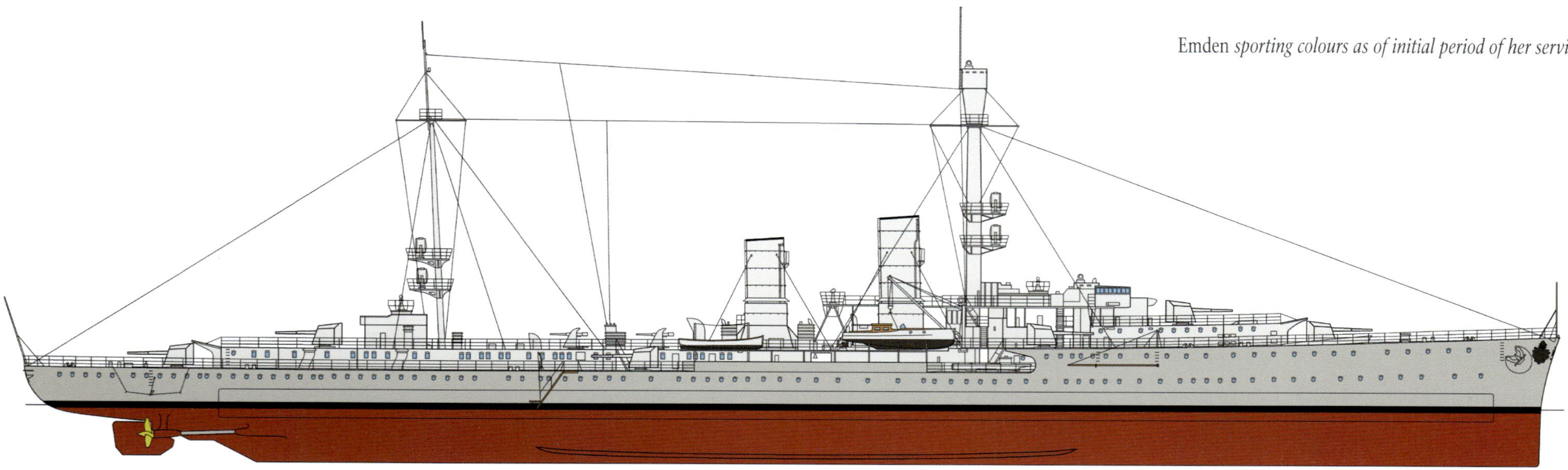

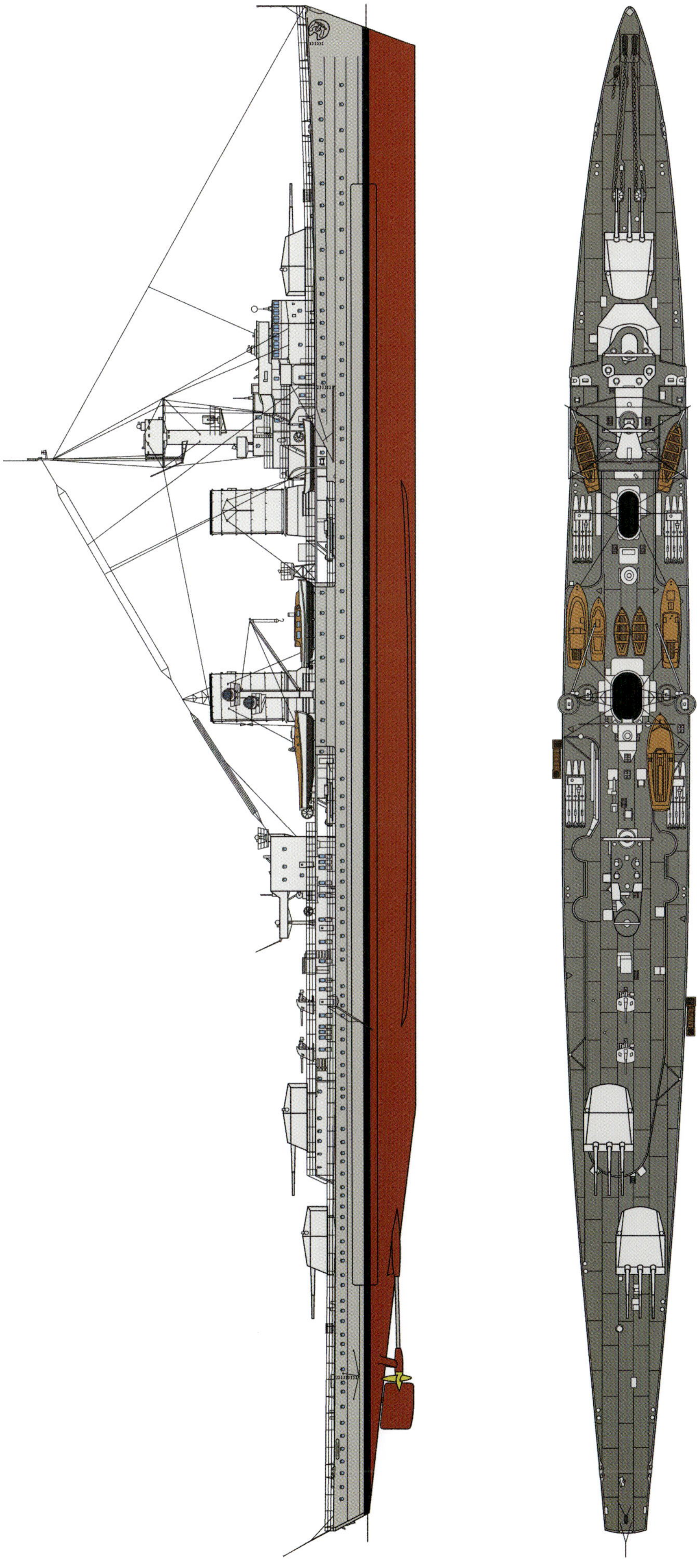

Königsberg *in her peacetime paint scheme.*

The cruiser Karlsruhe *sporting the camouflage pattern applied after her modernization.*

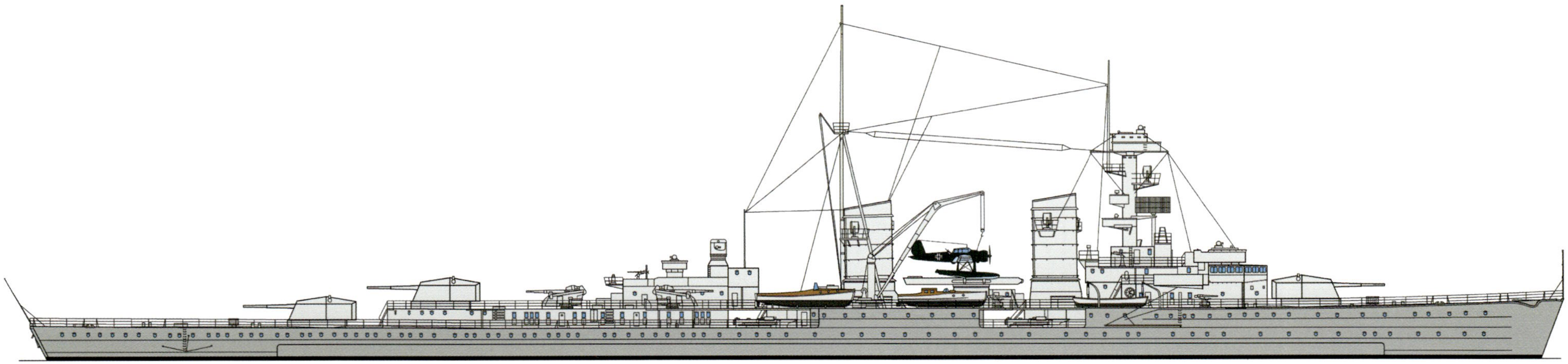

The painting scheme of Karlsruhe *from the initial period of her service.*

The *Köln cruiser in 1941 livery.*

Köln sporting the camouflage pattern from the initial period of her service.

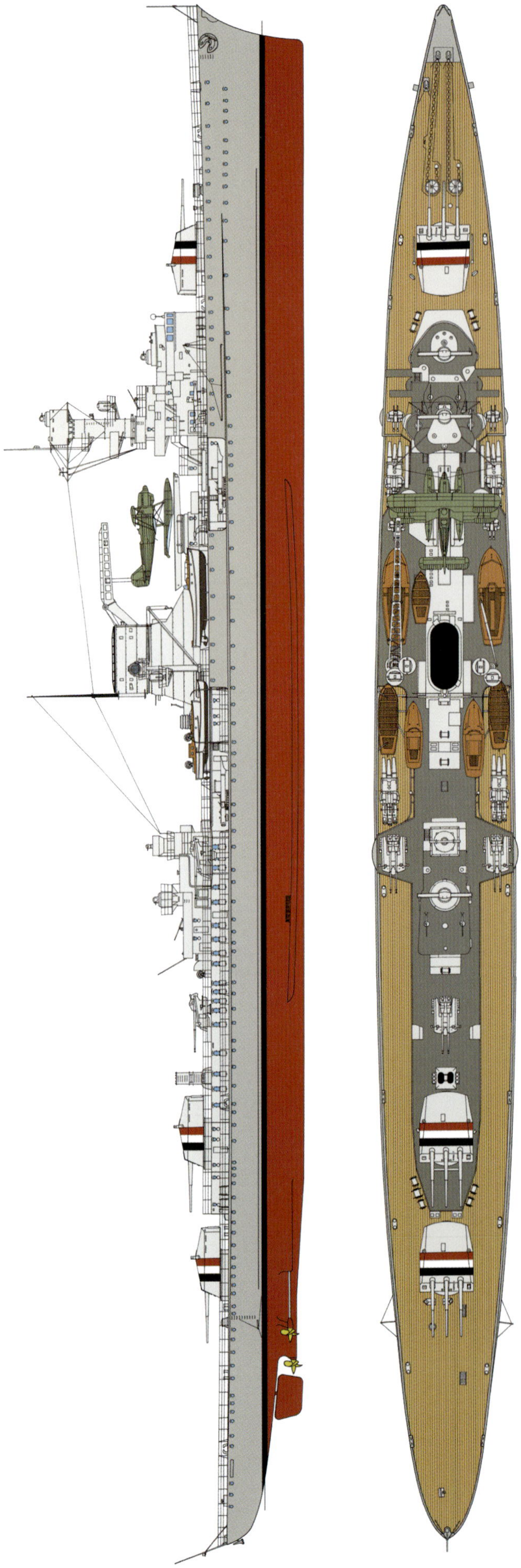

The Leipzig in the paint scheme she sported while operating in Spanish waters.